THE
PAPER
ECONOMY

THE
PAPER
ECONOMY

David T. Bazelon

237419

GREENWOOD PRESS, PUBLISHERS
WESTPORT, CONNECTICUT

Library of Congress Cataloging in Publication Data

Bazelon, David T., 1923-
  The paper economy.

    Reprint of the ed. published by Random House,
New York.
    1. United States--Economic conditions--1945-
I. Title.
[HC106.5.B38 1979]   330.9'73'092   78-11587
ISBN 0-313-21001-2

Reprinted with the permission of Random House, Inc.

Reprinted in 1979 by Greenwood Press, Inc.
51 Riverside Avenue, Westport, CT 06880

Printed in the United States of America

10 9 8 7 6 5 4 3 2 1

Acknowledgments

Portions and versions of the writing here appeared earlier in an essay in *The Reporter*, "Facts and Fictions of U. S. Capitalism" (September 17, 1959) and an article in *Commentary*, "Portrait of a Business Generalist" (April 1960). Sections of this book have also appeared in *Commentary* for September, October and November 1962, and *Partisan Review* for Fall 1962. Acknowledgement is duly made. The author also wishes to note his appreciation for various assistance received from interested persons at the Center for the Study of Democratic Institutions in Santa Barbara, California; and particular thanks for particular assistance are due, and hereby rendered, to Arnold M. Grant, Esq.

This book is dedicated

to all the people who helped,

including my mother and father.

CONTENTS

"In time, immutable rules of conduct enforced under progressively changing conditions should logically result in a muddle."

—THORSTEIN VEBLEN, in *Absentee Ownership and Business Enterprise in Recent Times* (1923).

THE
PAPER
ECONOMY

1

INTRODUCTION TO THE PAPER ECONOMY

NEW PROPERTY FORMS and old ideologies are the subjects of this book, along with other modern appearances of our politics and power. The purpose of the book is to convey to the ordinary educated reader a descriptive impression of the new American property system and its political significance —to correct the existing impression, which is hardly descriptive of anything at all. There are immense changes under way, as everybody senses; but through this whole earthquake alteration of circumstance, our ideas about the structure of our society have hardly mellowed, much less developed in a rough tandem with events. The muddle is upon us, and the days grow shorter.

In the past few years, the existence of Russia as our Grand Competitor seems to have become the main reason in America for thinking seriously about anything. One imagines that if it were not for the looming fact of Russian power, most Americans would be content just to live it up some more, continuing the postwar holiday—and literally ignore the circumstance that our society, even abstracted from the rest of the world, is a dynamic, dangerous collection of human invention and mis-invention which requires a great deal of talented attention just to keep clanking along. We could continue to abuse our historically granted super-privilege to do the wrong thing or nothing at all. And that might not be so bad, since the inevitable restructuring of our society could then continue at a more natural pace and in a more conveniently irrational manner. But as more and more of us are becoming aware, the available time-pockets are being used up and the big crisis is nearly here. It is also becoming clearer that this crisis will be domestic—profoundly domestic.

The essence of the approaching crisis is that we have not been able to make our great power felt by non-military means, either at home or abroad. The domestic source of this impotence derives, for example, from such ritualistic activities as budget-balancing, devotion to the supposed stability of the dollar, fear of inflation, and accompanying under-use of productive facility and talent. Under-use and mis-allocation of our great industrial and technological power, except under and by virtue of military purpose, all flowing from the predominant bookkeeping considerations which go by the names of money, profit, price, return on investment, etc. —that is, *existing property rights, all of which and the system comprising which I will here call "paper."* Taken as seriously and devoutly as it has been and still is today, the paper system is inadequate to ensure full production at home and to fight the cold war on non-military terms. So this is the nature of the domestic crisis: we must achieve a political posture whereby we can take the Paper Economy less seriously in order to be able to modify it according to non-paper considerations, or else we will surely forsake the promise of the future and also fail in the cold war—or worse, trap ourselves into fighting it out on military grounds, which could well be the end of all of us.

Important elements of our ruling elites, including the President and his administration, are very quickly coming around to an in-public comprehension of the special meanings in our special circumstance. For example, there was a speech by Douglas Dillon, Secretary of the Treasury, delivered to the National Press Club on June 20, 1961. A man who comes by his financial acumen with the best family and educational credentials, Mr. Dillon is one of the most broadly representative individuals in high position today—bridging, as he does, the traditions of Washington and Wall Street. As if to gild the lily, Mr. Dillon is a Republican serving in a Democratic administration. In his speech, this exceptional Secretary of the Treasury asserted the principle that deficits in the Federal budget were necessary and allowable for the purpose of underwriting the full use of our productive capacity. This is the hard-core economic point underlying much current discussion: What will we do and what will we not do to ensure full and purposeful production? A leading investment banker has now committed the Federal government—on principle—to the Thing-side of the ledger, whatever the Paper-side consequences may be. Note that this principle goes beyond standard popular Keynesianism, since pump-priming as practiced has been limited to leveling out the troughs, not ensuring rises to the crest. In justifying the approaching budget deficit, Mr. Dillon pointed out that the kind of inflation we are concerned with is the administered wage-price kind which "operates outside of budgetary influences." He made it clear that we do not have to fear supply-demand inflation, the classical kind, because "we are no longer in a time of shortages." He added:

> There is unusual—and underutilized—capacity everywhere in our land today; in steel, in autos, in housing, in textiles, in chemicals—indeed, everywhere we look. We also—and unfortunately—are underutilizing our labor force, which stands ready and willing to operate the unused capacity of our industrial plant.

Once the principle of full production is accepted and acted on, however, we are apt to grow at such a rate that budget deficits to underwrite the whole process will become administratively unwieldy and eventually too expensive, besides being inequitable. But that would be years later. Meanwhile, national policy has been shaped by budget-mongers since the War, and Mr. Dillon's statement constituted a major departure—at least in principle.

The basic ideas of the Paper Economy are being taken less and less as immutable objects of devotion by more and more important people. They are being approached—although queasily, almost as an act of sacrilege—as the ticklish but crucial problems they in fact represent. This is because the confrontation with the Soviet Union has forced upon the elite groups in our society the realization that there must be policy and purpose beyond money-making—just as if we were at war, because we are. (Neither hunger nor technological opportunity were ever able to accomplish this.) The idea that money-making—*any* money-making by *any*body—does not by itself properly confront all human problems, is a freshly upsetting notion for our leading groups. We have never as a nation been seized by such notions except on the occasion of war—and even there, who knows what would have happened if, faced with the necessity of winning a war, it was discovered *en passant* that the process was not profitable? Fortunately for the national psyche, it was realized early that wars are highly paper-productive.

If we could only fight the cold war as if it were an old-fashioned World War II affair. It would be over in a few years, we would of course win it, everybody would get terribly rich all over again, and the worst lasting consequence would be the usual permanent damage to a rising generation and a few hundred billion dollars of extra government paper. (The former would be suffered in the usual way by parents and other lovers; the latter would be tongue-clucked over in public, but in private it would again be duly appreciated.)

The traditional way out is no longer available to us. For one thing, you don't win the cold war (unless you are Senator Goldwater); you just keep the nuclear holocaust from occurring. For another thing, it is increasingly obvious that the war in which we are engaged is not to be fought with military hardware: the military part of it is simply a stand-off operation which allows the true conflict to go forward elsewhere and by other means. We could mobilize the economy for a World War II-type effort of several years duration. *But to mobilize the social economy for the kind of conflict in which we are actually engaged requires structural changes in our society, and these changes will be per-*

manent. Indeed, they will be continuing and cumulative. There's the rub—to accept or resist this new experimental form of mobilization.

America is not prepared culturally to make a choice of this magnitude. But on the other hand, who is? Some of us will have achieved our greatest contribution to this effort merely by acquiescing in it; others in considerable numbers will be required to participate with consummate devotion. But most of all, it is up to our leaders to notice the true contour of the crisis, which in the first instance requires them to abandon reliance on the military illusion, and to present the non-military issues to the public—to outline a road for social survival. They have every reason to do so, since favored class position is no longer any special insurance against personal disaster. In this sense, the Bomb has democratized our society as nothing else has ever done—not even free Western land. There are no longer any privileged roads to survival.

It is a hard irony of history that calls upon the conservative leadership of the most conservative great nation in the world to choose freely the pursuit of a permanent social revolution. Analysis and reflection reveal over and over again and finally compel the conclusion and re-conclusion that this *is*, however, the contour of the crisis—and that just such an unreasonable demand is now being made by *our* history.

A cruel fate for the nice Americans.

This book is an attempt to get at some of the considerations underlying the crisis. There is not one image transposed here from a Utopian drawing-board. The only touch of Utopia indulged is the presumption that irrelevant but revered ideas may be put (or pushed) aside in favor of descriptive insight. The real point for us now is that we have overindulged the God-given right to forego concern with changing circumstance. So I have continually insisted upon the facts of the matter, and have allowed myself considerable irreverence to ancestral ideas.

The point has been made that we are culturally unprepared for this crisis. So is everybody else in the world. The crisis has been occasioned by the awful advance of technology, before anybody realized well enough that the technology which has not been prepared for (or is not soon accommodated socially) is no blessing at all, but the deepest ironic disaster of the human race. The human being today stands poised to be destroyed by his primary biological blessing—his propensity to develop and his capacity to use *technique*. There is a direct line from the prehensile thumb to the nuclear bomb. But there has never been a direct line between the thumb—or the Bomb—and what to do with it. There is no help for this: it is our fate. But oh, how much time the human race has wasted discussing the philosophy of the relation between means and ends, never learning to live with the obvious fact that there was no relation at all that was not insisted upon by an acting individual. Means are winning out over ends because that is our essential biological nature. Notice children playing: their main concern is whether or not "it can be done" (safely, they think); if it can, do it. That is how the world has developed, and that is how and why it may end.

But we were talking about our cultural unpreparedness. Take, for example, business ideology—the root source of our cultural embarrassment. Its key idea is that if you have Competition—sometimes called Free Enterprise—you don't need Government, either to create or maintain the economy or justice in the economy. A good part of this book (beginning with the next chapter) is devoted to arguing against, disproving, ridiculing, and on occasion screaming at this notion—and insisting that what we have gotten and inevitably would get under it is Private Government.

Our chief assets are our great business institutions; our primary liabilities are their ideologies and the advertising culture they sustain. America is a business civilization, for sure: it is the Paper Economy. But the tension between the two sides of this balance sheet of our business way of life has become extreme. We have lived by all the Paper values—the belief in money, the devotion to paper profit, the ungodly worship of the balance sheet. All this commitment is now fading into the twilight area of madness, and what is sane and human in each of us refuses to follow. It is a very real crisis we are in.

In the big 1902 anthracite strike, George F. Baer, representing the Wall Street interests in the coal and steel industries, made the following statement:

> The rights and interests of the laboring man will be protected and cared for—not by labor agitators, but by the Christian men to whom God in His infinite wisdom has given the control of the property interests in this country.

We do not have this sort of thing any more; but notice that it was uttered only a half-century ago. The change in everything has been so rapid. We really do not know what has happened at all, it has all happened so quickly. There has not been anything like the time needed to balance the books of modernity. And it is just we who are living this immediate and unaccounted-for life, with almost limitlessly irrelevant cultural resources, who are now called upon to institute the most intelligently directed social revolution ever conceived. Sustaining our unpreparedness, we have this business-fostered mass culture—a wonderfully crude and human outpouring. If we were in better shape, if the world were easier to live in, we would all laugh at it. But it isn't, and we don't. (I have felt that the day I see a dying man smoking Kents, I will have had the transcendent vision of the power of American advertising.)

This book is decidedly *not* concerned with the capitalism/socialism way of understanding things. It is an argument here that this is no longer a very live formulation. Many great historical conflicts were fought out in terms of this rhetoric, and numerous of these persist as vital historical issues, certainly. But the idea that something called socialism just had to replace something called capitalism was based on one very wrong idea—or, let us say, one particular confusion. The great historical issue had not to do primarily with capitalism, really, because the great issue was and is the new technology—the new power of the human mind to fashion reality. Capitalism just happened to be there when this terrible new freedom occurred—and it has restrained at least as much as it has expressed this fundamental historical force.

Because capitalism and its paper world were based on true existing scarcity, the drama of the system was to contend heroically with the scarcity of things in the world. (That is why property—the primary scarcity concept—was so important to the capitalist system.) But the whole point about the new freedom, the new technology, is that it has made scarcity absurd. The problem of history is now changed—it has become how to learn to live with the new technology, and live in increasingly large and complicated aggregates. (Veblen was perhaps the first to comprehend this factor; although he was a radical libertarian critic of society, perhaps the most perceptive we have had in America, he never worked up much interest in socialist ideology.)

The following pages contain the frequent assertion that capitalism has been decisively altered from the inside, to the point where it is question-begging to continue to call it capitalism. Socialist ideology was always mostly an inverse image of capitalism, and consequently it either changes with changes in the capitalist order, or it shares the irrelevance of traditional capitalist ideology. Unfortunately, it has participated in the faults of its antagonist. But that is a problem for the American socialist movement, if any. The purpose here is to attack traditional capitalist ideology as a necessary step in opening up a more useful perspective on the technological and organizational reality before us.*

The evangelical heart of socialism was pierced by the betrayal of the German Social Democrats in 1914, and by the nature of the Soviet power created after the Bolsheviks took over in Russia in 1917. The first demonstrated that high moral professions are no safeguard against the excessive practicality of the human being in critical circumstances, but indeed are partners to that survivalism—a perennial lesson learned and re-learned throughout history by highly moral people. The lesson of the second is even more

---

* There is much to suggest that traditional socialist theory in Russia, for example, serves to obscure the industrial and political reality just as capitalist theory does in this country. In writing about America, one reveals the power behind the property forms; in Russia, one would uncover the property-like interests behind the power.

instructive for our day: the Russian experience indicates that classlessness cannot be achieved by an act of human will, that to destroy one ruling class merely prepares the way for the creation of another and not necessarily better one. As a consequence, the nature and theory of class struggle have necessarily been altered in essence. It is no longer a sufficient perspective to contemplate the destruction of a ruling class; it is much more important to consider ways and means of living under and with *some* ruling group or other. Rulers we have always with us: the ruled must want to and must learn how to tyrannize over those who rule them: it is not enough to kill them.

Socialism assumed a perfect understanding of the essential nature of capitalism. With the disappearance of capitalism hardly noticed by the traditional socialists, this understanding is exposed as something less than perfect. Socialism—or a new libertarian movement under another name (something beyond Depression-bred liberalism)—may regain its evangelism one day, but only after it has become sufficiently relevant to re-entitle itself to the great dream.

One can sum up in this way: it is not that socialist theory was so wrong about capitalism; what the socialists were wrong about was socialism, meaning the future. They really didn't have a very good idea of it. Meanwhile, some of it has arrived. And just now, we are very hard-pressed to understand the present, much less dream again a great dream of the unarrived future. We are picking our way down a very dangerous road.

Money is not real. What made it *seem* real for so long was its scarcity. Since money is supposed to be spent on things, its scarcity can truly reflect reality only when that reality is made up of a general scarcity of things. It no longer is, except mostly by intention. Since the imagined scarcity of money no longer mirrors an existing scarcity of things, and since money that is not meaningfully scarce is not exactly money, the whole nature of the symbol has changed profoundly.

The main thing in America has always been money (or at least we always thought it was). Since we are the most productive society in history and consequently are daily threatened by cumulative non-scarcity, one can imagine the amazing richness of the money-idea. Also, money is not just a dollar bill—as a matter of fact, however we peasants may feel about Federal currency, it is an almost insignificant form of money. A much more common form —about ten times as common—is the piece of paper we call a check. And the check itself is almost insignificant compared to the entries on the books of account of a bank; a check indeed is nothing but an instruction to a bookkeeper somewhere. And all this common money, which is spent right away, is not nearly as important as the bookkeeping entries elsewhere which are not spent right away. The latter, usually known as debt and equity interests or bonds and stocks, are in fact either money or nearly money. They can be distinguished from money, but only in the utter practicality of a time-series, and generally speaking I have not bothered with that in this book. (Many economists bother with little else.) These value-symbols are typically represented by a piece of paper, and that is the occasion for the title of this book. Money is always paper, paper is always nearly money (near to it in time, that is), and both are symbols rather than facts-of-the-matter. So also, increasingly, is Private Property itself. Meanwhile, more and more values are translated purely into paper, and the volume of paper grows mountainously.

The difference between money and credit is hardly worth discussing for our purposes, and the argument in these pages concerning the difference between money/credit and private property is mostly directed to showing that this difference also is not particularly worth our attention. The basic property in the country more and more becomes great industrial complexes and the training of the personnel who run them. This property is not private. Under modern American property forms, "private" no longer means "individual"—if you are talking about the significant productive property. The word "private" in private property has become a euphemism for "non-state" and, too often, non-responsible: this is property owned and controlled by great organizations which, in turn, are not owned and controlled by any individuals. But these organizations do create great quantities of paper of all varieties, and much of this paper does end up in the eager hands of private individuals. In this sense, you may if you insist on it, consider our economy deeply involved with *private paper*. It is certainly founded upon modern technology and the *devotion* to private paper.

All this paper represents *value*. Now ever since Marx used Ricardo to expound his famous labor or surplus theory of value (a thunderous moral statement), traditional economics has noticeably lost interest in what was formerly the central problem in economic theory, the problem of value. This retreat from the discussion of value was so precipitous that most people did not recognize that Veblen made an original, non-Marxist and uniquely American contribution to it. It was also a little difficult to understand

Veblen's statement about value because he said it was an illusion, in the business society, being based on the businessman's belief that the value represented by a dollar is stable. He pointed out that if it were, it would not serve its purpose as a dollar—namely, identifying the current state of the illusion. (This is all expounded somewhat more clearly hereinafter.) People also did not notice what Veblen was doing because he was such a terribly witty person: finding an absurd illusion at the very core of society, he described it with truly magnificent irony, which I think is both excusable and appropriate. Anyway, when you talk about paper you are talking about value—whatever that is and whether or not it is an illusion—and I have relied substantially on Veblen's original thinking about credit and capitalization in America.

In a brochure about the Security-Columbian Banknote Company, one of our leading engravers and printers of the kind of paper I am talking about, it is sonorously stated:

> The system of commercial enterprise can be said to have begun when first the goldsmiths of medieval times issued written receipts for gold deposited with them and accepted written assignments and transfers of these receipts. Written paper began to represent and symbolize stated value great or small. Today the immense value [etc., etc.].

The brochure continues: "Pieces of paper suitably inscribed and decorated are the evidences of ownership in" almost everything. "These symbols of property must be perfection in print, artistically conceived . . ." etc., etc. Some of them indeed are very pretty. On the other hand, some very valuable ones have been perfectly represented by scribbled notes. But all paper.

I beg the reader not to be discouraged by this high-level discussion of the kind of money and property he will never see, and indeed only infrequently reads about. It is extremely important even if you never get close to any of it: the paper system described in these pages structures the circumstance in which we live out our lives. We have to understand what a billion dollars is, how it comes about and how it is managed, although the gods will never let us have any of it. (I once touched a certified check for $20 million and, apart from certain irrational impulses which shall be nameless, the event did not add much to my efforts to imagine what such a sum really is.)

There are other reasons why we thing-oriented consumers should try to understand the poetry of money. The things that money buys can seem unspeakably more significant than they truly are: the unanalyzed power of the symbol transfers itself to the things themselves. So that the rituals of purchase take on terribly meaningful qualities —which they could never have if one thought only of material need and material satisfaction, unmediated by the powerful symbolism of the Dollar. This is so true that even Madison Avenue knows about it—and uses it. As a matter of fact, it is probably a quality of all meanings in the world of Appearance. Which proves how terribly important poetry is in the first place.

In 1961, a substantially unpoetic study of some of the Paper was completed and publicized. This represented three years and $1,300,000 worth of effort by the Commission on Money and Credit set up by the Committee for Economic Development. Directed by a group of leading leaders and drawing upon research papers from more than a hundred scholars, the study was announced in 1957 as the first full-dress examination of the U.S. monetary system in half a century, that is, since the studies which led to the creation of the Federal Reserve System. In the *New York Times* report of June 25, 1961, it was resoundingly noted that: "Among more than eighty recommendations, only one innovation is proposed" by the commission—and that was not a new one. In other words, even the *Times* noted that the study was dull (which is probably more of a landmark than the thing itself). The report represents a painfully arrived-at consensus of conservative opinion, and is consequently not very interesting. It *is* rather interesting, however, that the vice chairman of the commission, Mr. H. Christian Sonne, dissented from the report, in the preparation of which he had participated for three years, because it was merely a tabulation of established opinion. The *Times* said:

> Mr. Sonne is critical particularly of the commission's failure to examine the changes in the nature and quality of the assets underlying the money supply. To his complaint could be added the commission's failure to make any direct examination of the spectacular growth of "near-monies"—the short-term holdings of businesses and individuals that may readily be converted to money.

The alternative to this kind of effort at elevated tinkering might possibly be a very low-level and even grass-roots opposition to paper money as such. In the late nineteenth century such a group was formed in New York, whose program was opposition to paper money *and* monopolies— it was called Locofocos. The point of view peddled herein is neither that of the Commission on Money and Credit nor of the ancestral Locofocos—there is not even much reliance on William Jennings Bryan.

To tranquilize the confusion I have just created, let

me suggest that it is helpful to view business as a *political* system—based on dollars, instead of votes, say. Business is a political system, and money isn't real. That's almost enough of an Introduction to the Paper Economy.

The paper system is conceived in terms of scarcity. It is founded upon that concept. Since scarcity no longer occurs naturally in this country (unless the Paper Economy just as it is today is considered "natural"), we are quickly approaching the point where the nation will have to make a fundamental decision about whether it can do without the whole baggage of historical ideas which were outgrowths of previously existing scarcities. There is probably no more profound personal issue that any of us will ever have to face than this one—can we stand prosperity? can we give up the scarcity idea?

J. K. Galbraith in his influential *tour de force*, *The Affluent Society*, assumed existing abundance in order to press his great argument about our obvious (and potentially disastrous) misallocation of resource. To date, that has been the most effective presentation of the anti-scarcity position. Another important presentation has been the rate-of-growth discussion—the one that candidate Nixon's ill-advised ghost-writers tried to exorcise with the phrase "growthmanship." There are two delightful kickers in this discussion. "Growth" used to be capitalism's biggest sales message—now it has become a challenge to the system itself, the primary assumptions of which have been turned inside out. And this half-hidden irony: without building another factory or a single additional machine, our "growth" could show an amazing advance within a matter of months simply by using the existing capacity. In any event, the effort in this essay is to discuss this great issue of non-scarcity from a somewhat different angle—as a comprehensive impression of the whole property system.

David Riesman believes we are burdened, psychologically, with a "scarcity view of man." Under the heading of What Are We Going to Do with Our Leisure? we had a discussion of something like this many years ago, but it was curtailed by the Great Depression. Since there will not be another Great Depression, we can assume that the discussion now getting into high gear will not be similarly curtailed. I think there is no question that man's sense of himself, and the traditional psychological notions about human nature, all have been substantially conditioned by the previously existing scarcities. So the final result of the technological revolution will be a new conception of man.

This need disturb no one, since economics has always been based upon a psychological image of man—on some model of motivation. In this sense, what we are faced with is a revolution in motivation, and the conservatives don't want it, because they see it as an attack on their personalities. Indeed, it *is* frightening, as well as exhilarating. What in God's name will we do with ourselves if making a dollar loses its allure? If things of all kinds are not very hard to get? If "hewing to the line" no longer really matters? If traditional sacrifice of the present becomes fatuous? (The reason President Kennedy keeps asking for "sacrifice" from the nation is not that any real ones are needed, but because he shrewdly understands that the nation yearns for the mood.) How, then, will we ever face up to the prospect of a decent life? In the previous history of the human race, only very small aristocratic groups were ever confronted with these delicate questions. And unfortunately they didn't solve them—either at all, or usefully for a democratic mass.

What we are going to do about this problem, either domestically or in its world setting, is still largely undetermined. The Marshall Plan was a very generous program, but it was aid to "our own kind," it was conceived as being a program limited in time, and it had the further advantage of appearing to be a continuation of the interests and commitments of World War II. The remainder of our worldwide aid has been mostly military and mostly propaganda. The issue of providing the capital, both intellectual and material, for the technological development of the whole world—and the alleviation of human misery more or less wherever it occurs—still has a dream or nightmare status in this country. We have not yet managed to bring gross poverty under control even within the continental United States. We have not yet accepted prosperity as a common matter.

Our consumer-gluttony is infamous. But whatever can and has been said about it from a moral-esthetic point of view, it is important not to forget that we would have almost no realistic contact with the technologically productive reality if it were not for this demand on the part of the American people. However, it is providing a way of life, for a large portion of the population, which has at best a temporary charm to it. We cannot continue forever devoting our lives to the newest model refrigerator. (At least, I don't *think* we can.)

Whatever our difficulties with affluence here in America, the rest of the world—in all its variety and with its more deeply traditional societies—is apt to have even more. (Unlike everybody else in the world, we were *born* to be rich.) As an extreme but illuminating example, a scholarly geographer reported to the *New York Times* (August 20, 1961) the growth of "cargo cults" in the Pacific islands. It appears that the natives have taken some indications of manna from heaven—they were informed about manna by missionaries interpreting the Old Testament to them—as referring to a return of American LST's bearing "tons of canned meat and fish, tobacco" and so on. They experienced these religious realizations during World War II when brimming LST's were a ubiquitous American emanation. Other native populations have different dreams enticing them into the new world. A report from the Australian territory of Papua (*New York Times*, April 17, 1960) states: "It is common to see Papuans walking along jungle trails listening to transistor radios. . . ." (This is strikingly similar to the behavior of Manhattan natives.) In the *Times* of November 26, 1961, a report from Canada revealed that the Eastern Arctic Patrol was surprised on its recent annual visit to the Eskimos: whereas the members of the Patrol were accustomed to rush ashore to take pictures of the Eskimos, on their last trip the Eskimos were waiting with their own cameras to take pictures of them.

A final introductory word on my method. First of all and most importantly, the effort here is a speculative essay —not a scholarly study. It would have taken a whole Harvard to study the matters essayed herein. The work here is quite different: it is an attempt at a synthesis of numerous factors and trends concerning the modern revolution in society which have been noticed by many observers, and elaborated by some at great length. If it fits into a slot, it is the kind the academics call "journalistic." (I am not sure what the journalists would call it.) It is an "essay," meaning an *effort*; and, I repeat, the effort is at synthesis. It is also an essay in that any chapter here could have been a book

2

IDEOLOGY
AND
PRIVATE GOVERNMENT

THE PICTURE that business presents of itself in America is somewhat out of proportion. It is both manly and nervously delicate; it expansively embraces the future, but may not last out the third quarter; it chases profits as a religious devotion, but a second later exists only to make further sacrifices to the all-powerful public it serves. And mostly it would like to be left alone to continue its mission of building this best of all possible worlds.

American business prefers to call itself The Free Enterprise System—or even more expansively, The American Way of Life. The latter is so true that it leaves nothing to be discussed; but the former is a Big Symbol that can and has in itself—and many of the subjects essayed have in fact been written about to the extent of large library sections.

If your desire is for molish information or official opinion, you have probably bought or borrowed the wrong book. I am not an expert on anything, and I speak for no one but myself. Some years ago, I think I was an expert on the SEC proxy-fight rules—but that lasted for only a few months, and there isn't more than a paragraph or two on proxy fights in these pages. I was adequately trained as a corporate attorney; but again, I have grown rusty in the past few years and cannot claim any particular qualification because of that. Really, my only qualification for writing this book is that I have on occasion, for one reason or another, been aroused in wonderment by some of the subjects dealt with.

In the complex organized society, there are no adequate rituals of qualification. It is true that almost everyone is, unfortunately, an expert. But an expert is simply someone who has been doing a particular something for a long time (probably too long), or at least longer or better than most other people. A medical degree does not make a doctor, an LL.B. does not make a lawyer, and a Ph.D does not make a big thinker.

An editor once told me, very archly, "The greatest research tool is the telephone." I thought about that for a while, but finally disagreed: it takes too long to figure out whom to call. The greatest research tool—and full laboratory, library and proving-ground ever devised—is oneself. So I guess the purpose of this book, all in all, is simply to tell you what I think is the obvious truth about property, power and politics in America.

been discussed endlessly. This talkathon has been greatly facilitated by the fact that "free enterprise" as a temporal description of something happening between New York and Los Angeles cannot possibly be defined for reasonable people. For just one thing, it assumes a miniscule role for the Federal government—and everybody knows better than that. No, the only existential meaning of *enterprise* is what businessmen generally happen to be doing at the moment, and *free* is merely the accompanying demand that they be left alone to do it.

On the whole, popular business ideology is simply a table-thumping evasion of the facts of life. It ruled the roost before the New Deal, and it remains today as the most ubiquitously available view of What We Are Doing. But it has become defensive, and for some time its burden has been increasingly, What We Are Doing *Wrong*.

Everything good is claimed for the free enterprise system, and everything bad clearly lies outside of it. So it cannot seriously pretend to be a description of reality. It is more of a moral thing, and consequently makes for good screaming, but poor discussion. It is, as we are all aware, intensely nationalistic: in one of its standard postures, the free enterprise system is assumed to have only the flimsiest connection with English or European capitalism (or anything else foreign), having been born fully grown of native parents called the Founding Fathers.

A main point of this book is that the current image of the system and the obvious facts of the matter are incommensurable. A little dab of reality might not be amiss right here, before we proceed further into the overheated atmosphere of the myth. Industrialism, the network of technology and productive industry, is not to be identified with free enterprise or capitalism or any name for any control-system which at a particular historical moment stands astride and determines how and why men shall operate the industrial complex. Capitalism is not the same thing as industrialism, any more than capital means the plants, machines and other subjects and objects of technology which shape the physical world under industrialism. Capital is not Things—and neither are enterprises, free or otherwise. Capital is *assets*; and enterprises are more or less organized and purposeful collections of assets. An asset is a money-value— another symbol-on-paper, in this instance that *torah* of the Paper Economy, The Balance Sheet, amen. But you could spend a whole day walking through the mammoth Fairless Works of the United States Steel Corporation without seeing the slightest piece of balance-sheet profit perched expectantly in the vicinity of a furnace. All the pieces are hidden in the heads of the personnel—some heads more than other heads, but all of them in one head or another. In the early commercial days before machine technology got moving, capital referred to a stock of goods. But now goods can be produced so quickly by machines that capital mostly refers to the machines, while goods are called "inventory." They are now felt by producers to be as often a liability as an asset. You *control* the machines, but you just *move* inventory. Indeed, you *have* to move inventory.

In an article called "The Defense of Business: A Strategic Appraisal" (contributed to *The Harvard Business Review* in 1954) J. K. Galbraith suggested sweetly that business, by the stridency of its arguments, was alienating the more important part of its audience in order to gain the entrepreneurial masses who needed no persuasion anyway. He asserted: "The case for business must inevitably be a case for large-scale enterprise"—which it ordinarily is not. He also noted the lack of humor in business sloganeering and looked forward to the day "when an NAM president opens the annual Congress of Industry with some amiable jest about free enterprise." (I want to be there.)

In 1956 four distinguished scholars published a serious study-in-depth of American business ideology. The book was called *The American Business Creed,* and the authors were Francis X. Sutton, a sociologist connected with the Behavorial Sciences Program of The Ford Foundation, and Seymour E. Harris, Carl Kaysen and James Tobin, three leading economists, the first two at Harvard and the third at Yale. The method employed was to gather material out of business' own big mouth; the collection-technique was academically impeccable.

It seems there are "strains" in the social and occupational roles of businessmen, the authors say. The pressure of these strains makes many businessmen something less than judicious in their appreciation of issues like labor unions, the role of the Federal government, complicated economic matters like prices, profits, money, competition, bigness, inflation, corporate power, and a few dozen other similar subheadings. In order to account for these strains, they have created a big, beautiful, and mostly perfect view of The System in a setting characterized by considerable hostility. "The notion of a coherent, unique, and consciously designed American economic 'system' is the central concept of the business creed." There are some complicated matters recognized by The System, but as long as Outside Influences are held at bay they all come out all right because of a great big gleaming washer-dryer called Competition. If you have

Competition you don't need Government, so Government is first among the Outside Influences. (The main animus of the whole concoction is directed against the government—because it is the one effectively interfering agency.)

There are two basic strands to the ideology, the classical and the managerial. In its pure, classical form, The System is an invention of the NAM—an elaboration by that organization's paid ideologists of a nineteenth century miscellany: it would appear to be based on a selective misreading of Locke, Smith, Jefferson, Bentham, Mill, etc. The managerial version of the creed recognizes, in a cautiously vague manner, that big corporations are the core of the economy and that they are probably social institutions, not just delicate atoms in the free market molecule. So there is some talk of administrative responsibility to customers, labor, and suppliers as well as to "owners," meaning the paper-holders. In sum, there is a cloudy admission that men are managing things.

It strikes me as very important that the managerial creed, in its logical extension, is a rather thorough contradiction of the classical one. It is not logically extended very much in public, however: these popular managerialists go only so far with their notions of conscious, administrative responsibility for business functioning, and then, presto! rely as they must on any and all defensive items of the NAM potpourri. The corporate elite quite consciously uses NAM nonsense as protective coloration. (The NAM is in fact composed of small firms and paid for by the large ones. Dues are assessed according to net worth.)

We are in such bad shape regarding our conventional awareness of what's going on in the economy that official managerialism, puerile and pompous as it may be, constitutes a hopeful portent. It is a move toward sanity, which un-doubtedly accounts for its growth: it reduces the unbearable strain of fabrication as this impinges on the managers them-selves. But the "managerial creed is relatively silent on the question of power," and that is of course the main question. (Under the classical version, you never reach the question of power because—if you keep your foot on the government's throat—nobody has any, all they have is Competition.) On the crucial question of public as against private power-centers the managerial creed is not relatively silent, but quite noisy: Big Government is a terrible thing, whether one ob-serves its evil machinations from behind a haberdashery counter in Keokuk, or from the fortieth-floor aerie of a Park Avenue corporate emporium.

The authors of *The American Business Creed* also offer this delicately phrased statement: "The use of clearly mis-leading material is much more frequent in advertise-ments. . . ." (Big institutional advertising of and for business was an outgrowth of the War, when the usual products sold themselves.) Which suggests that perhaps the basic error of the Madison Avenue ideologists is that they have tried to sell Free Enterprise as if it were just another agency account like Sara Lee frozen pastry. They neglect the fact that just because it's sweet doesn't mean you can eat it.

The central idea of business ideology is Competition, because that makes all sorts of difficult, questionable and downright unpleasant matters come out all right in the end. As Professor Galbraith has engagingly put it: "Like marital fidelity, decent plumbing, or clean underclothing, competition is a prerequisite of respectability in our so-ciety."

Have you ever tried to suggest to a true believer that not all Competition is good, and that not all Non-competition is bad? It sounds like an obvious enough proposition, but he will immediately begin to get edgy, even though his lexicon includes some Bad Competitions like Unfair, Cutthroat, Chainstore, and Discount, to mention a few. It's the other side of the proposition that really twangs his nerves—probably because, *sub rosa*, he can't help thinking of a quietly rigged market as if the delights it offered were equal only to those of an expensive Parisian bawdy house. Even under the regular view of things, if you stop to think about it, perhaps only *half* of the businessmen are at any one moment happy about actual competition—the half that are competing to take away what the other half already have. And Non-competition is not all a state of runaway moral decay. There is such a thing as Positive Non-competition, as when during the War the government-as-big-purchaser said to the aircraft industry, "Give us fifty thousand planes a year." A few years later we were getting ninety thousand planes a year. This was accomplished by planning to produce, and carrying out the plan. You might say that the producers *competed* to see how many planes they could turn out. But that is not the kind of "competition" the theory talks about. The theory calls for balance-sheet competition, and as often as not that will require a shrewd curtailment of inventory. Indeed, the typical postwar disorder in our Free Competitive Economy has occurred when too many shrewd competitors started competing a bit too strenuously in non-production—in reducing inventory.

So Competition differs from competition decisively. The latter is not only sometimes good and sometimes bad, but it actually exists in the real world in a great variety of forms. And it exists, like everything else in the real world, along with other things. If you want to be reasonable about it, the issue is not whether something called "competition" (without further definition) is an effective factor, but whether it is always *the* chief effective factor and whether there are any other such factors which play a role in ordering our economic activities. Pretty obviously, there are—in the real world.

But in the world of business ideology, no. "The free market economy is self-coordinating and self-regulating, without master plan or central direction," says the Chamber of Commerce. And there you have it. (Read it over again, because that particular statement says it all.) Very simply, the creed refuses to distinguish between laissez faire and competition. But, as Sutton *et al* point out,

> the whole trend of economic science for the last forty years has been to cut away every basis for the belief that a competitive system automatically reaches stable equilibrium and avoids violent fluctuations in aggregate output and employment. . . .

A modern economic order is supposed to do two things, under any theory: to produce goods and to grow—to keep up with or even induce technological change, and to incorporate the same into the system of industry with a resulting increase in efficiency. Keeping an eye on these two obvious propositions, we stand a fair chance of restoring a sense of reality to the discussion of the uses of competition.

Take the first point, producing goods—in an established industry. General Motors, Ford and Chrysler do not compete in producing cars, they compete in selling cars. And even in sales competition, they do not struggle with each other to sell cheaper—which under traditional theory would lead to greater production. (It might also, incidentally, lead to the bankruptcy of Chrysler.) They compete among themselves in terms of style, gimmicks, and efficient psychological rape of the consumer, for shares in a limited market—about 6 million cars a year. In 1955 the big auto-producers made a terrible mistake—they sold 7 million cars. Which made a mess out of the 1956 market because, as became apparent, the big sell in 1955 had mopped up some of the following year's take. They are careful not to make the same egregious error again—it did, in fact, help to upset the whole economy. Where is the "competition" in all this? Or more pointedly, where is the *benefit* of the competition? If it exists somewhere, it certainly does not concern the production of automobiles. With no strain at all, and without expanding plant capacity, the automotive industry could produce well over 7 million cars a year—more like 10 million. We could give them away as birthday presents to the walking masses of Asia. Perhaps they could sleep in them—or build a religion around them, as we've done.*

Or let's take a "growth" industry where the connection between producing and selling is closer because the producers are still dealing with a market which has not yet been saturated with goods. Say, missile hardware and electronics. Now here you do have thousands of small, young, vital producers competing strenuously with each other.

* The discussion here unfortunately ignores the fact that there are already too damn many cars in this country. And the last thing the Asians need is for us to export our traffic and urban air problems to them. The point is that the productive capacity which *could* produce 4 million unnecessary cars annually could also, if rationally used, give us and the Asians what we really need, the fuel for life to assure our physical and mental well-being.

Why? Because it's cheaper and politically more expedient that way to build an industry which will later be taken over and operated, naturally, by the big corporations which are the only institutions we have for operating large-scale production complexes. And even in this early stage you could hardly call the situation *free* competition. It is highly organized, *managed* competition. The freight and overhead, all the basic charges, are paid for by the government—military procurement has created the industry. And the competition is organized by the big industrial giants in that every weapons system or other primary project is under the control of a GE, RCA, Westinghouse, Boeing, General Dynamics, etc., whose main job is to subcontract thousands of items and problems and bits of scientific hardware. They are massive purchasing agents for the Department of Defense.

Can anyone seriously contend that a half-dozen brilliant technicians with a converted garage and a million-dollar defense subcontract to make a new whatsis-diode to GE specifications, is "in competition with" major factors in the missile hardware market, including GE? The statement is meaningless: GE is GE, and the great majority of the enterprising scientists will, after working themselves to death for a few years, be back in the GE laboratories where they came from. The handful of successful scientific entrepreneurs—the ones who hook up with some business savvy before the government money gives out—will end up around retirement age exchanging their six-product operations for some GE paper. And that will be that. Competition? Certainly—like a Baby Parade on the boardwalk at Atlantic City, with benign parents happily controlling the whole show.

Perhaps it strikes you as unfair to discuss competition in terms so close to the Department of Defense's annual $50 billion or so. Then let's take real estate, a superbly disorganized market based on the freest, purest, most perfect competitive-type competition anyone could hope for. Our cities are falling apart in front of our eyes. Everybody who owns urban real estate is making money, some just by breathing regularly since the War, others more actively by renting ratholes to Negroes, Puerto Ricans, displaced farmers and other proper objects of Pure Competition. And there has been a lot of new building—some of it for corporations and the new rich, most of the rest based on government-guaranteed paper and Title One operations. Why, in New York City we probably have whole new luxury apartment buildings inhabited in large part by people who made their money out of the appreciation in value of other less luxurious apartment buildings. But adequate housing for the majority of the people that happen to be around, with the incomes they happen to be receiving—no, this glorious example of free money–competition has not quite managed to bring that about. And it never will. Finally the governments, over pained protests, will do it. But meantime, while the buildings we need are not being built, and to a considerable extent *because* they are not being built, a lot of wealth in the form of paper money will be created. At least we can be glad that a few luxury buildings are going up for the benefit of these new paper-holders. But if we took notice of Things instead of just Paper, we could have buildings for everybody—including better ones for our more competitive citizens.

The Idea of Competition asserts that competitive markets are the exclusive regulators of all practical and moral relations in society. With the result that all conscious human intervention in economic process, all planning, is too little and too late, accepted only as disaster threatens; and once its agonizing birth has been effected, the high priests of paper propriety revoke its birthright by denying or ignoring its existence. The Idea of Competition is one of the most mindless notions ever to dominate the supposed thinking of a society of grown men. It is a religious tenet of faith, because: 1) it requires that the evidence of one's senses be denied; and 2) it forbids non-ritualistic thinking. Since one *chooses* to believe in The Competitive System, the additional element of religiosity, free will, is included in the concoction. It is in essence a theology of militant mindlessness. With this idea as the keystone of The System, it becomes impossible to discuss anything rationally—What are we doing? Why are we doing it? Does it work? What are the alternatives? and so on. Instead of purposeful thought we have primitive magic—the mindless magic of Competition. As if we were committed to the proposition that the thoughtless life is the only life truly worth living.

The issue is not whether at some times and places competition functions as an effective allocative factor. It does, and if you want to be specially happy about it, feel free. But look at it this way. In any fresh, unorganized situation you are going to have unorganized activity—"competition" —until someone is able at last to organize the thing on some rational basis. Most of our great business heroes—Rockefeller, Carnegie, Morgan—were men of capacity who dramatically carried forward this process of organization. They recognized that competition was a dangerous form of internal warfare, of benefit to no one, and exactly the kind of senseless feuding which it has been the role and the justification of the state since time immemorial to suppress. So they suppressed it, and did a very good job of it for that time and place. Of course they were not the state *de jure*, but that was not a matter of much consequence.

For example, around the turn of the century Morgan was engaged in trying to bring some better order into the railroad situation. The railroads had been built, and it was then a question of organizing their paper structures on a more reasonable basis, as a prelude to operational integration. He had a scheme for a holding company designed to bring peace to the industry over a large area—which unfortunately has gone into the history books as the Northern Securities Case, one of Teddy Roosevelt's trust-busting victories. When the case became active, Morgan was quite annoyed at the President, and impatiently said to him: "If we have done anything wrong, send your man to my man and they can fix it up." But TR believed in Competition and never sent his man around, with the consequence perhaps that the railroads never achieved the order of organization of, say, the steel industry, one of Morgan's big successes.

It is no accident that business ideology, based firmly on a theology of militant mindlessness, is also distinguished by being profoundly and even violently anti-intellectual. Sutton *et al* report this as a dominant characteristic of the creed. (In the managerial version, this is clearly an untenable duplicity, since so many of the managers are highly trained intellectuals.) The mixture of fear, hatred and contempt which many businessmen will express toward intellectual experts of various kinds—the same ones they so frequently employ—has many sources. For one thing, the executive suspects they may know something he does not. For another, the business administrator is not very clear about what he himself knows—all of his savvy is of a practical, unsystematic kind. He is very much like a politician in that no one really knows what he does or how he does it, but only that he gets it done. Also there is the horrid memory of the New Deal brain-trust and the hordes of college-bred OPAers and WPBers and so on during the War. (And now, President Kennedy's army of bright boys.) The businessman has become increasingly dependent on his experts—lawyers, accountants, publicists, engineers, management consultants, etc.—so that he spends a great deal of time "managing" the work of people who know a great deal more than he does about their field of competence. Indeed, the expert intellectuals—defined broadly to include anyone whose productive work draws on the capital of education—constitute a new class in our society. (See Chapters 12 and 13 for fuller treatment of this point.)

The "top" or "pure" executive largely symbolizes organizational authority. He is a politician. These executives don't want intellectual experts interfering with their System, and they don't want the government to interfere either. Which is psychologically quite appropriate, since without experts and the government their System wouldn't last out the week. They are *pure* politicians in that they do nothing but operate a power system, and they want nothing but to be left alone to operate it as they see fit, which means in the customary way.

But like the old-line political machines in our urban centers, business power is being undermined. And by essentially the same underlying social forces—the rise of the new class, the emerging revolt of the intellectuals, and the absolute need for the higher order of planning and organization which only this group, using Federal power, can accomplish.

Business has not and will never recover from its 1929 failure to run the society with a minimum of decency and competence. It had all the power it needed, and all the freedom in the world to use it—but the hand was overplayed, and the business system revealed itself once and for all to be incapable of resisting the easy exploitation of the money-credit-price mechanism. One is tempted to say that the financial giants of an earlier day would never have permitted the debâcle; but the truth is probably that the country had become too big and the system of industry too complex to be managed by any control-center wielding less than national governmental power. *Nineteen twenty-nine was the melodramatic end of effective private government in the United States.* It is interesting that the big-city politicians were the first to leave the mortally wounded ship on which they had lived so long and so well, and immediately to begin assisting in the creation of a new national government, this time in Washington, D. C. where many of the Founding Fathers had thought it belonged. And only a quarter-century before it had been confidently proclaimed that "in the course of evolution and a higher civilization we might be able to get along comfortably without Congress, but without Wall Street, never."

Business is bitterly embattled today. The business system is fighting a rear-guard action against the continuing transfer of power from private to governmental hands. That it is a cynical, hopeless, rear-guard action has been revealed by the recently lived-through eight years of "Modern Republicanism." It turns out that business interests are not counter-revolutionaries, but only determined saboteurs of a reasonable adjustment to the change. In pursuance of this petulantly amoral purpose, businessmen have introduced fresh qualities of dishonesty and deception into our national life which are destructive in the extreme, and far beneath their level and ours. It seems that they insist on being dragged—clawing, scratching, screaming each inch of the way—into the new world of rationally organized abundance. This is high historical stupidity, as many of them are beginning to recognize, since they have every opportunity to preside over an orderly and perhaps only partial liquidation of private government just by moving from New York to Washington and handing power to themselves. But in their largest numbers they lack the foresight and the courage, the deeper willingness to live with history, that such a reasonable maneuver calls for. Instead, they concentrate on their absurd rear-guard action, which will certainly ruin them and may very well ruin the nation.

An unprincipled rear-guard action. And as the business ideologists slap on the violent reds and awful blacks in the picture of government they are painting, one becomes uneasy with the suspicion that they are talking themselves into something, perhaps even threatening us with their overheated imaginings. Certainly one of the least hopeful signs for the future is that business organizations are now so authoritarian in structure, so much more so than many other bureaucracies in our society. At the very least one gets distorted training in them for a future based on an adequately organized society of liberal intention. Note these candid words of General Robert E. Wood, former chairman of the board of Sears, Roebuck:

We complain about government in business, we stress the advantages of the free enterprise system, we complain about the totalitarian state, but in our individual organizations, in our striving for efficiency we have created more or less of a totalitarian system in industry, particularly in large industry.

David Riesman has said: "We have been trained for a world of scarcity and we have developed an image of man under the psychology of scarcity." Our ruling business groups are extremely reluctant to modify the training or abandon the image. If they continue this reluctance (and let us keep in mind the authoritarian organizations on which their power is based), it is distinctly possible that in the approaching crisis, when their stop-gap notion of limited government will have to be abandoned and serious planning undertaken, they will just naturally apply "business principles" indiscriminately in derogation of democratic processes. Especially if they at all credit the nightmares of Big Government which they have been peddling to us these many years. We can only hope that they are coolheaded, outright liars, these Rear-guarders in defense of incompetent private government. The alternative is decidedly frightening.

The government has underwritten the entire functioning of the economy. That is what the New Deal meant, that is all it meant, and that meaning stands under Modern Republicanism. The traditional underwriters—investment and commercial bankers, utilizing the central banking authority of the Federal Reserve System, and allied with corporate power in key industries—were unequal to the task. They were not able to fulfill their obligations. So a new underwriter was called in: date, 1933. The terms of the new underwriting contract were stated generally, the details being left to future needs and contingencies, and "arrangements" with the former underwriters—as in any major bankruptcy. It is these details of the contract, of our new unwritten constitution, that make up the issues of our political life. But the remnants of private government are not negotiating in good faith with us, their creditors, nor are they acting reasonably with regard to the future of the common enterprise.

American businessmen, the legitimate heirs of Rockefeller, Carnegie and Morgan—they ought to be ashamed of themselves! The old men would never have behaved so irresponsibly.

Why don't they send their men around to our men, and let them fix it up?

THE
PAPER

3

WHAT IS PROPERTY?

UNDER OUR REGULAR IDEOLOGY, property is even more sacred than Competition, if that is possible. It takes two to compete, but the most beautiful form of property is *private*. We so revere Private Property that we no longer bother to revise our ideas concerning it. As a conglomeration of existential facts, property changes daily—but our received ideas about Private Property have not noticeably altered in the past few hundred years.

A good way to get started correcting this oversight is to apply the ancient Greek issue of appearance-and-reality to the concept of property, as follows: the reality of property would be a house, a car, a washing machine, the morning toast, the material part of New York City, the actual installations of the iron and steel industry, or the 2,974,726 square miles of land comprising the continental United States—in other words, *Things*, the whole complicated productive machine, all the identifiable matter that has been or may be appropriated to the process of production. Reading "appearance" to mean representation or symbol, the appearance of property would be the deed to the house and the mortgage, the bill of sale or conditional sales contract on the car or washing machine, the fact that the toast is on *your* table, the stock certificate representing shares in U.S. Steel, or the Charter of the City of New York which says you have the right to vote in municipal elections if you live there—in other words, *Rights*, entitlements in and with regard to Things: all the symbols, all the *paper* in our Paper Economy. (Including the sales-slip you received from the grocer when you bought the bread, or the paper money you used to buy it.)

Generally speaking, we refuse to distinguish between symbol and thing in regard to property, and have consequently not even allowed an appropriate language to develop which might facilitate our discourse. (But we have managed to stabilize our confusion on a high level of profundity.) So "property" is indiscriminately both Things and Rights, paper symbols are as real as the things they stand for, the capitalized future takes precedence over the here and now, and paper profit engages our affections much more than the actual production of goods. It is almost as if we really don't care about the important differences between appearance and reality when it comes to economic activities. We *like* the confusion, apparently—it makes our "reality" both less real and more important: a newest model car, for instance, is never just a means of transportation, but *is* how much it costs in paper money, just as it *is* what we read and hear about it in our symbol-sustaining mass culture. All of which softens the actual automobile's dangerous, expensive qualities, its harsher reality, by adding imagined meanings which the-thing-itself does not have and would not in itself evoke. But a central consequence of all this is that we end up with symbolic lives—and the symbol-system which conveniently leads our lives for us is over-tightly organized around the one perfect paper symbol: Money.

The ordinary idea of property implies a mental reference to Things. A man's property is what he owns—and he looks about him and sees a house, some furniture, clothes in the closet, a car in the garage, and his mother's amber beads. *His* property. But wait a minute: there's an insurance policy, some cash in his pocket, a bank account, and maybe even ten shares of AT&T. That's property, too. But of a very different kind. He doesn't "own" AT&T but only ten out of many millions of shares—which *share* only after some billions of dollars of debt—and in fact his ten shares have to be carefully punched out on an IBM card not to be lost sight of entirely. The stock certificate, the deposit, the policy, the cash—they're all paper. He just owns the paper —he doesn't own AT&T, the insurance company, the bank, or the Federal Reserve System. So his property consists of some things and some paper. But wait a minute again: he lives in the house, everybody on the block will tell you it's his house, but as a matter of fact the Nickel Savings Bank of Lower Sandusky has a greater right to the house than he has —it's worth $15,000 and his equity comes to only five as against the bank's mortgage of ten. Likewise the car, and some of the mechanical trinkets in the house. (Maybe even the clothes on his back.)

So where does that leave us with the idea of property? Well, the truth is that if you are talking about things, you hardly need the idea of property at all—until somebody tries to take some of it away from you. Property is not the thing, it is rights in and to the thing. Consequently, the ordinary notion of property, with its quick mental reference to things, is almost exactly wrong.

Perhaps if I am going to talk like a lawyer, I ought to backtrack and explain how lawyers learn to talk that way.

One professor said, "As a thing apart property is only an academic norm." That may be true for academic economics, but not for the practicing lawyer and the as-practiced law. For him and it, property is the root idea of law under capitalism—it is just about all that he has to work with. Now when a lawyer talks about property he may use many different words and phrases. He will, for example, use the word "rights" or "obligations" (which are rights looked at from the other side) instead of property rights; he will speak of "contract rights," or perhaps just "claims." A favorite phrase is that someone owns or has "an interest in" something. He will say, "That's actionable," meaning that a situation contains a claim on which a lawyer can go to court. Many words and phrases, but they all add up to the same thing: a right, ultimately measurable in pecuniary terms, which a lawyer can imagine some court sustaining or enforcing. They all add up to Property. And none of them are Things. They are rights and interests and claims in and to things—including, incidentally, people. Most frequently, property ends up being a right to force someone to act or refrain from acting in a certain way toward a certain thing, or to pay for the privilege of refusal—pay in that biggest form of property, *money*, the great common denominator.

In a modern law school, some of the best all-round fun is had in arriving at a definition of property. The faculty considers it a first essential for the development of legal technique to tease the apprentice lawyers out of their ordinary received notions.

First off, the basic image of property—land and things—is pooh-poohed; then the search for a definition is carried through contract rights, choses in action (unrealized rights, including claims in court), and other intangibles. The class then thinks it has the answer: property is rights—called property rights or, in the short form, property. This is the point at which the modern professor enjoys himself most, and to confound the class completely he pulls out a case in which a property right is recognized and enforced by a court for the first time—a good one is the early radio broadcasting case in which a court first held that the right to broadcast a description of a baseball game "belonged" to the baseball club, could be disposed of by it, and could not be pirated by a party lacking contractual privilege from the "owner." Then the *coup de grâce:* did the court enforce the club owner's right because it was a property right, or was it a property right because the court enforced it? The silence thunders, a rainbow of a smile settles on the professor's face, and the pot of gold is indicated: property is a right of use or disposition which will be enforced by a court. On that day we are men; and the legal elite is then prepared to go out, tautology in hand, and grow rich creating and defending such rights.

But a whisper of doubt remains as older tautologies assert themselves: land is land, to own is to own, and all property, like land, is supposed to be owned. Yes, but less frequently nowadays by any one person. Take land, for example: the bank holds a first mortgage on the suburban home, the contractor has a materialman's lien, various governmental authorities hold tax liens, the niece of the guy who sold it to you is suing you because her uncle didn't have the right to convey it, and you hocked your equity in order to post bond for your brother-in-law. Who owns the house? Why everybody who has an enforceable right to its use or disposition; and all the possible rights in and to the home, the whole bundle, add up to *the* ownership of it. In our crowded, mobile society there has occurred a very extensive fragmentation of property ownership. This is a crucial characterizing circumstance in our society, and we shall return to it. Not only workers but capital as well has become profoundly alienated—the first from the product of their labor, and both from *the owned thing*, the tools.

The venerable Blackstone remarked in his handbook (which educated generations of lawyers): "There is nothing which so generally strikes the imagination, and engages the affections of mankind, as the right of property. . . ." He hardly had to remind the profession of this, since lawyers have always served as the *maîtres de chambre* in the eternal love affair between men and things. Indeed, in the service of the client's passion they have created fabulously intricate and elaborate objects of desire, that is, forms of property. There are wonderful examples of this in that period of history when the ingenuity of lawyers was called upon to adapt feudal forms of property tenure to the uses and purposes of the emergent bourgeoisie. The lawyers perhaps even more than the political representatives of the rising merchant class (many of whom were also lawyers) played midwife to the birthing of the modern world. The politicians served as ambassadors of the new class, but the lawyers were the true heads of state. And I rather think they were the type of practitioners old J. P. Morgan was looking for when he said, "I don't know as I want a lawyer to tell me what I cannot do. I hire him to tell me how to do what I want to do."

The formal structure of American society is more or less the product of the legal mind. Both Edmund Burke and Alexis de Tocqueville commented on the major role of lawyers in the early years of the Republic. Lawyers have in fact been the dominant professional element in our state legislatures and in Congress throughout our history. But their greatest achievement in fashioning American society has been the invention of the corporate system—which is considerably more important to our way of life than that eighteenth-century rationalist document, the Constitution. Indeed, the American legal profession managed for some crucial decades to make of the Constitution a kind of carte blanche endorsement for the corporate system they were then engaged in building.

This was accomplished under "the contract clause"— which brings us back from the subject of the creators and caretakers of the property system to the idea of property itself. Because the generic form of property is a contract, an agreement, a promise. I won't bother going into the textbook definition of a contract—let it suffice that contracts are made up of mutual promises, with the added proviso that in law a man may "promise" by his course of conduct, without opening his mouth and uttering that ringing law-school phrase, which still raises the hair on my neck, "I accept!"

The right to enter into contracts "freely" is the substance of the free market concept—the latter being the place, or the habitual pattern by which contracts of purchase and sale are supposed to be entered into freely. Economists have always been blinded by the glamour of the equilibrium of the free market; but when you look at the same phenomena from the point of view of freedom of contract, the lawyer's point of view, you are much more apt to see this freedom for the lopsided license to steal that in large part it was. This point is substantiated by the fact that freedom of contract rather than the free market was the first grand bastion of defense to be raised by business and then to fall in the course of the popular onslaught against unbridled capitalist plunder in the nineteenth century. Freedom of contract justified almost any predatory practice; the free market serves mostly to justify unfettered pricing power. The main reason that freedom of contract has never been as free as advertised—and it is a painfully obvious reason—is that sellers and buyers are not equal in bargaining power. So the terms of sale will simply reflect the power, or lack of it, that each party brings to the market place. So a market is also a financial slaughterhouse, where the strong chop up the weak.

The right of the dominant seller or buyer to his dominance in the market place is enforced by the state. Indeed, this is one of the chief functions of the state under capitalism. This big fact has been obscured in a big way by the historical circumstance that the bourgeois state supplanted autocratic monarchies, and in this struggle the bourgeoisie developed a non-state or anti-state, almost anarchistic, ideology. For the early bourgeois ideologists, final governmental power was always something the other fellow had. So their ideology had not much positive place, theoretically, for the role of the state. But when control of the state had been achieved, and the "other fellow" was nowhere to be found, the new ruling class did not pursue its own anarchistic principles (to say the least). It used the state power it had finally inherited—and used it not just negatively, although negative use too can be as much of an effective power-play as any other: "A system of property is an abridgement of the liberties of the persons excluded." If the state does nothing but enforce the exclusion, it has wielded its power mightily.

But the state in the service of private property did much more. It created the whole system which was based on the effective power of the state because the state recognized, defended and enforced the millions of "interests in" which made up the system. Adam Smith was quite candid about the matter: "Till there be property there can be no government, the very end of which is to secure wealth, and to defend the rich from the poor." Or Jeremy Bentham, much to the same effect: "Property and law are born together and must die together. Before the laws there was no property; take away the laws, all property ceases." It is a shameful bit of sophistry to argue, as is still done today, that there is a choice between private property *or* the state. It is not a "little" government that ensures that property interests, and primarily property interests, shall rule men's lives. It was necessary that the middle classes create the modern nation state as a condition of their private property system. (Morris R. Cohen: "Modern property exists only in the modern state.")

In the beginning there *was* a theory of private property which appeared in some degree to bypass the power of the state. That was the natural rights theory, most closely identified with the name of John Locke. At the end of the seventeenth century, just after the Glorious Revolution, he gave the ascendant bourgeoisie the ideological package for which they had apparently been waiting. Relying on the "property" in one's own person and labor power in a state of nature (not at all a new idea), he found a *natural* right to property which it was the duty of the state to recognize, protect, leave alone, interfere for, and so on. He said, ". . . labour, in the beginning, gave a right to property." The fact that he was talking about an imagined early state of nature, and that he recognized that property in society had to be based on convention and law, was conveniently forgotten. The property-based merchants had what they wanted—a justification of their possessions and their activities, derived from nature rather than the state. People have always described what they want as a natural right when they are struggling against the established order to get it. But also the established order itself is tempted to derive its rights and prerogatives from nature (usually at the height of its self-confidence, as when old John D. Rockefeller said God had given him his money). So for a while they had it both ways.

But all this turned out to be an untenable burst of enthusiasm by a newly victorious class. It could not last much longer than that eighteenth-century hiatus when the property owner also worked in the counting-house or was a kind of foreman in the factory. Because the right to property was tied, by the theory, to the right to the fruit of one's own labor. That served the merchant (soon to evolve into a capitalist) and the craftsman (soon to become a factory-owner and industrialist) well enough in his battle against feudal prescriptions; but it quickly became clear that the idea that the laborer had a right to the product of his labor could become a severe embarrassment to the propertied classes. So the whole bundle of natural rights theory was dropped by the powers-that-were at about the same time that it was picked up by the more radical-minded members of society.

In the nineteenth century, it was Marx who used the labor theory in his radical attack on private property. The capitalists who bothered to justify what they were doing came more and more to rely on Bentham's utilitarianism: "Rights are . . . the fruits of law, and of the law alone. There are no rights without law—no rights contrary to law—no rights anterior to law." The property system was justified because it fostered the accumulation of capital, on which progress depended, and therefore worked out to the greatest good for the greatest number. "Free enterprise" in America still claims this beneficence for itself. But today the more important argument is that something called Private Property has been once and for all welded, by pro-property steam-fitters, to something called Liberty. (We shall see about that, in Chapter 15 and 16, for instance.)

The title of this chapter is taken from a famous book of the last century by Pierre Proudhon. His answer to the question was: property is theft. Now there is no doubt that, historically, a great deal of it has been. But this statement is mostly moral, and fails to get one very far along the road of understanding. R. H. Tawney's comment on this thesis (he too was a strongly moral writer) is very neat: "Property is not theft, but a good deal of theft becomes property." Under a commercial system, probably the greatest source of property accumulation is what the economists call "profit." But

not all of them are quite sure what that is. Professor Frank
H. Knight has written: "In the idealized society of equilibrium theory, there would be no occasion for assigning the
distinctive name of profit to any type of return." That is,
everything would be either interest, rent, or wages, including the capitalist's wages of superintendence. Professor
Knight is very revealing on this subject, and quite relevant
to Proudhon's proposition, when he says that "all income
represents a mixture of a more or less accurate evaluation of
services in the broad sense with force and fraud. Since
violence and fraud belong to the sphere of criminology,
economic analysis of profit must center around" the evaluation of services. Which is quite a statement, when you stop
to think about it.

So on one far side, property is theft; and closer to
home, it is not a proper subject of study for economists.
Perhaps the most telling achievement of the established order
of thinkers has been this obscurantist isolation of the so-
called subject of economics from the rest of life as we
recognizably live it. In line with isolating the subject by
tearing it out of context, it has also been necessary to isolate
the occasional brilliant minds who have approached the
matter from a more robust point of view, particularly Marx
and Veblen. But this is too large a subject: meanwhile, a
main point of this essay is to assist in de-neutralizing the
subject of economics so as to afford means for seeing it
again as the essentially *political* activity that it always has
been, and still is.

*In economics, everything other than the purely techno-
logical is mostly a matter of social politics. No item of the
received economic ideology should be allowed in any way to
inhibit democratic political activity directed toward the use
and disposition of our magnificent productive system.*

And a big key to unlock the *papier-mâché* doors behind which our political and productive energies have been imprisoned is the idea of property—as used every day by the few thousand key managers who run the system with the ever-helping guidance of their intellectual valets, the lawyers. The principle to be employed is this: we will notice more particularly what the managers do—how they go about making a "profit" and creating property—rather than being overly impressed with what they say they are doing. Tawney, writing forty years ago, was a bit melodramatic when he underlined the fact that the owners were not speaking publicly in candid accents, by saying "the lords of the jungle do not hunt by daylight." It's not reasonable to expect that they would. But today things are not nearly so mysterious; and even though we never get full reports of the crucial discussions at the Duquesne Club, we see the results readily enough in the various maneuvers of the steel industry. The prior Duquesne staff conference would make fascinating material for a novel, but we can put together a pretty fair picture of the American property system and its managers without any such tidbits. All we really need are the daily intellectual tools of the lawyers, who run the show in a structural way.

But a warning: many economists who are not lawyers, and most lawyers who are not especially conscious of what they are doing, see the world of production and things as controlled by the encompassing universe of money and credit—the independent concept of property may be lost somewhere in between. This is unfortunate, because the truth is that money-and-credit are simply the most generalized and so most obvious form of property. It is the *whole* property system, not the money-and-credit system alone, that decisively represents our society's attempt to control and rationalize the real world of things and the people, *pari passu* thingified, who live in it. It is in the property idea that law and economics meet, and from this meeting emerges the critical context for the perception of social organization. And beyond that, an approach to the ultimate social problem, the mystical one, *the problem of power*—the capacity of one man to direct the existence of another.

We needn't be embarrassed by plunging ahead without a nomination to the Duquesne Club or the blessings of academic economics. The first is not obtainable, and the second is not necessary—since the economists tend to disagree among themselves rather excessively, despite the new sainthood that all have assigned to the late Lord Keynes.

A nice bas-relief of this disagreement is contained in the responses to a questionnaire which the Subcommittee on Economic Stabilization of the Joint Economic Committee of Congress sent out in 1958 to 1500 economists in 150 universities in all the states and the District of Columbia as well. Most of them, apparently, were too busy patching up holes in their theoretical models to be able to respond at all. Of the 40 per cent who found time to answer the dozen or two multiple-choice questions, the highest order of unanimity—85 per cent—was achieved on the proposition that "the Federal Reserve authorities . . . should follow a flexible policy" in open-market operations rather than continuing the discredited "bills-only" policy (that is, trade in long-term as well as short-term Federal paper in controlling the money supply). It has since happened.

More typically, they split 50 pro and 40 con (with no-responders on the order of 10 per cent) on whether wage increases beyond productivity increases have boosted prices in recent years. Sixty per cent, regular fellows all, believed it was "feasible to achieve simultaneously both relatively high employment and relatively high stability of the general price level in the short run," but 25 per cent, all young Turks, held this to be impossible even in the long run. Surprisingly, 67 per cent favored standby authority for direct rather than monetary controls; but most of them were thinking of controls over the amount of consumer credit—this is a favorite daring-conventional opinion, since the Reserve had this power for a while after the War and, contrary to expectation, Truman did not become Emperor. (The same standard three-fifths or so felt that the need for such direct controls would be lessened by Vigorous Antitrust; but of course everyone knows that Vigorous Antitrust, like Hadacol, can cure anything.) Finally, forty-nine old folks were still looking for the ultimate restoration of free domestic exchange of dollars for gold. I can just hear them muttering in quivering tones that *they* certainly would never put Keynes on the same shelf with Marshall or any other *real* economist!

It must be noted that conventional economic theory, in its broad phase, is frighteningly irrelevant today. It doesn't even handle its old job of justifying vested power—the corporate managers stand forth ideologically naked, and whatever wispy covering they are able to clutch around them has been supplied by public relations men, rather than serious-minded academics. In the massive corporate economy, the old market equilibrium theories are thoroughly bankrupt, whether or not supplemented by Keynes' money-manipulation notions. (Keynes' theories, as applied, are not adequate for a full production economy: he was an exceptionally clever and completely English dialectician who modified received theory no more than necessary for his purpose at the time. He did *not* revise economics in the light of corporate market power; he accepted existing theoretical baggage and then merely outlined a role for the government to save the whole works—in special circumstances—by monetary and fiscal maneuvering. And he buried the Gold Standard, that shining relic of pre-1914 confidence in the rightness of all things.) This market theory—which at best offers a passable description of certain aspects of the eighteenth and nineteenth centuries—is, along with Keynes' techniques for keeping a depression from downright destroying us, the basis of fateful governmental policy. It gives one pause.

To corroborate, let me call upon Dr. Gardiner C. Means. As co-author with Adolf A. Berle, Jr. of *The Modern Corporation and Private Property*, he helped initiate the discussion of corporatism. Dr. Means also carried out the basic statistical study of the inflexibility of prices in areas of the economy dominated by major corporations, thereby providing the factual basis and the name for the very widely discussed issue of "administered prices"—currently one of the liveliest flies in the unctuous ointment of standard theory. So I call to the stand a highly qualified (if controversial) expert witness.

He says the whole thing needs re-doing—"a major part of our economic theory is built on an obsolete base, and another part has been disproved by events." The main thrust of his criticism is that the conceptual models of the economy are derived from past societies—whether Adam Smith's atomistic trading society made up of individual producers, or the nineteenth-century factory system based on "free" wage labor. But there is no adequate model of an economy such as our present one in which the essential major production "is carried on by great corporate units." He christens this new model-to-be as follows:

> With the separation of ownership and control comes the possibility of great aggregations of productive activity. We now have single corporate enterprises employing hundreds of thousands of workers, having hundreds of thousands of stockholders, using billions of dollars' worth of the instruments of production, serving millions of customers, and controlled by a single management group. These are great collectives of enterprise, and a system composed of or dominated by them might well be called "collective capitalism."

In such a model, the bureaucratic decisions of the managers, rather than the supposedly automatic operation of a market mechanism, are at the guiding heart of the matter. Not only are prices administered under this kind of system, but also wages, the allocation of resources, and the creation and maintenance of markets. So the tail now wags the dog, and we need a new theory to account for this—"in which the unseen hand of Adam Smith will be replaced by the visible hand of business bureaucracy."

"Ownership"—the very word has a warm, embraceable feel about it. *Mine, all mine!* As if by utterly appropriating a little piece of the "things" of the world we give ourselves a pinpoint of reality on which to build a fantasy of relation with the whole universe. Ownership—the identity in depth between self and thing. Such a pure and wonderfully childlike emotion—the way the whole unknown world must have felt in late infancy when the growth of ego, that technique for acknowledging the distinction be-

tween the individual and the rest of the world, was more of a threat than an accomplished fact. Mine, all mine—oh, the grand coziness of it! No wonder we so believe in property, especially when it's "private."

Of course it is not very rewarding to throw your arms around ten shares of AT&T, or cuddle up for an evening's bliss with the cash-value of a life insurance policy. So we don't "act out" these fantasies any longer; but they are just as real as ever in the inner temple of our affections. Especially in the United States. As Adolf Berle has remarked, we are "the most violently private-property-minded country in the world." Which brings the whole subject to a kind of ironic perfection, since typically in this country we do not own the more important things around us, and just as typically what we do own is not nearby or even a thing.

In 1898 Veblen published an article in the *American Journal of Sociology* called "The Beginnings of Ownership." It is one of the more enjoyable aspects of Veblen's writing that one is often not quite sure whether or how much he is kidding. I am still not certain about this article. He starts out by referring to the notion we have already encountered, which he notes is held by capitalists and socialists alike, namely, that "the legitimate basis of property" is the "productive labor of the owner." Then he says:

> This natural-rights theory of property makes the creative effort of an isolated, self-sufficing individual the basis of the ownership vested in him. In so doing it overlooks the fact that there is no isolated, self-sufficing individual.

Which leaves a problem—what are the origins of ownership?

Veblen then refers to the fact that private property

must have grown out of early communal society, which does not itself give evidence of this institution. He suggests and then rejects the idea that it might be derived from the savages' "quasi-personal fringe," that is, nail-parings, clothes, likenesses, etc. Things of daily use nearby are an extension of personality, not alienable "property." But savages invade the personalities of members of other tribes, and come away with scalps or whole heads, and also objects we would call property. So the beginnings are based on "exploit, coercion and seizure," and the first form of ownership is "tenure by prowess"—predatory acts and then war plunder. But all this is still seen by the savage as appropriations of the person, not the products or properties of the person. You might say it's a way of insulting people, not of exploiting them. True property—the right in one person of the fruit of another's labor—he finds in one particular item of primitive war-plunder, women. Captured women, and the resulting "ownership-marriage," are the earliest source of the ownership of private property. First you own the person, and then you just naturally own what that person produces. (Certainly the largest amount of property in the infancy of our species was other animals, including people.) Today, the existence of paper money and so on makes it possible "to own" in this sense without being burdened with specific title either to people or their particular products.

Besides women and men, almost everything imaginable has been subject to ownership and held in sacred possession. Tawney says: "In the past, human beings, roads, bridges and ferries, civil, judicial and clerical offices, and commissions in the army have all been private property." (It has even been said that the purpose of clerical celibacy was to

keep intact the property of the church.) Indeed, so much of
the paraphernalia of social living have been thus denominated at one time or another in our long travels that he
calls property "the most ambiguous of categories." Perhaps.
But nonetheless important. For instance, the author of the
article on "Property" in the Encyclopedia of the Social Sciences, referring to the role of the Supreme Court prior to
1937 in its outrageous interpretation of the due process
clause of the Constitution, says quite acutely: "It is incorrect
to say that the judiciary protected property; rather they
called that property to which they accorded protection."
That's a good definition, and that's the way sensible lawyers
see the concept. Property is never for long anything more
or, really, anything different from what some politically appointed court says it is.

With a *caveat:* lawyers always think of what may happen if the issue goes to court, even if the question is whether
the president of the corporation can take a week in Palm
Springs during a crisis; but the better they do their work,
the less chance there will be of wasting any valuable time
in a courtroom, with all that mess of "figuring" a particular
judge and pasting together sophistical briefs. One of the
nicest examples of work-in-avoidance of courtroom messi-
ness is the history of convertible instruments. These are
debt that contain an option to be converted into stock, or
stock of one kind that can be changed into some other
security, and they have been very important in the history
of corporate finance. A convertible security is a hedge—
better protection if the earnings go down or go smash, and a
ride along up with the equity if the business booms. So they
were important in the early days, and also as a promotional
device in the boom market of the fifties. Now undoubtedly
billions of dollars of convertible securities have been peddled

in the course of the three-quarters of a century or so of fancy finance, but there are precious few court decisions interpreting the "law" of these valuable forms of property. Because the legal (and I suppose also the practical) work was done so well, the issue never got to court or went to decision at all often. That's *private* property.

But not the kind of Private Property that Thomas Jefferson, we are so frequently reminded, was thinking of a century and a half ago. I don't quite understand all the holiness currently connected with Jefferson's ideas about private ownership and its intimate kinship with individual security and liberty as against the state. He was talking about farmers. Today, farmers are the sickest, most feckless business element in the whole economy. It costs billions a year just to keep the whole enterprise from going under: American farming has been much too successful in production, and as a consequence has been socially bankrupt for decades. It lives on handouts. Is *this* the ideal image of men solidly plunked down on the glorious institution of Private Property? They wouldn't even be much of a political force if it were not for the political atavism which enforces a nineteenth-century distribution of power based on a nineteenth-century farm population which has long since moved to the city. And even so, it was Jefferson who, in choosing the words for the Declaration of Independence, decided to Americanize the European slogan of "life, liberty, and property" by having it read, "life, liberty, and *the pursuit of happiness*." And you know, as I understand America, he may have been right after all.

In comprehending the demise of the private-property system, it is helpful to remember to think of property as being of two kinds—"thing-property" and "rights-property." The former would be the plants, machines, railroads, buildings, etc., most of which are organized in great corporate units. The latter would be pieces of paper, like stock certificates and bonds, representing certain direct entitlements relating to such property. Now we have to complicate the picture a little by indicating a third, hybrid form of property—liquid capital organized in huge blocks, mediating between corporate thing-property and personal rights-property. A clear example would be the $20 billion–plus in mutual funds. The point here is that a mutual fund would be capable of exercising ownership control over thing-property, but no one could exercise ownership control over a big mutual fund. The same would hold true of many banks, insurance companies, and pension trusts.

Now, as a consequence primarily of the raw fact that corporations and big-money funds get bigger and bigger, there is observable an increasing fragmentation of rights-property and an increasing accumulation and concentration of thing-property (and hybrid-property). Rights-property remains private, but it is just paper—somewhat like money, except that it earns and more radically changes in value. Most thing-property is not private, because it is not owned by private persons and, as we shall see, it does not exist, in the last analysis, for private purposes.

But we still favor a Robinson-Crusoe view of property, although in a material way it has been some time since this continent could be conceived as anything like a desert island. This primitive sentiment is exactly wrong in that it assumes property to be things, and it assumes that ownership is always accompanied by control. We own paper, but the only things we control are consumables. The world of productive things is largely not owned at all—it is merely

controlled and administered by its controllers and administrators, its managers.

To continue in our circumstance to speak of private
property as meaningful and even fundamental, much less
as the *only* basis of our liberties, is clearly an intellectual
scandal. Most of us are job-holders, paper-holders, and consumers—we control nothing by property-ownership. And
our present powerlessness is based on and daily reinforced
by the idea that we do. As a consequence, we are trying
quite unsuccessfully to deal with a runaway technology
within the framework of an archaic business-profit system.
The result, we will see, is under-used and misused plant
capacity, a circumstance covered over—just barely—by a
puerile public relations culture which is almost impossible
to bear, even by its beneficiaries. And lost opportunities piled
one upon the other into an infinity of disgust.

Business and money are based on a fantasy. No active
people has ever taken as seriously as we have the childish
idea that each individual can be self-concerned to the final
degree, and that such devoutly pursued indulgence will end
up creating the best of all possible worlds. It is the present
system of paper that enthrones this presumption. And the
children among us, including many Leading Citizens, really
believe it. We have created our image of society on this
basis; and we seem fully prepared to continue to mess things
up in order to demonstrate just how firmly and faithfully we
subscribe to it. This childish know-nothing egoism is the
Rock of Unreality on which our world stands.

We have sown a dream, and are reaping a whirlwind of
paper.

4

MONEY/CREDIT
AND
OTHER MAGIC

MONEY IS A DREAM. It is a piece of paper on which is imprinted in invisible ink the dream of all the things it will buy, all the trinkets and all the power over others. A kind of institutionalized dream which, along with its companion dream-institution of Success, constitutes the main fantasy on which our way of life has been built.

Most of us who are not outright losers in the Great American Scramble love money much more than any of the things it will buy. It is not a means to an end for us, it is a passion. And I rather think that the main significance of the incidental fact that money can be exchanged for things—that this act of spiritual betrayal is ubiquitously possible—is that it obscures the dreamer's madness from himself. He likes to feel that because he can stop dreaming on any street-corner by buying something, he is not really dreaming at all, not really as mad as in his soul he knows himself to be. As a matter of fact, all of us, when we are uneasy and nervous, go out and buy something in a pathetic effort to get next to reality again. Especially women, who are the keepers of the flame—technical managers of the Dream. Its latent content, as Freud would have put it, is of course all of the forbidden desires to do and become which are lost in the onrush of eternal postponement which our way of life demands. We are a nation of dreamers, and it is adventitious or even treasonous whenever we do or become anything that is not a certified image in the national dream. We should never be anything, according to our scripture, but absolute potential.

The greatest sign of national vitality or health to which anyone can point in the United States today is the childlike pleasure with which millions of dreamers are awakening and acquiring things as if that act were a new discovery revealed to the natives by Columbus returned. The new consumer is so completely taken with the available hardware that he actually prefers to acquire it the most expensive way, by debt rather than cash, as Whyte pointed out in his loving portrait of suburbia. (Installment buying also and absurdly affords the delicious feeling that you are getting something without paying for it, which of course enhances the beauty and perhaps even the frigidity of a new refrigerator. Anyway, the two acts of paying out money and acquiring things are beginning to separate.) This amounts to a revolutionary abandonment of the dream. A whole new class of avid Americans prefers things to paper, and all the strenuous effort of the New York Stock

Exchange to create a fresh status symbol out of the direct ownership of a few shares of stock will not stem the tide. We are faced with a national hunger to reclaim the real world of things. The old money-dream is dying. We are passing through a purgatory (or, if you prefer, a child's garden) of fantastically shaped automobiles and ineluctable electric can-openers, and what our new dream will be no one knows. But at least, before we begin again, we will have touched down for a time and even have lived a little in existential reality.

Meanwhile, the high priests and other devoted functionaries of the old dream have not become willing apostates. For them, money remains the Reality of Realities—the transcendent dream of God's favor, and Heavenly justice besides. Since they still run things to a considerable extent, and can hardly be dismissed as idle dreamers (backward certainly, but not idle), we are obliged to put them on the couch and interpret the dream.

The main point is this: the money that figures so prominently in the dream of money is not money for spending. You don't ever buy anything with it. It's for earning more money. And after you really get moving, you don't even buy anything with the money you earned on the money you used to earn it, and so on.

At this point, if you don't have any more money than I do, you may be tempted to think that this chapter is being written for somebody other than yourself. But no, it isn't. Because everybody knows that money is important, and I want to talk now about What Money Really Is—about the moneyman's money, not that mere spending stuff. So let's put to one side for a moment our healthy impulse to define ten dollars as a six-hour pass to get away from the television set, and think about un-spending money, the big money, the real money, the money that runs things. (But just remember that in a society founded on the quaint notion that money will buy Anything, and anything money won't buy is hardly worth bothering with, the scope of the under- lying dream is enormous—as is also the difficulty of ex- plaining it to the dreamer. *Or* his national bedfellows, for that matter.)

To make things very simple, let's make believe there are three kinds of money corresponding to three uses. Money One is the paper you have to have to walk into a drugstore and get a carton of cigarettes, or to buy the tobacco and pay the staff that makes the cigarettes. Money Two is the paper required to build another factory because so many misguided teenagers are developing the filthy habit, or because the cancer scare has scared the manu- facturer so much that he is diversifying into ethical drugs. Ah, but Money Three! That's *real* money. It will never buy anything except more money or more profitable money. It feeds on itself in a narcissistic ecstasy; sometimes it eats itself up in the wink of an eye (as when the market drops); more often it appears as if from nowhere and then seems vital and virtuous (when the market goes up again); and it disdains to be spent—the vulgar re-entry—as the plague. It exists only because of spending, but it is not itself spent; it is a charge on all spending by others, whether for ciga- rettes or cigarette factories or factories that substitute for cigarette factories. It is pure paper: the dream of dreams.

Money Three insists on its return whatever else hap- pens, and it doesn't care where the return comes from, just so it comes. In the usual course, it is not recognizably dis- tinct from the other kinds of money, especially Money Two, investment money. It usually makes up a part of investment funds. It accompanies genuine investment like a pilot fish, and it is in all instances an added charge on the right to invest, as it is on the right to produce, as it is on the right to consume. You might say, it is the tollbooth on the superhighways of our Paper Economy. Money Three is that final, decisive part of money or the price of money that never gets spent and never gets invested in anything real or productive.* In our day it is particularly made up of old paper—inflated capitalization and debt—which in the natural course of things would have been washed out in bankruptcy or panic, or some other deflation, except we don't believe in or practice deflation-of-consequence any longer. (Or it is paper that has been well-protected.) It is, in effect, the clammy hand of history on our shoulder. The history of all our paper excesses. The greatest surviving form of ancestor worship in the world today. And I would guess that millions more of it are being created hour by hour, day in and day out.

But what is the generic thing itself—what is money? Well, it is not just a dream. It is also not wealth, which exists in reality and is not merely a symbol. (Of course the particular *value* of a piece of wealth is necessarily bound up with one form of symbolism or another, and not all of these symbols are rational or operational. But wealth is still things of value to human beings, and it is very important to remain clear that it is *things*, even though you may have to delve deeply in the irrational souls of men—as well as noting the character of their rational technology—in order to understand the *value* of the things that make up their

* Under usual theory, no large distinction is made between "savings," from whatever source, which are used to buy existing paper or to buy new plants—both are indiscriminately "investment." But some people are impressed with the difference.

wealth.) The paper in the world of paper we live in is supposed to order the creation and use of our wealth, but it is not itself wealth. This is an essential point, and is probably the most difficult idea to come to terms with in the whole discussion of property, money/credit and the Paper Economy. We are talking about a social and political system based on law, and the habits of human beings in society who by choice or otherwise more or less live up to this law. It is difficult to comprehend because it seems contrary to all our training, but money—and all the paper—is profoundly irrelevant to existence. To pick an analogy out of the air, the paper bears a relation to reality similar to the relation of human will to the vital, spontaneous animal behind it or under it. Paper and will both direct and distort the course of action. For either to become anything more than a technical means is deadly, and unfortunately we have allowed just that to happen. So we suffer from a rigid will, and are experiencing the death-throes of an absolutistic paper system.

For one thing, money is a contract—the freest, most gorgeous contract of them all. Money is somebody else's promise to pay, to give me what I want, when I want it. What a magnificent conception! The fully alienable contract for anything, anytime, anywhere. If you are at all aware of the history of contract law, you will realize what an immense historical achievement modern paper money represents. Whatever else history may ultimately record of the Western bourgeoisie, this honor most certainly must be accorded them: *They perfected modern money, which is a contract with parties unknown for the future delivery of pleasures undecided upon.* There must be hope for any group of mammals that could invent anything that marvelous. To so honor the self-indulgence of strangers—only a race of men with great reservoirs of hospitality could ever have conceived the possibility of it.

So money is a contract. But are all contracts money? Potentially, yes. Actually, only to the extent that they are accepted as such or are exchangeable for something that is accepted as such. *Which* contract rights become money is a perfectly conventional question, unless some higher authority than convention successfully intervenes and insists, as the government does today, that *this* particular piece of green paper with silk threads in it is the first money, superior to all other paper of whatever color or composition. And even then, in the shadow of the majesty of the law, this money merely becomes the measure of all other paper. It is a kind of *home-base* paper used as a benchmark by paper manipulators and their expert mechanics. Federal Reserve Notes and Treasury Silver Certificates are merely base-line money hardly used any more today than gold itself was a hundred years ago. You and I may approach this green paper as if it were something important, but it is really just paper for the peasants. It is *dumb* money in the sense that while its value changes, it does not earn other money. And money that does not earn other money is just not with it.

Gold as cash is irrelevant (except internationally, because we are so primitive in that arena); cash is paper immediately and universally exchangeable, also called currency: currency is a contract right currently accepted; and all such contract rights are based on credit of one kind or another (you only enter into a contract with someone you "credit" with the capacity to fulfill the contract.) Therefore money is credit. And credit is based on reputation. So money is a function of reputation. And everybody knows what reputation is. Reputation, as a matter of fact, is what everybody knows about somebody. There you have, quickly, the story of money.

Too quickly? All right, let's go slower. The modern Keynesian economists and marginal-utility fellows talk about "liquidity preference." What they refer to is the length of time it will take, and the success that can be expected, in exchanging a particular kind of paper ("interest-in": see Chapter 3) for cash. You venture away from cash in order to earn money on money, but you are ever aware of the line of retreat from your paper-pushing derring-do. Thus, liquidity preference—the delicate, nutty balance-line between going forward toward more money on money, or backward to real and regular money. How far forward you go depends on the state of your "confidence" —so this is one of the biggest words in the vocabulary of business.

We needn't waste much time on gold or any other commodity-money. Gold is yellow and it's pretty; it has earned its place in the history books; it is highly irrational money, suited only to primitive stages in the development of a money economy. And one of these days, when the system of international exchange becomes somewhat better organized, Fort Knox can be turned into a great dental laboratory devoted to improving the teeth, say, of the British lion, which would be appropriately ironic in the perspective of history. If international arrangements for loans to underdeveloped countries progress as they ought to, there may very well be enough good international paper around in a few years to relieve the world of its atavistic fascination with our Kentucky horde.

Cash or currency—mainly Federal Reserve Notes, which it is true bear some devious relation to the Kentucky pile—is more and more used in our domestic economy the way gold or U. S. Treasury Gold Certificates are used in the international economy, to prove on occasion that you got what it takes. Except for small incidental payments, our most common money is bank deposits and our most common paper is checks. Now most people, I should imagine, accept checks as money because they are under the impression that banks are loaded with *real* money. It is true that you can take a check to a bank and get some engraved paper for it, if you want to be fancy, but it would be one hell of a long day for the fellows operating the government printing presses if any large number of people had this idea at the same time. No, banks are mostly just like us—all they have is bank deposits. Where do they get them from, you ask? They create them—that's their business. Nice business, you say? Yes, it's not bad. It used to be rather nerve-wracking, but the New Deal took all the worry out of it. (I suppose that's why bankers loved FDR so much).

For the Serious Reader who would like to probe the intricacies of how banks go about creating money, the Board of Governors of the Federal Reserve System in Washington, D. C. gives away a nice introductory volume called *The Federal Reserve System: Purposes and Functions.* It is readable and entertaining and I recommend it. I won't try to describe the rather intricate mechanism: but just in a few distorted words, banks create money by making loans. These bank loans could be taken in cash by the borrower, but that is considered very backward, and would probably end up as bank deposits somewhere else anyway. Usually the loan is made by crediting a shaved amount thereof to the borrower's deposit account in the lending bank. All that happens is that a couple of bookkeeping entries are made in the right places. That's how banks create money. Their license to do so is limited, however, by something called "reserves." Most banks, especially most of the important ones, are members of the Federal Reserve System—America's eccentric form of central banking—which controls and manipulates the bank-money supply by acting on this special pile of paper (really, bookkeeping entries) called "reserves." The Federal Reserve Board can prescribe the amount of reserves a bank must have and if this is, say, 20 per cent, then all the banks together can create an optimum of four dollars for every dollar they "really" have. The FRB does not generally manipulate the supply of money, as it could, by raising or lowering the reserve requirement. Most often it enforces contraction or allows expansion by buying or selling government securities. Briefly, when the Reserve buys government paper the net result is to increase bank reserves and thus also the bank's capacity to create money by means of loans. When the Reserve sells this special paper (or anything else), the reverse happens—it soaks up money, and old loans have to be called or new loans limited by the banks. That is very roughly the way it works.

It is very indelicate to speak lumpishly of "bank deposits," as we have been doing, because when you are talking about important sums the distinction between different kinds of deposits can be crucial, and possession of cash can be very expensive. If big transfers are being made, Federal funds are more desirable than Clearing House funds —the former can be transferred and deposited by wire, thus saving a day's interest. There is centered in downtown New York something called "the money market" which has been "broadly defined" by an official writer to "include all forms of short-term credit, as contrasted with the capital market which deals in long-term obligations and equities." (The capital market is just as much a money market as any trading center in short-term paper, and if you get broad enough, is so defined.) So now the cat is out of the bag: money is credit, and the important distinction is not between money and credit—there is no good one—but between money/credit that earns other money/credit 1) not at all, 2) a little, but quickly, or 3) a lot, and over the long run. Where paper is concerned, time is of the essence. Time and reputation. Those are the main things.

Short-term credit which is not cash has been called "near-money." Banks have what is in the general run for most of us the "nearest" money. But they don't have anything like a monopoly on money. Because money is just credit, and credit as one writer says is "another name for debt." Every IOU is money, if anybody will accept it as such. Since almost everybody nowadays can go in debt, everybody can create money. *Isn't money wonderful?*

The whole show began historically with two great events, both growing out of the emergence of trading in Europe, the medieval fairs, etc., etc. The first event occurred when the first seller transferred his goods to a buyer who at the time had no goods to trade and no gold to substitute for goods. This pioneer seller said to his buyer, probably in disgust, "OK, give me two pigs or one gold ducat next year—and if you don't show, I'll come and get you. And write it down on this piece of paper here, so there won't be any argument." The second great event begins like the first but adds a new twist—which turns out to be a creative act on about the same level as the invention of the wheel. Same scene, same characters, but when the seller goes home he's still boiling because he's stuck with a "worthless" piece of paper, his buyer may be dead next year, or impressed into military service, or go into another line of business somewhere else, or any number of things. He feels maybe he's been took, and as so many people before and subsequently have done in that uncomfortable circumstance, he looks around for somebody to take in turn and so cut his loss, resolving firmly in his heart never to be taken again. Wonder of wonders, he finds a real patsy (he thinks) who is willing to take the buyer's paper in exchange for a half-ducat of gold payable immediately. This "patsy" happens to know that the buyer is a big man in a far country, vigorous and powerful, and well-respected: *a man of good reputation.* The gold is exchanged for the paper, and the Paper Economy is born.

We traditionalists in the law deal with the science of paper exchange mostly under the heading of "negotiable instruments" (which incidentally leaves us somewhere in the eighteenth century halfway between the London money market or the Federal Reserve System of today and the last of the two great events I have just reconstructed for our mutual amusement). A negotiable instrument is a piece of paper representing somebody's promise to pay—like a note, a bill of exchange, or a check—which runs in favor of anybody who holds the paper. The important thing about this marvelous invention is that once the paper has been "negotiated"—passed through more than one hand—the fellow who promised to pay has no defenses against the holder. The latter is called a "holder in due course" and the gods smile on him. In other words, the apples in exchange for which the note was originally issued may be wormy or otherwise worthless, and still the purchaser has to honor his promise to pay any holder who was not in on the rotten apple deal in the first place. The paper is good, even if the apples were not: he has to hunt up the seller and sue him to get back what his paper cost him. Another wonderful thing about a negotiable instrument is that if the honored holder in due course is not able to collect from the original promisor he can turn around and collect from any endorser; that is, any earlier holder. So the more names that are written on the back of the check, the more glorious the paper becomes, even though the apples were lousy and the purchaser never had the what-with when he bought them.

Modern paper money derives more from negotiable instruments than from bullion. I don't know that money is any less equal to credit because there is some gold behind it somewhere, but in any event our money is paper, not gold, and the history of paper concerns *promises* to pay rather than any magical "payment" this side of a sequential purchase. That is the whole point of paper: it actually dispenses with payment, which is an unnecessarily rigid requirement interrupting the flow of exchange. The point of gold or any other whatsis serving the ritual of payment is merely the hit-or-miss *test* of the validity of a particular piece of paper. Just as in a love affair one lover will act badly toward the other just to see if the other's love is still there and still strong enough to absorb poor behavior—so paper-holders use symbolic "payment" to test the strength of the promises which constitute the world of paper, this being in effect the outward manifestation of Western man's financial love affair with himself. Instead of payment so-called, you have the unending creation, destruction and exchange of paper. Except when somebody unbends and actually buys something and thus re-enters the world of things for a moment or two.

Once we get past barter—the direct exchange of things —we are stuck with gold or something like it until men begin to write down their promises and accept these instead of gold. But gold is a very limiting factor—there never was enough of it—so it was absolutely necessary to create something "as good as gold." *The closest thing to gold-today is gold-tomorrow, and that's how the system was born.* All of our paper today is ultimately gold due in a tomorrow that never comes. And just as well—there isn't enough to go around.*

The promise of gold—the promise of "payment"—is a particular type of contract called a "debt" (which is another name for credit, as we have already been informed). You can make a lot of fine distinctions between different kinds and classes of paper—as for example that preferred stock is "basically" different from a debenture, or a Federal Reserve Note is "much better than" my check—but one of the many points of the argument of this book is that *all* paper is interrelatedly similar. The differences may be crucial for individual paper-holders, but they can't see the forest for the trees. The idea of "money" as a very special kind of paper can be overplayed—there is only a hazy line between money and other paper, and the distinction can never be absolute (unless you limited the definition of money to legal tender, which is silly on the face of it; nobody dealing with

---

* It might be noted however that, as Keynes pointed out, the pure golden belief in gold—the glorious Gold Standard—was a necessary theoretical and emotional basis for the incredible notion, the once-solid rock of the whole capitalist ideology, that the proper regulation of credit was "automatic"—like free competitive markets. Adam Smith's "unseen hand" was supposed to ensure that there would be exactly the right amount of paper at any particular time, but in fact it was rummaging around in the bourgeois pocket—and that's how financiers were born.

money does). All paper—meaning contract rights and property interests, which are usually represented by paper—is potentially money of one kind or another. The only questions intervening between paper *x* and monier money are: 1) how long will it take; and 2) the value of paper *x*, and therefore the price of exchanging it for monier money.

R. G. Hawtrey, one of Keynes' co-workers, wrote the article on "Credit" for the Encyclopedia of the Social Sciences and therein attempts manfully to distinguish between credit and money. He says there are two kinds of credit: for borrowing—notes and bills of exchange; and for payment—checks and banknotes. Then he says legal tender is money, but banknotes may or may not be money. He admits that at this point, "The distinctions between credit and money then become obscured." For sure. There may be some reasonable or even useful definitional distinction somewhere, but it is not apt to be very important for our purposes here. We might define money as that paper or the measuring paper of that paper which is the means of fulfilling the ritual of payment, but that wouldn't get us far because payment is still just a ritual. Money and payment are intramural aspects of the paper world—and it is all the paper in the world that directs and distorts, that *controls*, the real world of things, processes and men, not just money or the means of payment or even credit. For instance, absentee ownership has so completely triumphed that the difference between ownership-paper and debt-paper has faded, as far as I am concerned, into meaninglessness. The primary difference, rights on liquidation, doesn't come to much because there hardly are any liquidations.

Hawtrey considers debt more important than money, and he says that the "assignment of debts" is basic to the history and theory of credit. (In medieval Venice, payments were made in person at the bank by the transfer of debts in an actual book of account.) But contract is a bigger word than credit, unless you expand the scope of credit as I am inclined to do to its root meaning—"belief or trust"— and not limit it, as Hawtrey says it is now limited, to "trust placed in a debtor." In which case it would be a quality of all contracts. Anyway, debt is only one kind of contract, and credit creates only one class of paper (in the confined definition). But *all* contract rights, not just debt, can be assigned, and therefore *all* the paper must be considered in any attempt to regulate the Paper Economy. Keynes, or at least the official Keynesians, believe the whole show can be kept on the road by manipulating the supply of money and credit, mostly that. Relying on Veblen, I disagree. I say with him that you have to shoot for the paper moon, to hit anything in this Barnum & Bailey world.

So how does a bank begin? Most of us would imagine that it begins when a few people leave their gold with an exceptionally trustworthy fellow for safekeeping. One line of banking did start out that way in Europe with the gold-smiths—although rich people delivered their gold to be made into plate and other baubles rather than merely for safekeeping. Anyway the goldsmiths knew all about gold, they had a lot of it in their possession one way or another, they bought and sold the stuff and therefore were market-sensitive. And so they just naturally became bankers as the popular belief in gold and the need for banks joined to provide *one* basis for the money/credit system without which capitalist-exchange would have remained a gleam in our forefathers' eyes. But all this was insofar as gold was available in excess of the amount needed for coin. And the place had to be where the rich people who owned the gold lived.

But if you are rich, or people think you are, they will assume you own gold or something "as good as gold," and such individuals became bankers, too. If they had a sufficient air of affluence, the banking customers-to-be did not bother to demand to see the color of their coin, but assumed it was a full, rich yellow. In any particular area, the richest-seeming man would just naturally be nominated by the towns-folk for banker. Often he would be a commercial type, a trader whom everybody could see sitting on the high stool in his counting-house, surrounded by bales and bags and bundles of desirable commodities. A great deal of this valuable merchandise arrived by ship—shipping was notoriously the most profitable form of endeavor—and it was commonly known or rumored that Mr. Big regularly outfitted and owned interests in the (so the gossip went) lucrative voyages of the *Mary J.*, the *Johnny G.*, and even, some housewives said, the *Suzy Q.* That man was called to banking.

But Mr. Big did not have much gold around the house —if he had any at all it was certainly out working for him— so his stock in trade became gold-tomorrow. *All you have to do to become a banker is to go into debt.* Mr. Big's promises to pay gold-tomorrow circulated as money, especially when endorsed by other leading citizens, and that's how banknotes were born. Then people began to leave their gold with the banker for safekeeping, or they asked him to collect from out-of-towners on merchandise sold and delivered (bills of exchange), or to discount out-of-town paper that had come into their possession; and they left all these funds with him because he was a nice fellow and he paid interest. When everybody found out that everybody else was leaving all his "money" with Mr. Big, he became Big & Co. for real (and even later it was Big and Sons, Inc.). If enough people leave their money with a banker, his notes can circulate at par without being endorsed by other wealthy men—the deposits are endorsement enough. At this stage of the game, bankers can engrave their notes on special paper and we are well on the way toward the fantastic shambles of nine-teenth-century American banking. And not a moment too soon, either, because all the gold, faith, deposits, hope, paper engraved and otherwise, and pure charity that the new banker-merchants have sopped up and agglomerated will hardly be enough gold-tomorrow on which to build the railroads, the steel mills, and the rest of our great industrial establishment. The people engaged in that enterprise will, besides, find it incumbent upon them to print their own money. And even that won't suffice: they will unfortunately find it necessary to steal from the government and even, on very black days, from each other.

It was not until after the Civil War, when unsecured banknotes became illegal, that bank deposits moved by check became the primary currency. But it was not until the twenties that the peasants were let in on this soft money (at about the same time, interestingly, that installment credit secured only by employment status became widespread for peasant-consumers). The peasants screamed, of course—the Greenbackers tallied a million votes in 1878, and Bryan tried three times to return to the fundamentalist farmers of America the God-given right to manufacture money—but all to no avail. The great financial interests who were run-ning the country at the time were determined that what had to be done would be done on their terms or not at all—and moreover when they were good and ready to do it.*

* The Gold Standard was a noble flag to carry into battle, especially for its effect on the opposing troops, but what lay behind it was not

So they played out the hand, and everybody in on it got very rich. But they wanted central banking in some more viable form than that offered by the House of Morgan. After enough of the wrong people had been hurt in enough financial panics, and after Congressman Pujo's investigation of the banking system in 1905 had smelled up the atmosphere, the quaint Federal Reserve System was allowed to enter the union in 1913, half-slave and half-free, a compromise use of government power on behalf of private banking. Thus the paper created in the course of raping a continent was canonized. You might say the policeman waited in the hall until he was needed.

As one gentle economic historian (George Soule) has poetically put one aspect of it:

> And when the recurrent cycles of speculation and crisis had left railroad companies bankrupt and had brought huge losses to investors, large and small, the roadbeds, the rails, the rolling stock, the yards, and all the rest of the railroad property was still there, ready to transport goods and passengers.

And so was the surviving paper still there, ready to release nevermore its clutch on the udders of the iron cow, and thus with that stream of milk to support subsequent peccadillos, and the creation of generation upon generation of new udders. Until 1929, that is.

---

a devotion to yellow metal but a determination to preserve credit or soft money, and the attendant inalienable right to benefit from inflation, for the uses and purposes of the raucous gentlemen of the East. Chauncey Depew and his fellow club-members of the New York Chamber of Commerce might raise a cheer for "honest money," damn Western silver, and rise to a solemn toast to the Gold Standard at the annual banquet, but this was all play-acting. At least I *hope* so. Wouldn't history be awful if the people mis-running things had no good selfish reason to do so?

5

MORE PAPER MAGIC

———————————————

The phenomenon of credit is one of the most profoundly engaging in the whole rainbow range of social life. Its significance, once grasped, is truly startling.

There is a lot of talk these days about status in our society. Well, compared to credit, status is about as exciting as Calvin Coolidge in deep thought. Because the point about status is rather obvious—the details can be fascinating and funny in revealing our nonsense to ourselves—but the thing itself is just there. Status is static, but credit is dynamic. As a matter of fact, credit is the active arm of status, it is status on the go, status in current use to effect some purpose in the world besides mere display: *credit is status capitalized.**

* It is worth while to stop and realize that Veblen's most famous book

Everybody knows that it is a fact, but have you ever asked yourself just *why* it is that the rich get richer? The answer is really very simple: the more you have, the more you can borrow. (That's why all rich people pay their bills quarterly when the coupons fall due, and in England—with its gentlemanly institution of the overdraft—it is considered bad form, I am told, to hurry payment to one's tailor. Even the tailors think it's bad form, and they won't venture to nudge you for money until a year or so has passed; but of course they don't cut cloth for just *any*one.) Let's say credit is the existence of an individual capitalized—that is, dynamically projected into an unending future. If we grant this we can then get beyond the simple, orderly, utterly wrong idea that credit is merely the socio-economic distance between selling and buying. It is so much more than that. There is, we must remember, Money Three (or something very much like it).

Under capitalism, the reputation of individuals has been commercialized—literally turned into money. Indeed, that is mostly what money is. Under prior aristocratic societies, all power felt to be necessary was achieved or maintained by

---

was *The Theory of the Leisure Class,* a very perceptive and amusing cartoon on the subject of status, but that his most important and brilliant work all revolved around his insights into the function of credit in America—what he called the price system. The fact that the cartoon has impressed the American intellectuals so much more than his epochal thinking on credit does no due respect either to them or to Veblen. It is intellectually easier to laugh knowingly at a secretary's high heels and white gloves than it is to urge one's imagination on to comprehend the intricacies of the money/credit/price system which has determined just about everything really important in American history—and that fact of ease may help to explain the historical misuse of Veblen, but not to excuse it. The secretary's painfully awkward effort to type with long fingernails is the *least* of the effects on her life of the status/credit complex administered by the leisure class and its hired managers.

the display of status, by a grand here-I-am gesture, and it was not the usual thing actively to "trade on one's reputation." To trade on one's reputation is to secure credit on it—that is, issue debt—which means to commercialize or capitalize it. It is to use it actively to get more and more of something. That is capitalism—and it says more about the nature of leadership thereunder than all the stately volumes of the *Dictionary of National Biography*.

It is the reputation of individuals and institutions that holds society together, and makes the wheels run. Reputation is what-a-thing-is-known-for. That is, what it is believed to be. There has never been a society based on what-a-thing-is, and the closest approach to it is the society of modern physical scientists, the creators of our technology; or the tiny society of you and me when we are in agreement, and so can dispense with the troublesome distinction between what a thing is and what it is known for, and go forward on the basis of what we agree it *shall* be known for. (Physical scientists don't agree on anything—they allow only experience to confer the blessed quality of agreement.)

The rich get richer because they own money-making property on which they "can get credit," which means their money-making property is just naturally worth more than other money-making property on which the credit-givers are not so willing to give credit, especially since credit is given on personal reputation even more than on any knocked-down property values. For purposes of credit valuation, there are two aspects of reputation to be considered: 1) what you appear to have; and 2) what you appear likely to get. It is the second—expected flow of income to the debtor—that is far and away the more important.

You can capitalize a well-reputed entrepreneur at a considerably higher rate than you can a collection of buildings and mechanical equipment. The latter just turns out commodities, but the former is the darling of the business world —he makes paper-profit.

One sometimes wonders, however, what the leading people in our society think they have achieved by so completely commercializing their reputations. Most of the money they get in exchange for the respect due them is not for buying anything, and a great deal of it does not even lead to the creation of real national wealth. The heart of it is Money Three. So the process becomes circular—reputation creates money and money creates reputation, and not enough happens in the meanwhile. Where do they think that is leading them? In past societies, great reputations fulfilled a much more creative social function. I think this hollowness at the center of the money-circle is what impels so many money-successful men into philanthropy and other assorted forms of community jitterbugging—most of which is beneath their stature and in many cases their vital talents as well. The successful businessman in his fifties who is finding business stale and women uninteresting or inexpedient is a sad sight indeed. Especially since he is the certifield torchbearer of our civilization. This disproof of the reputation-money complex by means of fulfillment has posed very sharply for us what is possibly always the fundamental problem of any society, that of leadership. Meanwhile, the intellectual experts are coming up strong on the outside—and they are publicly more entertaining, certainly to each other (their numbers grow daily) and also to large sections of the neither/nor group which always provides the backbone of any society.

Before we proceed further with our wayward parable of money-reputation and aspects of its contribution to the Paper Economy, we might pause in all fairness and note that *all* reputations are traded on in our society, and that it is not at all necessary to issue certified paper in order to carry on this common line of commerce. To bring the point uncomfortably close to home, I will refer candidly to the literary and professional worlds. Reputation is current—and achieves a form of currency with which one can acquire things—when the quality of pre-belief referrable to it (also unkindly known as prejudice, in long-term issues) is both common and immediate. All ideas are more readily accepted as true, worthwhile or even interesting when issuing from "an authoritative voice." People get let in on good things, get invited to parties, are accepted at face value or better, and so on, according to their reputations. In any literary society, for example, there is a finely perceptive market maintained by a number of skilled brokers in the relative "price" of these exchanges. And "value" is determined—calculated and re-calculated periodically—just as informed and uninformed opinion jostles to decide upon the going price of shares of General Motors or some dud on the New York Stock Exchange, or 90-day Treasury bills or even Federal funds on the New York money market. The same is true, for example, of the reputation of lawyers—except that the counters of the game are paying clients, not actual consumption items. (The literary world probably constitutes the most primitive society—based on crypto-barter—surviving in the modern world of big, smooth exchange.) But in the one as in the other, the most substantial collateral for further credit is a recent success. That's what you get when you win anything—creditable collateral: the pre-belief that you will win again.

This question of collateral is fundamental to the whole marvelous business of borrowing, and consequently to the story of the Paper Economy. We all love money (or currency, metaphysically conceived), and money is debt—but *who* gets a leg up on going into debt? That is the question. The answer begins by reference to this idea of collateral—the what-with behind the debt. Now recollect that you *earn* on collateral, and *pay* on a debt. But you are allowed to get into debt because you have some kind of collateral. That is hypothecation or capitalization (as a matter of fact, that is life-as-hypothesis or capitalism). In the typical case, first you make a profit (earn) or appear to be doing so, then you capitalize that apparent profit-making.

Note the similarity of bank reserves to collateral. We have what is called a fractional-reserve banking system; that is, a something-percentage is supposed to stand behind all of the created or make-believe money. That is the law, and that is the practice. These reserves are as much paper as any of the paper up front of the reserves, but this Big Twenty Per Cent (at present) is *unusable* paper. That is one of the big differences between types of paper—paper that is used and paper that is not used. Indeed, that is one of the main things that stands between us and absolute madness: some of the paper is neutralized, and so cannot be used as a 100 per cent basis for creating more paper. If there were no reserves, no neutralized paper, banks would lend make-believe money in any amount to any reputable business that wanted it when times looked good. But only banks are subject to this fractional-reserve requirement as a substitute for the fact that, since gold-tomorrow took over from gold-today, the ability to go into debt has no firm relation to any arbitrarily limited quantity of collateral. And banks aren't everything.

A basic principle of life under capitalism is that only a slowpoke fails to collateralize—that is, use what he has in order to get more. If you have a house and don't mortgage it, you are unimaginative, or at the very least un-American. If you can borrow money at 5 per cent, there is something wrong with you if you don't scramble around looking for a place to lend it at 6 per cent. Now it is true that there are a lot of lazy people like you and me in this country, and some of them are stick-in-the-mud businessmen; but we slow-pokes do not set the pace of the system. As a matter of fact, our backwardness just makes life easier for the smart boys who play the larger roles.*

They hock everything. In recent boom days, most of them had already borrowed to the hilt on every last guess as to what might be the fact five years from now—*vide*, the recent state of the stock market. To limit themselves to borrowing conventionally against collateral security like things would be much too pedestrian. Their standing (read, *status*) as successful buck-chasers substitutes for any realer collateral—just as in England the gentleman's overdraft is a loan secured by collateral no firmer than his proper gentle-hood. Whether or not, in this process, engraved paper called stock or bonds is used is a matter of indifference. What is being collateralized or hypothecated or capitalized is a

---

* They are in fact quite dependent on us, because our inactive paper serves—in the larger view of things—as a collateral-reserve against their fast paper.

reputation for making money. The engraved paper simply makes it easier for the lender in turn to sell the debt or borrow against it. Because that debt is now money, if anybody will accept it as such. And if your name is General Motors, they certainly will. (That's how consumer financing was born.)

You may have noticed a sleeper in the story of the last few paragraphs: it is rather crucial that the profit on investments be greater than the interest on loans. It is, for the people who count—otherwise the system wouldn't work. That's why we have a stock market, a place where values based on capitalized earning capacity have room in which to outrun the rate of return on credit. Now in order to accomplish this feat it is repeatedly necessary to raise prices on goods in order to increase profits in order to make borrowing worth while. But everybody understands this necessity, and the important people involved are even quite knowledgeable in noting exactly the proper moment when the existing game has been played out at a particular price level and another boost is in order. If necessary, production can be induced to drag its feet for a few months, everybody gets nervous about a possible deflation, and the Federal Reserve Board finally loosens up the process of creating money, thus making a rise in price absolutely irresistible and, with a national sigh of relief, prices are once again upped. The ante having been raised, a new hand is dealt. The better technique is to raise prices when required for credit reasons by blaming the unions, because in that case it is not necessary to frighten everyone to death by sabotaging production; but it appears that this bit of public relations business has about had it.

Until you start capitalizing human beings, the only

possible reserve against or collateral for the paper is existing things—the producing and consuming plant. Proper book-keeping that made reference to real wealth rather than paper-profit, would have to capitalize human beings—on the producing side for their education and training, and on the consumption side for the capacity of their gut, viewed figuratively. But as it is, human beings, especially in the form of corporations, are capitalized on the basis of their profit potential. And some people seem to like it that way. Certainly makes for a lot of paper, though. And paper-chasing as a way of life.

The beauty of a bank is that in pooling reputations it creates a new and more glorious reputation for itself, without tying up absolutely the reputations collected in the pool. These are still more or less free to be used elsewhere. Notice how wonderfully circular this can become: in-dividuals lend their reputations to a bank, which can even use the reputation thereby created to guarantee the paper of these individuals, its depositors—*vide*, cashier's checks, banker's acceptances, etc. So I think central or fractional-reserve banking, which exists in one form or another in all advanced capitalist credit economies, is a form of under-writing. The central bank and its depositors underwrite each other's promises.

Underwriting is the greatest credit invention of them all, after alienable paper itself (gold-tomorrow). We have already come across it in pristine form in the endorsement of negotiable paper. That's really all it is, endorsement or guaranty—one man's credit standing behind, "written under," another's. Here, reputation becomes superbly gen-eralized—nothing at all is promised, that is, put on the line, except the promise to pay if the first fellow doesn't. It tones up the quality of the paper something wonderful (and it can be quite lucrative for the underwriter, too). The more people who put their names on paper, the better it is; and the bigger their reputations (for paying when due, or earning all along, or just plain having it), the better than better it is. That's underwriting, and it doesn't cost very much unless everything goes to pot. And of course that doesn't happen anymore. One of the great principles operative in our life today is that if somebody is deeply enough in debt, he cannot be allowed to fail: too much paper involved. The creditor/underwriter will step in actively to save the situation. The old technique of defaults, whereby paper is wiped out, is not much used any more. Too crude. Nowadays, the over-extended losers are taken care of, and if necessary somebody raises prices somewhere to cover the loss. Of course, if the debtor is small enough to be dumped without rocking the boat, well enough, over he goes. But that's small potatoes. Nobody big goes under any more. The situation has been organized. (In ordinary language, an underwriter is either someone who writes insurance or buys an issue of securities from a corporation and resells it to the public, thus guaranteeing the sale of the issue. My use of the word here is much broader, since it includes the central banking function and all important endorsement.)

The biggest underwriters in the world used to be the moneymen in the City of London. Then their American correspondents, like Morgan, took over—at first in America, but later being called upon to shore up the mother lode during the First World War. Finally, Morgan and other similarly situated underwriters defaulted in 1929—the situation had gotten out of hand—and then the central government of the United States became the primary underwriter. It still is today. Now when you underwrite one-half of the civilized world, you do not accomplish this task by endorsing a check. In principle, yes; but the actual process is much more complicated. The greater magnitude of the present operation should not lead us, however, to denigrate the complexity of the maneuvers so successfully carried out by Morgan *et al* and the consequent honor due them, when they were running the country more or less by themselves. After all, they carried out their stewardship without an army at their immediate disposal—and damn few police, as a matter of fact.

Today, the Federal government stands behind all of our paper—and like any competent underwriter, it intervenes in the actual processes of reality on occasion (when it can) in order to ensure the validity of all the make-believe promises concerning that reality. It particularly intervenes, by specific guaranty or even *de facto* receivership, in all unprofitable activities which are nevertheless necessary for the functioning of the economy. After all, that's why we have a government—to distribute the chips and brush down the green-felt in preparation for the next role of the dice. I think we all understand that.

Standing behind the credit of the Federal government, which credit stands behind all other credit, is the right to tax without mercy, to intervene in the processes of reality with the full power of the modern state, and even the capacity to use force against recalcitrant debtors or creditors —or to blow up the whole world if the situation becomes hopeless. You can't beat it. It's a wonder nobody thought of it before. But now *everybody* needs the government, to hold everything together. This Paper Economy is nothing if not complicated. It is the true and ultimate form of American togetherness, because it is nothing but the extension into the future of all that we have thought we were.

A special word about corporate paper, the basic kind (before we go on to one of the biggest subjects in the Paper Economy—the omnipresence of inflation and continuing strange absence of its former opposite number, deflation). Big corporations, being in control of the actual production of goods and administering the prices of same according to their own convenience, are in effect their own best underwriters. They are the ones who underwrite paper by actual reference to their dominant position in existing social reality. So they are the great source of new paper, or the increase in value of old paper.

Probably what happened during the twenties which made the situation unmanageable and led to the default of the financiers was that the basic creative power in the business system had, without anyone's clearly recognizing the significance of the fact, shifted decisively from the old paper centers to the producing corporations themselves. Major corporations in key industries, run with a view to balance-sheet profits, turned out to be fantastically paper-creative—profitable—beyond anyone's premonition. When Morgan took a 50-million-dollar bonus for putting together the paper structure of U.S. Steel a half-century ago, that looked like really big business. But it was quickly dwarfed in the avalanche of paper-value that the corporation itself was able to generate year after year. It turned out, to everyone's surprise, that the profitable production of actual goods on a mass scale is the greatest collateral of all. The financiers made fortunes launching the big corporations—and their

activities were considered the height of paper-sophistication
—but they were as nothing compared to what the big babies
were able to do after they began to walk upright on their
own feet. As financial institutions, the corporations ended
up making the big banks look like corner grocery stores.*

Writing in the early twenties, Veblen said:

> In effect, assets are now capitalised on their earning-
> capacity regardless of cost or tangibility; the corporation
> is rated or capitalised at its value as a business concern,
> and among its valued and ratable possessions is its ability
> to borrow.

If you understand that it is capital that stands behind the
paper, and that capital is *not* the plants and machines but the
"capitalisation of earning capacity"—all this magic becomes
somewhat more explicable. As Veblen pointed out in the
same book—"In the business world the price of things is a
more substantial fact than the things themselves." The great
power of our great corporations is not their magnificent
capacity to produce goods, but the taxing authority inhering
in the power to raise prices. If the purpose of their power
was to produce goods—to create real wealth—then they
would just produce and produce and produce, as they did
during the Second World War for a few years, and there
would be so much wealth lying around that the bother of
dumping it in the ocean would be so great that the alternative of distributing it "unprofitably" to the people who
could use it would become downright attractive. In order

---

* Of course, some of the earlier corporations, like the railroads, had
been bled into a state of perpetual anemia: but that was because they
had been so paper-raucous in their early days that their right to tax
the general population by means of continually raising prices—which is
the primary paper-creating power of big corporations—had to be somewhat circumscribed in order to preserve the Union.

to avoid such an unpleasant alternative, the big corporations act more reasonably and view their essential power as the princely prerogative to create more paper-value. This is done periodically by raising prices, and continuously by not lowering them as costs are reduced—which they continuously are under modern technology.

Take the stock market, for example—that paper bawdy-house where billions of dollars can be diddled away in a few hours, and just as quickly revived. There are a lot of factors and indicators and so on that market analysts and operators use in their blindfolded efforts to "feel" which way the market is likely to go, but behind them all is one primary tautology called the "price-earnings ratio." This is the "gold" of the market, the final measure of all things. And it is nothing but a guess as to other people's guesses! The price-earnings ratio is the basic calculation in the Paper Economy since it is the conventional way of stating the price of expected profits: if a business is earning a million dollars a year, and the ratio is decided to be nine times earnings, then the right price for the business is nine million dollars. Of course, Polaroid or IBM have sold at something like 100 times earnings—but they were believed to have glorious futures. Other companies may sell at three times earnings, but who wants to talk about them? And universities don't sell at all: no earnings, it is said.

Here is an expert technical analyst stating his views for the benefit of one of the better intuitive market-interpreters:

> . . . I feel that I should clarify my position and perhaps that of other stock market technicians.
>
> First, to my way of thinking, the price of a stock or the price composite of an industry group, or even the level of the market as a whole is determined by three variables

—earnings, dividends and investor psychology (the latter is generally called the price-earnings ratio). The fundamental analyst is concerned with earnings and dividends, and projections of these figures by our analysts meet with a fair degree of accuracy. However, when it comes to determining the proper price-earnings ratio, the fundamental analyst generally asks himself—What multiple of earnings and what yield have been given to this stock in the past, and in view of the current price level of the market or industry, what multiple of earnings would the potential investor be willing to pay now? Since investor psychology can swing widely over a period of time, you can see that this could leave room for a considerable margin of error. Think back to as recent a time as 1950, when the economy had vigorously come out of a recession. Based on the Standard & Poor's Industrial Average, stocks were selling at about 7 times earnings and yielding in excess of 7.4% in dividends. At the end of the third quarter of 1959, however, although earnings since 1950 had increased only 20% and dividends only 25%, the S&P Industrials had tripled. What happened? Investor psychology had changed, and these same stocks were selling at 17.3 times earnings to yield 3.1%. It is the technical analyst who seeks to bridge the gap between what should happen based on facts and what actually happens based on psychology. After all . . .

And so on. Then, on the basis of stock values determined in this frightening fashion, the stockholder can get credit extended—and so can and do the corporations themselves.

Now does anybody doubt that General Motors could circulate its IOU within a large area as a substitute for Federal Reserve Notes? Or that General Electric could completely displace them in Schenectady, for instance? I should hope not. Because I rather think their paper is a bit better than the government's since they don't have to ask the permission of any elected Congress to raise taxes.

The bridge between the make-believe world of money/ credit and other paper, and the real world of the production and exchange of things for other things, is *price*. The paper system rests absolutely on the price level, and the rational control of the price level is the only way out of our paper-chasing madness. Veblen misspoke when he said "credit is . . . indefinitely extensible and stands in no quantitative relation to tangible facts." Credit is based on price, and the power to set prices is a tangible fact—a complicated fact, a political fact, but nevertheless a tangible fact of social reality. Veblen called our mad way of doing things "the price system" and this couldn't be truer; but he made an epistemological error in assuming that human beings live in a non-symbolic world of things and mechanical processes. They don't: their basic reality is social, and the central issue for them is not power over nature but power over each other—the former derives from the latter, and is no longer much of a problem whatever its derivation. Price is a part of this power issue—probably the crucial part at this stage of our development.

In the business lexicon, price-control is a particularly unpleasant form of sexual perversion. It is immoral, unhealthy, and if you play with it too much you can go crazy. But also it works very well, and by means of it a society like ours can turn out a truly incredible stream of merchandise, as we did during that eye-opening historical episode, World War II. When it looked as if we would need a passel of new equipment to fight the war, Roosevelt—sounding just like his bushy-haired New Dealers—called for the production of 50,000 airplanes a year. Who ever heard of such a thing? Everybody thought he was nuts. A few years later when the war ended, we were turning out 90,000 airplanes a year. It's a good thing the war ended when it did, because God knows what we would have done with all those complicated machines in their pretty aluminum packages if it had gone on a couple of more years.

There is an Extra Big point to be comprehended about the mechanical significance of price control—even before we get to the essentially political issue of *who* controls prices and for *what* purposes. If prices are held steady, demand can be fed into the economy until the limits of supply (short-term) or technological capacity (long-term) are reached. The result is full production—full use of our productive capacity. The "demand" referred to is easily created by printing presses: it is just paper. Prices are not supposed to go up until demand, of whatever source, outdistances supply-capacity—and it just doesn't any more, except rarely and in special circumstances. The reason prices go up anyway, thus ensuring under-use of our plant, is that the people controlling them want them to go up. They prefer profit-paper to demand-paper—and they control the printing presses of the Paper Economy, so to speak.

One of the most important intellectual executives involved in devising and carrying out the wartime system of price controls was J. K. Galbraith, in his pre-affluent days. He had been asked so often, What happened? that in 1952 he published a brilliantly instructive little book called *A Theory of Price Control* to supply a readable answer. To begin with, there had never been an effective price control system previously in this country, and therefore academic theory and its flame-tenders were, as to the possibility, unprepared, unwilling and unbelieving. Like Keynes politely explaining the irrelevance of gold to a similar audience a couple of decades earlier, Galbraith sets about dulcetly to apologize for the "unexpected workability of price control." It seems that the reason price control worked was that after the quixotic administrators set it in motion they immediately became aware of the unsuspected prevalence of "imperfect markets," that is, markets in which prices were not determined by simple competition. Or, to sum the matter up in a neat phrase, "it is relatively easy to fix prices that are already fixed." And these were the leading prices. Also galloping to the aid of the OPAers was the phenomenon, especially in retail trade, of "conventional pricing," that is, prices set and held steady by nothing more theoretical than habit; in other words, not all haberdashers have read Adam Smith. (It could have been guessed.) Galbraith opposed the precipitate removal of controls in 1946 because this act amounted to an eager invitation to inflation, consumer goods of all kinds being in very short supply at the time; but his course did not prevail, with well-publicized consequences.

For the other side of the story, let's listen to the First National City Bank of New York mumbling to itself on the subject of the Congressional investigation of "administered prices" (in its monthly letter of May 1959). Much, we note, may be achieved by the simple expedient of sloppy definition. The subject under discussion is defined as "the failure of big manufacturers to jiggle their prices around all the time"; and what everybody does—"The Government Printing Office sells a report on the evils of administered prices at an administered price of sixty cents." Administered prices, says the bank, are prices set by a seller after considering certain matters: "Putting the right price on a product is a difficult task," we are informed. Also, Roger Blough is quoted to the effect that prices are administered in the chewing gum and fireworks industries as well as steel, which conclusively proves the absurdity of Senator O'Mahoney's proposal to require steel and other "dominant corporations" in "heavily concentrated" industries (the bank's quotation marks mean the wrong people are using these terms) to give the government thirty days notice of intent to raise prices. Price review is only somewhat less disgusting than price control. "Let the nose of the 'reviewers' under the tent and inevitably the whole 'camel' of controls, herded by a burgeoning bureaucracy, would barge in." They have a point: If a new bureaucracy burgeoned, where would the existing herd of business camels which reviews, administers and controls prices find room to burgeon and barge? Under what tent, O Allah?

There is, however, a nagging little point that this high-level discussion neglects to consider. Namely, that the whole business system is based on the idea of price competition, and supposedly derives its validity, as well as its workability from this "fundamental" notion. That, according to received opinion, is the Number One logical reason that the government need not and should not concern itself with pricing, in any way. Notice the bank's slip of the typewriter in the use of the active tense, as in "manufacturers *to* jiggle." But according to regular theory, manufacturers don't do the jiggling, they *are* jiggled—helplessly, eternally, and to the greater glory of the Free Competitive Market. *The* competition is *price* competition, and that has gone to heaven; meanwhile, down here in the mud, there are numerous forms of non-price competition burgeoning and barging—as for instance, advertising, merchandising, and assorted forms of salesmanship. All of which become increasingly necessary as the recognizable differences between products (and their prices) diminish in utility. (Pierre Martineau, one of the less hidden persuaders, informs us: "There are precious few products that can be sold today on the basis of a demonstrable product superiority. . . .")

The whole awesome structure of conventional theory, including the sterilized Keynesianism of the FRB, is based on the assumed ubiquity of *price* competition. But in the most important sectors of the economy—especially where the big manufacturer stands astride the raw material supplier and the ultimate consumer—there isn't any. And wherever there is, the deficiency must be and is made up—as with subsidies to the farmers, and a Robinson-Patman Act for the corner druggist and other Independent Businessmen.

The Paper Economy is like a balloon, which is why the key terms are inflation and deflation. The hole where the air goes in is labelled "Price—Blow Here." And they sure do. During the fifties, it has been figured that the dollar lost value at the rate of 2¼ per cent a year—while the rest of the smart paper gained. Among other things, this process added about two hundred billion dollars to the value of stocks listed on the NYSE.

Now there is a great deal to be said on the subject of inflation, and most of it has already been said more than once. Fifty "distinguished scholars and leaders in public affairs" identified by the Committee for Economic Development tagged inflation as the Number One economic problem on the domestic scene through 1978. Other thinkers have suggested that it is, like nuclear warfare, a true problem of survival for democratic industrialism. It is also like the Bomb in being the ultimate source of destruction in our domestic cold war, the Armageddon of paper against reality. The

Official Morning Line on inflation is simple and clear-cut: governments spend too much and workers get too many raises. Since governments and workers are the best spenders-on-things and the slowest creators-of-paper, the Official Morning Line is exactly wrong—and one can only hope, as usual, for better post-time comprehension.

For use in understanding the course of this Momentous Discussion, I would like to urge two propositions, both frequently neglected by all parties concerned: 1) in order to have inflation somebody has to raise prices somewhere; and 2) there is no inflation in the real world of things, only allocation. Real values do not get inflated, they get allocated; only paper and balloons get inflated.

The Official Morning Line suggests that the paper be kept out of the hands of the spenders, and left to the safe-keeping of the paper-creators. In this way, it is said, we will get a "stable dollar." Maybe so. But then we will also get fewer things produced and consumed. This is the road to the poorhouse, because only things are wealth, while the "stable dollar" is the figment of a disordered imagination. No one's ever seen a stable dollar, and no one ever will. It is, in fact, a contradiction in terms. The dollar—stabled, off-and-running, or about to be shot—is neither thing nor paper, but merely the tautological measure of the supposed value of *all* paper—and all of this paper, we have seen and will see some more, has no reasonable or necessary or measurable or measuring relation to true wealth, namely, things. It is gold-tomorrow, referable only to gold-today; and the value of gold-today depended on its supply and the demand for it as an item in the ritual of payment. Payment is not a "real" measure of value: it takes place entirely within the universe of paper.

Gold had a different meaning in the past when it served

as a non-rational but natural limitation on the amount of paper that could be created. We were then future-oriented as far as the creation of things was concerned: our markets were not saturated with goods. But you leave gold behind sometime before you catch up with your future, and gold-tomorrow only a little later, simply because there is not enough of the stuff to clear all the paper that covers all the things. Now tomorrow is here, and consequently pure gold-tomorrow has become somewhat dated. The only way you can clear the paper with a "stable dollar" is to curtail the production of things: what you "stabilize" is production. But the whole purpose of paper—promises to deliver things in the future—was to induce the greater production of things. And there you have something of a contradiction.

Inflation is the very essence of the paper system which capitalism has never even dreamed of living without or even significantly altering except in moments and for moments of extreme crisis, like the Great Depression and World War II. Inflation is raising prices (it is *not* any particular theory as to why they are raised). Prices go up, they don't go down: since the thirties they haven't even dipped very much. This used to be called progress and now it is called inflation. The difference is that now it has become frightening even to those who benefit most from it. Inflation, we were told endlessly in business advertisements, is the "cruellest tax of all." So was the previous progress, also known as the accumulation of capital. But now business opinion comes out and identifies pricing as the private taxing authority it has always been. And it is of course a really brilliant piece of *chutzpah* for the managers of a price-and-profit system that exists at all only by virtue of a steadily increasing inflation of money-values (and an increasing substitution of such values for all others) to campaign righteously *against* inflation. It shows they are really at the end of the line, and are reaching for daring expedients. But even so, they would not have attempted this *volte face* just now if our elite labor unions had not, since the War, so completely compromised their position by lending themselves as the regular excuse for unnecessary price rises. Besides, they have only called a temporary halt to see if they can control the pace of inflation. They will be quite bankrupt intellectually when they discover that they cannot—without central price control. Then watch out—business may find it necessary to take over the government. But we can hope that American ingenuity will come up with some mixed private-public institution like the Federal Reserve System for the central control of prices in key industries. Then capital as well as labor will be tied to "rises in productivity."

We should recognize that an impressive collection of political issues of real democratic magnitude, involving structural deficiencies of the whole paper system, are being gathered under the fighting slogans of Inflation. I would like to note a few of these before proceeding to take a snapshot of the other face of inflation—the discarded practice of periodically letting the air out, *i.e.*, deflation.

1) Most thinking on this subject, including practically all official thought, assumes that nobody wants inflation, which is wrong; that inflation is caused by too much spending-money, whereas in fact it is caused by too much paper demanding to earn more paper; that the cure for it is to curtail the availability of money that will be spent on things —which spending causes more things to be produced— whereas the stepped-up production of all possible useful

things is probably the best direct means of curbing inflation, since it puts something solid behind all the paper; that the businessman is helpless to keep from raising prices, which is patent nonsense; and that the most major of major causes of inflation is that money wages increase more than "productivity," which assumes that money wages can only result from the increased production of goods—an exasperating assumption in the arguments of the spokesmen of a system that never even conceives of trying to produce all the things that it can. If you give workers more "money" they will buy food, which is in frightening oversupply, clothes, which are likewise, go to the movies, which are a depressed industry, buy consumer durable goods, of which we can produce as much as we like at any time, and housing, which we simply have to produce in any event, and the lack of which has nothing to do with any short supply of building materials or labor.

2) Inventory is important in understanding inflation because it constitutes a sensitive contact-point between the two worlds of paper and things. If the price of an inventory-thing goes up, it is better to have a lot of it; if it goes down, money is better. Now most of the postwar recessions have featured inventory-panics among businessmen. (These substitute for the financial panics of our early capitalist history, the last one we shall ever see having occurred—along with much else—in 1929.) Why should this be? The more inventory we have, the more "backing" there is to all the paper that's around. If inflation is blamed on too much spending money and not enough things to spend it on, then why, as soon as there are enough things, do we have a recession? Because either more paper to buy the goods must be handed to those who will use it, or the price must be lowered so that

the goods can be moved with the given quantity of purchas-ing-paper. But the price cannot be lowered without dis-turbing the value of all the non-purchasing paper which is sustained by it—and for the same reason there is a reluctance to raise either wages or taxes, which would also increase the quantity of purchasing-paper. The new inflation-recession cycle results from the continuing chase after paper-profit in a circumstance where too much product is too easily pro-duced. The paper system is simply not adequate any longer to the job of clearing the shelves.

3) In the Paper Economy, inflation is caused by the desire to *make money* (literally) by taking advantage of every increase in production to manufacture paper-value and blow some air in through the price-hole. Prices go up further, or maintain their previous height, because of de-mand alone, without reference to supply: the latter is ad-ministered in major industries. It's so much easier and safer to "make it" this way—by further capitalizing production and raising prices—than by actually producing and exchang-ing goods. And why not? The money so made is not going to be spent anyway—it's just going to be used to make more money. And around we go. Take away the magic of Money Three, achieve full production, and there would be no infla-tion except temporarily in areas of short supply, and that minor problem of real allocation could in fact be handled by controlling the amount of money available to specific buyers. But in the absence of the two qualifying clauses, the attempt to achieve purposeful allocation by partial ma-nipulation of the amount of paper, without plugging up the price-hole, is doomed, hopeless, and I dare say insincere.

4) Inflation equals rising prices. How then is it possible

to deal with inflation without controlling prices—that is, keeping them from rising?

5) The whole game is based on scarcity—and that's as scarce as its symbol, gold, used to be.

The other face of inflation is deflation, and that's like scarcity—it's in short supply.

There are no losers any more. Prices don't go down, they only go up. Important quantities of paper-value are not wiped out any longer.

The Federal government has underwritten the Paper Economy—and the underwriter will not permit a really effective deflation. No more defaults, no more financial panics, no real bankruptcies, no more depressions—hardly any lackadaisical breathing-spells. Just an occasional coffee-break. The Federal government is not interested in making money; its only actual or permitted interest is somehow to hold the system together. It is reality-oriented. And it is operating under the most unprofitable underwriting contract ever written.

We have "recessions" every once in a while, of course, when things are going too well in the real world. They are a kind of retreat from the unreality of the dream—an attempted flight back toward the world of "solid" values, the long-lost spiritual identity between dollars and real wealth. But no go: everybody remembers the last debauch in 1929; the morally devoted underwriter steps in, slaps a few wrists and hands around some fresh paper to play with; and after the tremor of wayward desire has passed, on we go, ever upward. These recessions are nothing but daydreams, really —the office-worker with a hangover staring out of the window at about 4:10 in the afternoon—which is rather conclusively proved by the fact that nobody takes them seriously enough to bother lowering any prices. It would be fun, but . . . no, the last one nearly killed me. Well (*patting a middle-aged paunch*) those were the good old days, but like the fellow said, they're good and gone.

The old days were wonderful. Somebody yelled *Cheezit, the cops!* and everybody started to scamper around frantically trying to collect all debts at the same time. Quite a sight. The show amounted to an heretical worship of the ritual of payment—sort of a financial Holyrollerism —in which everything is going smoothly on Beneficent Wednesday but on Black Thursday it is arbitrarily decided that the "tomorrow" in gold-tomorrow is knocking at the door like Banquo's ghost. All the paper that can be called is called for clearing, and balances have to be settled in gold-today—right away. And nobody has the what-with to lend any more. Well, there never was enough gold for *that* kind of religion (if there were, then gold would not be gold—it wouldn't even be as good as gold) and the fact became clear even to the High Priests themselves in 1907, when everybody was frightened by the mass passion to be paid in yellow metal. Thus the Federal Reserve System. There have to be limits to religious frenzy in any well-ordered church—you have to keep the True Believers in line. (Financial panics were also encouraged by the fact that markets—*i.e.*, the domination of the consumer—were imperfectly organized: some real competition here and there, and as a consequence prices could on occasion be forced down faster than costs, which brings the whole related paper structure tumbling down with a loud *Whoosh!*)

We have not yet figured out a workable substitute for the ritual of bankruptcy and other forms of price reduction and deflation—for letting the air out of the balloon. Meanwhile the air is getting fairly stale inside, even though we keep blowing fresh air in through the price-hole. But really, how high is up? I would say that so long as the underwriter keeps us at our task of producing and passing around real wealth, and we continue developing our primitive system of real allocation, up is forever. After a while the balloon of our money religion will begin to look pretty foolish, but that's a matter of social esthetics. Drawing on my faith in the human race, however, I predict a considerable growth in apostasy. Eventually the point will be reached where the people laughing at the balloon outnumber the people holding the ropes, the latter will loosen their hold in the confusion of their embarrassment, and away it will go into the high scientific yonder, there to circle the earth forever in the company of forgotten Sputniks.

The problem could be stated this way: how can we deflate without interfering too much with the non-paper area of employment and production? The answer is simply to try as we have been trying—to manipulate the mass of paper (but not just bank deposits) with a comprehension of its basic unreality, and to keep our attention focused on important matters, like real wealth and its rational allocation. It will take a little imagination and a bit of doing, but I think we'll make out. The alternative—a real Old Religion type of credit liquidation—is really out of the question. That couldn't happen without production slowing down disastrously. We have had a steady government-underwritten (and business-benefited) inflation since 1933, with a special and unnecessary spurt for 1946-48, and all the old and new paper protected, and we're stuck with that system. Only crackpots seriously propose that we go back beyond the

New Deal to the depths of the Great Depression, and do the whole thing over again, but this time the Right Way—with a full, natural, uncontrolled destruction of paper-values. The American people would not stand for it—I know I wouldn't. That would be like trying to cure a madman by urging him to rave on more loudly.

But the fact that we live in the Age of the Big Underwriter, that prices don't go down, and that paper is never seriously deflated, is brand new, decisive, and changes the entire nature of our system.

On this question of deflation I leave you with the following reflection: How can bankruptcy (as the basic symbol of classical deflation) have its old meaning and old function when a corporation deeply in the red—with a big loss on its books—is by that fact alone, under modern tax laws, transformed into a valuable piece of marketable property? And what are we talking about if there's no bankruptcy? See what I mean—you *can't* lose any more. It's just not allowed. There were too many losers in '29. The price of prosperity is success for all.

I am about to wind up this interminable discussion of gold-tomorrow, but first I will keep faith with the hardy reader by addressing myself to the question which has probably nagged him throughout this chapter: *Are you trying to tell me that money isn't worth anything?* No, I am not. My point has been that money is worth only what you can buy with it, when and if you ever buy anything with it, a simple but neglected proposition; and anything that you can buy things with is money when and if you buy them, a somewhat more complicated proposition. But you are considerably farther along the way if you keep in mind that money is Einsteinian: it exists in a space-time continuum, as is suggested by the word "tomorrow" in "gold-tomorrow." Moreover, all that glisters is not gold, especially the "gold" in that hyphenation. Tomorrow can come on with the *zoom* of a supersonic jet, or it can approach with the impetuosity of a Steppin Fetchit hurrying to open a door for his employer . . . and sometimes tomorrow never comes at all.

Because the value of paper is all in the head. The capitalization of earnings (the price-earnings ratio) is compounded of guesses about the future—and in an active paper market, all guesses are created equal, the shrewdest and the most stupid. A few years back, United Fruit's earnings fell off and it omitted a dividend. In two days the stock lost 5½ points: on a dividend omission of about $4½ million the loss in value was about $48 million. Until that happened nobody knew that that dividend had been capitalized at ten times its value—and "nobody" was sure of the fact afterwards, either. In the market of recent years there have been a good number of trading days when stocks on the Big Board lost two and three *billion* dollars between breakfast and the cocktail hour. But no one jumped from Number One Wall Street: as a matter of fact, the paper loss wasn't very important—interesting, you understand, but not important.

What is so obviously true of equities on the NYSE, is true in varying—that is, slower or quicker—degrees of all paper, including the "dollars" to which the businessman so avidly sacrifices his life. Veblen: "Men have come to the conviction that money-values are more real and substantial than any of the material facts in this transitory world." And: "The businessman faithfully views the dollar *sub specie aeternitatis*, even when he knows better." And finally: "The fabric of credit and capitalisation is essentially a fabric of concerted make-believe resting on the routine credulity of the business community at large." Veblen nicely characterized the businessman's belief that the money-unit is stable as "the spiritual precipitate" of the price system (or the Paper Economy).

The money-unit is not stable and it does not measure all things—it merely measures all paper. The value of the dollar has to shift in order for it to do its job. The fact that it no longer shifts upward (opposite to price movement) is unfortunate, and of course makes the system of paper-value increasingly intramural. But the true historical purpose of the paper system was never to measure the value of all things (that would have been an impossible task); its purpose was to value a future-with-more-things-in-it more highly, much more highly, than a present-deficient-in-things. It certainly achieved that purpose—effectively, although not equitably. What has compromised the paper system is merely the superfluity of things in the present. The future has arrived—but the paper-chasers refuse to join the welcoming committee. The urgent point of this book is that somebody ought to get out there and welcome it anyway.

Let's put it another way: I can buy as much scrambled eggs with a stolen dollar, a counterfeit dollar, a borrowed dollar, any one of a thousand kinds of windfall dollar—or a piece of kleenex accepted as a dollar—as I can with a hard-earned dollar, whatever that is. Where then is a theory of the *real* value of paper to come from? Note that the scrambled eggs and my appetite for them have not changed at all in the course of this flurry of choosing paper—although not only my attitude toward eating scrambled eggs, but indeed the basic emotional quality of my approach to other people and life itself, may be quite decisively affected by the *kinds* of dollars I am in the habit of acquiring and spending (or keeping).

If value-paper is a symbol is a language, then pretty clearly it is even more difficult to speak the truth in this tongue than it is by use of word-symbols. Especially for the lack of good literary criticism. Among the conventions of literary criticism there is included the proposition that a novel is *about* life but is not the thing itself. The novel is frequently referred to as "an imagined world," and then the literary critic explores this new territory, remarking on relations to other similar areas, and even on occasion to Life Itself. All symbol languages should have their literary criticism, and all should proceed on the assumption that any language is for talking about life, but talk is not the same thing as living—no matter how nice that might be in the premises.

Economics is concerned with values, real or make-believe, and therefore it is not so painful to realize that psychology lies at the basis of both the theory and the practice of the discipline. All the great systems of economic thought rest lightly but firmly on various assumptions as to human motivation. At crucial moments in its exposition or application, any economic theory will read like an excursus on life as a system of incentives. Too many of the little economic Freuds of our day are unnecessarily abstract, unfortunately unimaginative, and too frequently wrong. Their notorious model of the economic system is not nearly so blameworthy as their even more rigid and worthless model of Man behind and under it.

Moreover, not everybody's psychology is equally considered: a fellow called the "entrepreneur" gets an untoward amount of personal attention, especially when he is not a person at all, but a big bureaucratic body called a corporation. The bigger and more bureaucratic this entrepreneur becomes, the more he loses his nineteenth-century manliness and takes on the characteristics of a neurotic Hollywood actress. Particularly his "confidence" must not be disturbed, otherwise he might not be able to go on camera at all until later in the year. This is nicely put by Sutton *et al:* "The economic system, sometimes depicted as stable, tough, and impersonal"—in its manly posture, one might say—is in its nervous relation to the government "pictured as so fragile a web of mutual confidence that an unkind word from the White House can cause collapse." The things we are told repeatedly that must be done to preserve, maintain, restore, increase, or just generally refurbish "business confidence"! You'd think that was the whole point of economic policy— and some economists do.

Confidence in what? In their guesses as to the profits that will be made. And if, Heaven forfend, they should lose a spot of confidence? Why, then everybody picks up his Private Property and the game is called for lack of confidence. Of course, nobody has seen anything like this happen since 1929; and there are, besides, the rather crucial considerations that: 1) you can't pick up Private Property and put it in your pocket; 2) all you can do is leave it there and run; 3) the farther you run, the less it's worth; and generally speaking 4) this particular game of marbles, whether or not played with confidence, happens to be the only one in town.

That the Paper Economy should have to rely on the stale notion of "confidence" as its key psychological concept is, to say the least, discouraging in a cultural way. Why couldn't they talk about "business passion" or "paper-moon hunger" or "the ecstasy of a five-point gain"—anything besides confidence, confidence, confidence. Who cares? You can make a lot of money these days in a very depressed frame of mind. Why all this whining about the state of their confidence? I think it's all threat, to keep us so concerned about them that we never have a moment's peace to think about ourselves—the same psychological gambit a possessive wife or mother will use to try to keep you in the house, or make sure you don't enjoy yourself if you do manage to get out.

The Official View of Life attempts to explain some of the vagaries of paper not only by categories like confidence. For example, there is the exquisite fine line between speculation and investment, which only those with years of habituation in the farther recesses of financial morality can even begin to understand. Under this bit of Zoroastrianism it is said that paper is just concerned with something called "savings" which are righteously "invested"—in other words, that all money is One or Two, and that Money Three does not and could not possibly exist.

To which the following rebuttal is made: What is the difference between one hundred dollars "saved"—even out of salary, or go further and say hoarded in Federal Reserve Notes—and one hundred dollars "made" by a one-point rise in a hundred-share smidgeon of Snappy Garter Inc., which rise, lasting only one day, resulted from an unfounded rumor that the Company's third-quarter earnings would snap back to 1961 levels? Freeze it in time, and you will notice upon dissection that all paper is created equal. Especially if, as can be done, you value it by discounting the money-cost of the space-time-institutional distance from shrewd thought to debt to stock to cash to dinner at the Ritz. Investment in *what?* The paper is in your safe-deposit box and the factory is over there in Pittsburgh, Pa. I think we have another tautology here: the theory is that you have investment when you own the thing, although by means of paper; speculation is when you just buy and sell paper, and never "really" own. Oh, yes? And how long do you have to hold the paper to "own" the thing, metaphysically? Six months under the tax law. And they don't wait a day longer before they sell it. (Before the tax law, nobody knew how long was long enough to transmute speculation into investment.)*

The whole ancient concept of investment assumes that *all* money is quicky spent on consumption or to build factories, and that there is necessarily a limited supply of goods. It confuses real wealth and the allocation thereof, with the irrelevant vagaries of paper. But by and large there doesn't happen to be a limited supply of goods (except as the producers create same artificially). Nobody has to "save"—that is, wait and work a year to get an automobile—so that General Motors can build another factory. That would be true only under full production—and we haven't experienced that phenomenon except in limited sectors and for limited periods since the War. Moreover, under full production—this is a very revealing fact—the paper system with its price airhole is utterly incapable by itself of rationally allocating materials and effort: to accomplish this, under full technological steam, reality as well as its conventional symbols must be consulted.

---

* With the national yearning for Capital Gains in the last decade or so, the fuzzy distinction between a fast income-or-capital buck has further diminished—considerably.

Paper is a useful and historically valid technique of accumulating capital, by means of a kind of privately distributed authoritarianism (relying on big banks and small governments), in those circumstances where the demand for goods is so great that all goods possible are actually produced and new factories besides. That was some time ago. Probably the reason the Great Depression was so great (as W. W. Rostow suggests) is that we had by that time left those circumstances rather decisively behind. Without, it may be said, bothering to modify the paper system, even in its basic banking functions.

The validity of paper in the absence of scarcity is unthinkable without conscious control of its quantity and/or value. When scarcity is in inadequate supply, so to speak, paper leads to a literal form of madness—a distortion or denial of reality in order to preserve the illusion of the absent condition. And when the power of great corporations is a part of the situation, reality itself gives way to the illusion—and a weird, glistening, new kind of scarcity appears, as an emanation from beyond the historical grave. It is Scarcity Regained—one of the ugliest of all human creations.

When we accept the Paper Economy at face-value, we willingly confuse reality with the bookkeeping system of business. This accounting order contains a complete metaphysical view of the nature and purpose of life on this planet. But is it really *your* view?

I suggest that the Paper Economy is nothing but a destructive perpetuation of existing power relations beyond their period of historical utility.

6

THE BIG DEBTS

THERE WILL NOT BE another Big Deflation in this Age of
the Big Underwriter—and there are some very Big Debts
that will never be repaid. For example: the national debt, an
obligation of our government with respect to past wars and
depressions running in favor of some of our more distinguished citizens and institutions; consumer hardware and
home debt, in one way or another effectively underwritten
by the government, for the benefit of producers, financial
interests and peasants alike; and some other more complicated paper configurations.

Very little is done any longer with mere spending
money. If we want to do anything nowadays, the first

necessity is always to "finance" the project. Unless it is a money-making project, it seems always to work out that the financing becomes a more enduring item than anyone at first imagined. Indeed, the debt usually outlasts the life-utility of the project—as with the Second World War. Or, if the debt should happen to be repaid at about the time the financed thing fades into inutility, as with an automobile, we discover that we can no longer manage to get along without it, and back into debt we go for a new one.

It is almost as if somebody somewhere with the power to accomplish it had decided that everybody had to pay a tariff on the right to get on with the business of living around here. As a matter of fact, that's about what has happened. Moreover, this taxing authority is not democratically distributed; banks and businesses have an untoward amount of it, and the bigger they are the more of it they have. Naturally, when a project has to be financed, it must get in line behind other projects that have to be financed, and the most profitable ones naturally get going first. This slows down the rhythm of life a great deal, especially when an artificial scarcity of the what-with of financing is created to maintain its price. It always is.

The quantity of debt in the United States has grown amazingly ever since we started to buy our way out of the Great Depression, which amazing growth has been paralleled, as previously noted, by unending inflation. Also paralleled by an unprecedented expansion of physical plant and attendant population. Here are some facts.

Total public and private debt has *grown* from $175 billion in 1935 to $883 billion in 1960, the biggest spurts having occurred in Federal debt during the War, and all other debt than Federal since then, especially during the fifties. That's just debt. To indicate the growth in other paper, the market value of all listed stocks on the NYSE "advanced," shall we say, from $47 billion to $308 billion in the same period—from a low of $23 billion in 1932. The value of this paper increased by more than $200 billion during the fifties alone. That's just stock listed on the NYSE—only 2 per cent of all domestic public corporations (but of course the big 2 per cent, accounting for 30 per cent of the total capital invested by private business, 35 per cent of corporate sales and *65 per cent of corporate profits*). Since we are just indicating, we won't go into other paper—like checks and the green stuff, insurance policies, pension funds, etc., etc.— and we certainly won't mention the increase in real estate values, because that might frighten everybody to death.

This increase in paper, debt and otherwise, has been accompanied by a certain increase in prices—necessarily. With a 1947-49 base, the purchasing power of the dollar (depending on what you were buying, if you were buying anything) was $1.70 in 1935 and $.79 in 1960. On the same base and for the same period, the Consumer Price Index went from 59 to 127. Also, to the extent that historical prices are supposed to have some relation to real values, they go up by standing still, because of our beneficent technology. But remember that the price system represents the *capitalization* of reality (whatever that may be) not the actual thing itself. So the historical value of the money unit, while important to consumers with memories, is much less significant to future-oriented paper-holders than is the over-all quantity of paper and the control thereof. Inflation may redistribute paper-power, but it does not necessarily weaken it structurally. The power still depends on who holds what paper—

and particularly who dominates what paper-creating and paper-controlling institutions.

This matter of capitalizing social reality is a political operation: that is, an exercise of power. For what purpose? Well, when the paper system was being created, the revolutionary point was to establish dual power in order to undermine the previous power system. Monarchs knew the value of gold and goods as a means of supporting their monopoly of armed force; but they could not—and did not—monopolize gold or adequately dominate the production and exchange of goods. The paper system was built on the latter, and it was a second basis of power which, under industrialism, became a much greater source of power than the state's monopoly of force. Much more creative. To put it another way, industrial technology is a much bigger thing in the world than armies; indeed, as everybody knows, the latter have become utterly dependent on the former. But grown to a certain point, paper-controlled industrialism can no longer do without the special power of the state: it is not armies that it needs, but the central command-capacity of the national state. Having reached a certain maturity, it doesn't work without this.

In Russia, the state attempts to extend its basic monopoly of force to include a similar control of the production and distribution of goods. In the West, there has been a peculiar and grudging attempt to share paper-power, rather than to dispense altogether with the paper system. That's what we are involved in now—working out the terms of that sharing. It's confusing, and it may not work; but one good look at Russian totalitarianism is enough to convince any reasonable person that it's worth trying. What I am urging in this book is that we really have to be somewhat more candid and critical in carrying out this effort. Otherwise it will not work—certainly not in time.

Which introduces a brief discussion of the Federal debt. My assumption is that we are engaged in a project of sharing power between public and private sectors—between two power-groupings, one stumbling along with the prerogative of using armed force, the other operating fairly successfully without that ancient privilege.

In the Paper Economy, the right to tax and set prices, and the privilege of going into debt or otherwise issuing paper, are the two distinctive sources of power. Both the private and public authorities have this right and privilege, and if you want to know what's going on at any particular moment with regard to the great Western adventure in the sharing of paper-power, all you have to do is to take a current slice of history and put it under a tax/debt microscope. For example, during the War and in order to prosecute it successfully, the government had to inhibit the private taxing authority in the course of asserting its own; but part of the deal was that it would not pay for the War exclusively by taxation, but would also borrow heavily. The difference is merely the subsequent tribute in interest which the government has since been paying on the war debt. Now what the government did with the money it taxed and borrowed during the War was: 1) win the War; 2) throw a lot of junk at the enemy for which it received no compensating monetary or material consideration; 3) feed, house, and clothe a group of persons about equal in number to the previously unemployed population; 4) create the greatest orgy of productive effort the world has ever seen; and 5) through various subsidies bring about a life-saving modernization and expansion of the nation's industrial plant.

When the War ended, the private authorities reversed roles with the government, reasserted their own taxing authority (price controls were lifted) and inhibited both the taxing and borrowing authority of the government. They then took full control of the refurbished plant—and were further heartened by the war-created debt, which placed a delightful pile of immediate money in the hands of the consuming population (remember cashing in your war bonds?). For the non-spenders, the war debt constituted a very satisfactory source of interest with absolutely no risk involved. That's been the shape of the situation ever since, except for a special paper-spurt at the time of Korea. That's the "new deal" after the New Deal and the War, and it is largely a disaster.

The existing Federal debt, even including the terrible waste of war—accounting for the largest portion of it— probably represents the shrewdest, most successful paper-investment in the long and glamorous history of the Paper Economy: just measure the distance between where we were when Federal borrowing began to be a significant activity, and where we are today—and then try to convince yourself that it all would have happened anyway. (The New Deal cost $26.7 billion in government debt—the War cost $212.3 billion.) The whole stream of nonsense about budget-balancing is twice-removed from anything like the real situation: 1) because every businessman borrows money in order to get a project going whereby he will make more money, and that is what all the proposals for Federal spending are and were intended to and did or would do, except that the government is most often generous enough to let somebody else reap the crop it has sown; and 2) it is not a question of borrowing or not borrowing, but *who* borrows and for *what*.

Since there are such grand misconceptions current about this debt, a few technical details concerning it may very well be in order. No one knows how big the debt "should" be. The only known principle for judging the proper amount of debt to be carried by an individual or organization is that the borrowed money should be profitably employed—that more money should be made on the money borrowed than it costs to borrow it. Also, that there be a chance to repay the debt when due: but that doesn't mean as much as it seems to mean because as long as profits outrun interest the debt can be extended or refinanced instead of "paid."

Since the government by and large is not permitted to make a profit on anything, you can understand the difficulty that right-minded people are having with this question. Their first and favored resolution of the confusion which has been created by their own lack of imagination is simply that a really *good* government, if it has to exist at all, certainly should not compound the felony and exist, like everybody else, by going into debt. The second line of defense is to assert that the government debt should not be more than its present amount, whatever that figure may at any moment be, and that besides it would be the essence of probity to "repay" some of it every week out of salary. In other words, this issue is met with all the resources of a disgruntled husband eyeing his wife's charge account.

The propriety of the size of the debt can be judged by reference to what the money is spent on; or by the difficulties, if any, in meeting the interest charges on it; or you can get very sophisticated and assume it to be the capitalization of the government's interest in the American reality, which it most likely is, and then its size would have to be discussed as a percentage of GNP, or as a percentage of all debt. At this point you would have to develop some tautological formula like the price-earnings ratio in order to express your belief about America's future and the government's role in it. Now wouldn't America look silly walking around the world with the 1917 debt of $3 billion or the 1932 debt of $19 billion? Can you imagine what this country would look like if the government had been engaged during the War not in this historical bang-bang effort but in underwriting domestic construction enterprises? (I assume the same *profit* to our, you should excuse the expression, Free Individual Private Competitive Enterprise System.)

The gross Federal debt amounted to $285 billion on June 30, 1959 (of late, it hovers around $300 billion). That compares to the top wartime figure of $279 billion (February 1946) and a pre-Korean low of $252 billion (June 1948). But the gross figure is highly misleading because it includes intra-governmental debt—the government's promises to pay itself. Of the $285 billion of Federal debt at the close of fiscal 1959, about $55 billion was held by Federal agencies and trust funds, and another $26 billion was in the hands of the Federal Reserve System. So at that time there was a *publicly held* debt of $204 billion, which represented an increase of only $9 billion over the comparable figure for the 1948 low-point (and about equals the 1947 figure). Meanwhile, back at the ranch, GNP has grown fabulously over this period and so also has net public and private debt. As a percentage of GNP, actual publicly held Federal debt has dropped from 87 per cent in 1947 to 44 per cent in 1958. Relating this detested paper to total debt, it has fallen over the same period from 51 per cent to 28 per cent. And it keeps falling as the other continues to go up.

So pretty clearly the national debt has *not* grown since the War, although everything else in the country—paper, population, and plant—has. The point is that it should have grown, and it will have to grow. The brave prediction made here is that if a national government holds the line on expenditures as successfully as Eisenhower's administration and Truman's Congress did, the cost and the frequency of our little put-put recessions will increase, and this by itself will force Federal borrowing. It is just not possible to live happily in the Paper Economy without creating paper. Not to do so is to lose ground, by which I mean power. The resisters, the economic Thoreaus, are plowed under, bypassed or just forgotten. Walden Pond is turned into a Naval Training Area, and the surrounding terrain plastered with installment paper. (Actually it has become a peanut-and-orange-pop picnic area.)

Now just a quick run-through of the other Big Debts that *have* grown, that is to say, skyrocketed, since the War. One of the sharpest paper-consequences of the successful damper on Federal spending has been a better-than-quadrupling of net state and local debt—from a 1946 low of $13.6 billion to $60 billion in 1960. (There is some method in this financial madness, since interest on this stuff is tax-free.) Despite this tremendous paper-effort, the *real* deficit —schools, roads, etc., that were *not* built and could and should have been built, plus increased salaries to upgrade institutional quality or keep it from further deteriorating, and more of the same—has probably better-than-quadrupled, too.

Net corporate debt has more than trebled between 1946

and 1960—from $41.3 billion to $137.5 billion in longer maturities, and from $52.2 to $157.6 in short-term paper. But this does not begin to tell the corporate story, because the big babies finance themselves mostly out of earnings, and this process is reflected in appreciation of shares rather than in new debt paper. We have already seen what this has come to with NYSE paper.

The most fabulous growth of all has been in non-farm mortgage debt created by non-corporate entities like you and me, which hovered around $26-27 billion during the War and stood at $173.9 billion at the end of 1960. The increase was about $100 billion during the ten-year period 1948-58. A crucial portion of this paper has been directly underwritten by the Federal government: according to the 1960 census, 57 per cent of the homes are mortgaged, and two-fifths of the mortgage paper is government backed—$23 billion of FHA-insured and over $30 billion of VA-guaranteed mortgages. This financing has accounted for what is probably the most impressive physical alteration of the American landscape since the forests were cut down, the farmlands occupied, and the cities built. All in all, as a number of people have mentioned, the creation of the suburbs and attendant physical, social and psychological paraphernalia is *the* domestic event of the postwar period.

And consumer credit—to equip the new houses, and provide transportation between the place of earning and place of spending. The total amount of short and intermediate-term credit outstanding topped $56 billion in January 1962, and is still moving up. In 1945, as the War more or less ended, the figure was a piddling $5.7 billion, down from $9.2 in 1941. And then *zoom!* the war bonds were cashed in and this credit climbed $3 billion or so a year: the

1945 amount had doubled by 1947; that doubled by 1951; and *that* doubled by 1957. Most of this was installment credit; most installment credit was for automobiles and other durables; and half of all consumer credit and two-thirds of the installment-credit paper is held by commercial banks and sales finance companies, the latter being a new form of corporate-consumer bank. According to the 1958 Survey of Consumer Finances, in 1957 "about 6 in 10 spending units buying cars and 5 in 10 of those purchasing furniture and household durable goods borrowed to finance their purchases." The Survey concludes: "Increased use of credit has probably been the most important development in the financing of durable goods over the postwar period." And there you have it. The peasant is being capitalized. By big corporations and other big banks.

So much for statistics—now let's get down to business.

What is unique about the Big Debts is that they involve an extensive capitalization of consumption: in effect, interest charged on the right to eat. It is new to apply the paper-creating credit mechanism on this scale to the "financing" of consumption and other non-profit–making activities. This now is a basic dynamic of our society, and it constitutes a kind of social revolution.

The dynamic is quite completely contrary to good sense, by which I mean business good sense. People with money have always loaned some of it to the government, and homestead mortgages are not brand new, and neither are pawnbrokers. But we are here dealing with another one of those modern situations where a change in degree has become a change in kind. The common man and his governments are being plastered with paper. This process can only accelerate. So there will be more and more paper the validity of which will be based not on profit-making, but on governmental taxing authorities and job-holding. Indeed, the former is also grounded on the latter—unless profit-making business itself would like to pay all the taxes. It doesn't.

Two big points emerge: 1) the business-and-paper system has become decisively dependent on rather full employment of the consuming population—day by day, it needs people "employed" less as workers and more as consumers; and 2) the present income-and-consumption level, already highly financed, clearly supports only the present level of production. If *real* deficits—as in "real" wealth, "real" income, etc.—in public-sector needs are considered, then even more paper will be required to sustain the current level since these cannot be handled without more borrowing.

The financing of consumption can also be described, and in all justice should be, as a democratization of credit. So describing it, we should refer as well to the greatly increased use of checking accounts (at one time—and even now in some other countries—this was a gentleman's privilege), charge accounts, credit cards, personal loans, "instant" money, and so on, as well as government guaranties, subsidies, transfer payments, and other general welfarism. In an important sense, business and government are "cooperating" in carrying out this social revolution. The idea that almost everybody took away with him from the Great Depression is that level y of production can only be sustained by level x of purchasing power. So everybody's for purchasing power. But the American business genius did not go to pieces under the strain of this apparently anti-profit notion—it has found numerous means of making money out of purchasing power (consumer credit costs about $11 billion in interest), just as it did out of production, now that it has been decided that both are necessary.

Ah, but the irony of it all! *The primary collateral of the New Financing is the job of the debtor.* That's his only source of income. He can't pay taxes or meet installment payments without one. The repossessed automobile or washing-machine is useless unless it can be sold on credit to someone who still has a job-as-collateral. So now we are really on our way in the grand adventure of finding paper means to distribute what we absolutely can't help but produce to the peasants who can absolutely use it. But this means the peasant has to have a job. And *that* contains a whole universe of consequential meanings!

The property system has been the basis of the money/credit system. With jobs-as-collateral, jobs-as-a-source-of-credit, you can easily see that we are becoming re-engaged with jobs-as-property. (This is otherwise indicated by the well-known fact that trade union members are more concerned about seniority and other on-the-job rights than they are about straightaway wage rises.) You might put it formally by saying that we are coming back to status as opposed to contract. The latter, at considerable social cost, was capable of creating the modern world, but not good enough to keep it going or make it livable. As pointed out in an earlier chapter, status is the basic source of credit even at the height of classic capitalism; so we might have to remind ourselves that, contrary to the textbook tale, freedom of contract never completed its ascendancy. But until the new American day, only profit-making and other bourgeois status was accepted as currency in the credit system. That's what Bryan was so incensed about.

We say to you that you have made the definition of a business man too limited in its application. The man who is employed for wages is as much a business man as his employer . . . the miners who go down a thousand feet into the earth . . . and bring forth from their hiding places the precious metals to be poured into the channels of trade are as much business men as the few financial magnates who, in a back room, corner the money of the world. We come to speak of this broader class of business men. . . . You shall not press down upon the brow of labor this crown of thorns. . . .

So the Paper Economy, by some weird maneuvering of internal tentacles, has grabbed itself by the throat and is now quite fully committed, for the least impressive reasons, to reasonably full employment, and to buying off the next depression which has replaced Hoover's prosperity as being eternally just around the corner.

But all of this creates an awful lot of paper—and an awfully messy situation behind and under it, because business doesn't quite believe it is doing what it is doing, and is no more (or less) committed to it than any dreamer is to his own nightmare. Notice that the logic of their situation would require business to support Walter Reuther's demand for a guaranteed annual wage for production workers since this would accomplish wonders in increasing the value of jobs-as-collateral—and allow for another burst of consumer financing. They are not apt to confront their situation logically, however: the struggle against the nightmare of Thing-Abundance is carried on with irrational ferocity. Our business rulers confront abundance with horror because it would reduce the power of the paper world; and our wealthy classes also face the awesome perspective of the cheapness of wealth with understandable revulsion. I think this may represent the most profound self-hatred the human race has experienced since the Middle Ages. Having built the modern world of technological industry, the owning classes and their attendants simply refuse to let the rest of us move in. They fear that if they did, money would lose its value. It probably would, since the essential element of its value up until now has been scarcity.

They just can't see their way clear to doing without the money-power. They can't stand prosperity, especially somebody else's. To make the money system a bit more rational and to achieve full production would, they feel, and I'm afraid they're right, diminish their power. So instead of getting the best out of the system, the purpose of the Rearguarders is simply the minimal one of keeping it from going utterly to pot. Five million cars a year would mean a federally expensive recession, so they shoot for six-and-a-half to sustain a dismal prosperity, instead of for the nine or ten that the existing plant could turn out. And meanwhile they suggest that everybody should "save"—money, that is—so next year they can get a new car. No! The real reason is so that money will retain its value as a symbol of scarcity for the benefit of their power and pelf. Just that. (One day we ought to leap forward and request that General Motors use its plant to produce something really useful, instead of just more tinnier cars. That's apostasy, of course, and I have been assuming *arguendo* with the rest of this misguided nation that more cars, or the same old junk sooner, would be desirable.)

They don't know what they're doing. For example, the same principles of credit and capitalization which governed the building of the paper houses of profit-making business

are sure to have their effect on the paper tents of non-profit–
making consumption. The dynamic is for more paper, and
a higher take on the existing paper. How can this be possible
without more jobs, higher wages and salaries, increased
governmental taxes, and so on? And where is all this to come
from except as a bigger slice out of profits and interest? The
whole thing has become too circular. And still we have no
really new commitment to full and purposeful production,
which would necessarily mean conscious modifications of
the whole paper system—like price-control, or at least restraint; penalty taxes for non-use of productive plant; more
direct intervention in the allocation of money/credit; or a
number of other creepy socialistic horrors.

Can anyone doubt any longer that what we are discussing is a religion of money-power? As a system of effective allocation of resources, the unmanaged Paper Economy
is palpably inept. To retain its validity at all it must recreate
or maintain the scarcity of real wealth which was its whole
historical point. But industrial technology is much too productive, so it can only accomplish this low task piecemeal
and as part of a rear-guard action doomed to defeat. The
paper-creating religion: Never do anything for its own sake
or simply because of its utility, but only if it is also an act
of devotion—a money-maker.

Note that the screams issuing from the Right-and-
Propriety sector are muted with regard to the increase in
mortgage paper, state and local debt, consumer credit, and
so on. But nearly everybody gurgles with pleasure when
there is a miniscule paper-surplus in the Federal accounts,
and a paper-deficit of a few billion incurred in underwriting
the whole economy is "fiscal irresponsibility," will destroy
the Western alliance, and no proper businessman would

countenance it for a moment. Except that business lives by that sort of thing. And all the business endorsements are as smoke written across the sky, without the underlying Federal guaranty that there will not be another depression.

Paired with its role as the Big Underwriter, the Federal government is also the Big Customer—with similar economic effect. Spending under the Federal budget, whether derived from taxes or borrowing, and whether through transfer payments or direct purchase, sustains—that is, underwrites—the given level of production. In recent years, this spending has accounted for something like 15-20 per cent of GNP.

This is not the place to attempt to convey the full scope of the Federal government's economic effect (see Chapter 10). The point here is to appreciate the general underwriting effect of the Federal budget in relation to the piddling debt that accompanies it. In doing so, please note: 1) that recent budgets and deficits have not sustained full production—nothing like it—but only the pale prosperity of the Eisenhower years of fiscal responsibility; 2) that the real deficits in education, housing, medical care, etc., have grown alarmingly while the Federal paper deficit has been manfully held in check; and 3) that meanwhile other paper (not called "deficits," for some reason) has increased fabulously.

Where will all this end? As long as we continue to allow reality to happen only in capitalized form, it is very clear indeed that the amount of paper will increase. Is this, in the long run, dangerous? No, not necessarily dangerous— more on the order of absurd. What is dangerous, every-where and always, is action or non-action based on the belief that the paper world is more real or more important than that other world we occasionally live in. If the increase in

paper means an increase in this belief, then it is of course
dangerous—in fact, terrible. But if as the paper grows we all
become somewhat more cynical about it, then all may end
happily after all. By cynicism I mean merely that objective
attitude toward the course of events whereby conventional
symbols are manipulated in view of their effects, rather than
vice versa. The pure, noble, and uncynical belief in a Sound
Dollar and similar religious abstractions can ruin us.

This isn't as awful as it sounds. Ostensibly, the Federal
Reserve Board money-magicians are engaged in just such a
manipulation of the money supply; and the government is
committed to fiscal manipulation in the form of contra-
cyclical redistributions of income whenever the nearness of
a down-swing is sensed. So major opinion is cynical as
described—the question is how much and for whom. The
answer lies not in subtle formulations—such as are engaged
in by so many professors and editorialists—but in political
action. It is purely a political question, and since we are a
great and glorious democracy, there are available a full
democratic rainbow of answers. The world has become very
complex: we have to think and plan in order to survive in it.
Is the Federal government to borrow more extensively than
state and local governments, than consumers and home-
builders? Is this borrowing to be devoted to education or
highways, health facilities or further subsidies for air transportation? Political issues all—and hundreds more like them.

The use of the Federal taxing authority, the participation of the government in the management of the money
system, and the amount of Federal debt the foregoing may
support, are all part of the paper side of the political discussion as to distribution of institutional power in our society.
Since the War, we have had a tremendous growth in private

and local debt and a well-held line on Federal debt. That was a political decision, and can be reversed. It better be. Otherwise we continue to limp along for another decade—and no gimpy nation is going to square off effectively with the Soviet Union.

The fact that paper-values are not any longer destroyed—that this is the profoundest meaning of the government's no-depression policy—has not yet sunk in. When it does, the revolutionary contour of our circumstance will be perceived, and it will become increasingly clear to all reasonable men that the government-as-underwriter—just as any underwriter previously—is entitled to a strong voice in the further creation of paper, the value of which it will also be called upon to guarantee. Moreover, since the government's underwriting activities are decisive for the whole economy, it is entitled also to selective intervention in allocative and other institutional decisions, as well as in paper-creating think-sessions. In the very long run, it cannot be an effective underwriter without exercising these prerogatives. In the very short run, it is a captive underwriter if it does not exercise them. And since it is after all *our* government—and moreover our only legal one—we are entitled to liberate it when and as we decide to do so. Another political decision. We have to decide whether the purpose of the government in underwriting the economy is to validate the paper as an incident to the production and distribution of necessary and desired goods, or as an end in itself.

The Big Debts, I have suggested, cannot be "paid back." They constitute an unconscionable charge on the right to live in the Paper Economy. But pay them off, and they become Big Money—in the hands of people who couldn't possibly "spend" it. Where would the money go?

Into building factories and such? There are already too
many for the Paper Economy, and they move goods as
much as they do only because of the unpaid Big Debts. To
pay back the Big Debts would be to stick a pin in the
balloon of the Paper Economy.

You might say that all of the lack of understanding of
the Paper Economy finds violent refuge in our enthusiastic
misconception of government paper. The Federal debt could,
for instance, be converted into non-interest bearing money
any time the political decision to do so were effected. Another nice way of doing away with the debt might be to
issue some long-term paper that has, say, double value for
the payment of estate taxes—this way it could be retired
eventually (if estate taxes were actually collected) and no
caviar would be taken out of the mouths of any living paper-
holders. Any bright paper-mechanic could think of dozens
of ways of paring it down or doing away with it altogether.
But it would just build up all over again—in the Paper
Economy. Wouldn't it be silly for an institution dispensing
a selfless $100-billion-plus cash-flow each year—and "own-
ing" great quantities of things, including $50 billion of real
property alone (all unmortgaged)—not to capitalize itself
in a society built on capitalization? Indeed, it ought to go
public and sell shares.

The Federal government is the most generous underwriter any ambitious entrepreneur could hope for. It takes
over all unprofitable but necessary activities; it pays for the
initial costs of the most risky endeavors, and as soon as they
look as if they may go, it demurely steps aside; it is preparing
to contribute decisively—beyond Service-connected training—to the whole project of education, which is the *sine*

qua non of a dynamic technological society; it directly takes over substantial quantities of the welfare charges of the producing population; and it absolutely guarantees to do whatever may need to be done to maintain a certain minimum level of production, and otherwise forestall a general collapse. *But it is not permitted to make a profit!* Since it creates so many profit-making possibilities for others, I see no reason why it shouldn't operate on sound business principles and ladle in some of the gravy for itself (that is to say, for the citizens themselves). It is very primitive, very poor PR indeed, to call all your taxes "taxes"—business never does. And when the government by its own efforts and expenditures creates a new industry, it is not anything that can be called "expropriation" for it to hold on during the profitable season as well as the risky early years. Also, if the government made some profit, citizen-businessmen would have more respect for it. All in all, I think it's a very good idea and should be studied seriously in graduate seminars in advanced universities.

The national debt is not a housewife's charge account. Paying for an adequate national educational system is not a supermarket Saturday. Rather obviously, the difference is between an individual family and a nation. At the national level, the only reasonable limitation on debt is actual resources, and the political decision to use them this way rather than that way. But not paper-considerations: never paper. Except to the present holders of paper-power. And they have no moral position to speak of, since their paper either wouldn't exist or wouldn't have much value without Federal underwriting. And there you are.

7

TAXES:
THE HOUSE'S TAKE

THE FREQUENTLY FRANTIC and always continuing effort to
"save money on taxes" has brought about a whole new lively
area of paper-manipulation in the modern Paper Economy.
This subject has such a bright aura of complication about it,
however, that we must pause briefly for an explanatory departure. But you will see that this is worth doing, both for
the importance of the matter and also its intrinsic interest.
Modern Federal taxes have quaintly but clearly revised the
nature of paper wealth in this nation—besides being the
basic underpinning of the New Finance discussed in the previous chapter.

Probably nothing reveals us to ourselves so terribly as

that barely believable document, the Internal Revenue Code. This bit of modern secular scripture now constitutes one of the most closely worked abstractions yet created by Western man. Although it was brought into being by a political process which has much in common with the drip-drip method imputed to modern abstract artists, it is distinguished from modern art and similar intricacies by having an always immediate effect on daily life. And even though the code is a magnificent abstraction, it is further distinguished by being written in a language directly derived from spoken English. The gloss upon this text, consisting of regulations, cases, rulings, bulletins, Congressional documents (and even dutifully noted oral innuendoes of highly placed officials of the Treasury Department) fills a nice-sized library and is only occasionally less complicated than the code itself. In 1958 alone, the Internal Revenue Service issued 45,000 rulings.

There is, to begin with, a literal riot of popularly held misconceptions about the tax system, and first among these is the naive faith in its progressivity. It is hardly progressive at all, especially when state, local and other taxes (both hidden and apparent) are thrown into the hamper along with Federal income taxes. It is quite true that some people pay more dollars as tax than other people: 20 per cent of $100,000 is $20,000, while 20 per cent of $10,000 is $2,000. The idea of progressivity, however, does not have to do with the absolute dollar amount of tax, but with a *rate* of tax that increases as income increases. The popular notion that taxes are progressive derives from the annual viewing of the horrifying rate tables which accompany the instruction sheet to Form 1040, under which if the amount on line 5, page 2, is not over $2,000, enter on line 6, page 2, 20 per cent of the amount on line 5; but if the amount on line 5, page 2, is over $200,000, enter on line 6, page 2, $156,820, plus 91 per cent of excess over $200,000. It's all propaganda, a kind of spiritual consolation prize to the 20-per-cent fellows. (Now truly, haven't you felt both innocent and relieved to find yourself in the $6,000-$8,000 area of incompetence rather than on the $20,000-$22,000 bright-boy level, with your "excess" knocked down at 30 per cent rather than 56 per cent? Sure you have, because the whole emotional trend of the annual tax-return travail is that income is a liability— even an expensive luxury.)

If the highest tax rate were 50 per cent rather than 91 per cent, the revenue loss would be about $800 million, well under 1 per cent of the total national tax-bite. But if the personal exemption down at the bottom were increased by only $100, the cost to the government would be about 3 billion dollars. That is because 85 per cent of all money received as income tax is collected at the basic 20 per cent rate —and that is the only rate applicable to two-thirds of all returns. As for the top rates, the big point is the distinction between the formal demand of the well-advertised tax table and the actual effective rate tolerated after a diligent reading (by experts) of the more difficult passages of the code. The average rate of tax on adjusted gross incomes of $100,000 or more was 46 per cent in 1956, although the table said $67,320 plus 87 per cent of the excess over (and $53,640 plus 75 per cent for happy split-incomers). The actual rate comes down to 35 per cent when you account for capital gains and tax-free interest. Also note that "adjusted gross income" is the figure you get *after* business expenses, but before personal exemptions and deductions. Business expenses, capital gains, tax-free municipals, depletion allowances, etc., etc.—great amounts of these are availed of above the 20 per cent rate. To put it mildly.*

Every once in a while a Congressional committee conducts a straight-faced "investigation" of the system of Federal taxation (a scholarly one, not the whose-hand-in-the-till kind like that of the King Committee prior to the 1952 election). The sober findings of these committees tend to be remarkably similar. The reason for this dull fact is that essentially the same situation is investigated each time, and by substantially similar people. NAM publicists, union spokesmen, and judicious scholars don't change that much, it seems. Even so, the detailed story is quite informative.

The last such was released to a public of several thousand moles, including myself, late in 1959. I refer to the "Compendium of Papers on Broadening the Tax Base Submitted to the Committee on Ways and Means in Connection with the Panel Discussions on the Same Subject to be Conducted by the Committee on Ways and Means beginning November 16, 1959," familiarly known as the Tax Revision Compendium of the Mills Committee. The Compendium is

---

* For the sake of fair statement it should be said that about a thousand or so returns in the $200,000-plus area reported only ordinary income, and so did not get in on the 25 per cent capital gains rate. I hope they had some tax-free bonds, and if not it just proves how dumb some people are. Also, the 223 annointed ones who reported AGI of $1 million or more in 1957 actually paid $231,648,000 in taxes on AGI of $447,528,000, which works out to a 52 per cent rather than a 46 per cent rate: but this AGI figure is *not* adjusted for capital gains, business expenses, etc., etc. Anyway, not 91 per cent as advertised. And I personally don't think it's so awful that these 223 taxpaying units forked over as much Federal income tax as the 11 million bottom units reporting AGI of $1,500 and under, to which I suppose should be added the 30 per cent of the population, dependents included, who for one reason or another pay no tax at all. As a matter of fact, I don't much care for an economic situation where one person financially balances out a few hundred thousand other persons. Do you?

a three-volume item of 2,382 pages containing 183 papers dealing in detail with almost all known aspects of the Federal income tax. It is comprehensive (twelve papers on depreciation, ten on percentage depletion, and even seven on the tax treatment of cooperatives); representative (mostly the leading scholars, but also Roswell Magill, senior tax partner of Cravath, Swaine and Moore, the New York law factory which represents U.S. Steel and so on, John C. Davidson, a high official of the NAM, Peter Henle and others of the AFL-CIO, and more); and is "a large storehouse of valuable information" containing "many thoughtful suggestions," according to Fred C. Scribner, Jr., a leading Treasury Department politician of the Eisenhower administration. The Compendium is clearly the most recently decisive few million words or so on Federal income taxation.

What is the tale told? Well, no one steps forward to defend the structure—the best said for it is that, contrary to all reasonable expectation, neither the collection system nor the economy have collapsed under the irrational weight of it. Everybody criticizes—not enough of this, too much of that —but there is a marvelously broad area of disagreement on what's "this" and what's "that." The political lines of cleavage are clear enough except when the fair-minded technicians let loose, in which instances it is clear enough that only the God of Logic would take the spoils of their victory. For example, a rational, equitable arrangement would require taxation of social security benefit payments as well as a guillotining of the infamous depletion allowance which has made Texas so important to itself. As to the first, even the union man would go along if the level of payments were raised so that there would be no actual loss of income to the old folks; and as to the second, the logicians suggest that if the Federal government wants to subsidize the oil industry it should do so with an item in the annual budget called "Subsidy for the Oil Industry." Net practical gain, zero.

The broadest agreement was reached in connection with the shared pessimism as to any possibility of realizing the purpose of the committee—broad tax reform. This here-we-are-again mood was most nicely expressed by Professor Walter J. Blum of the University of Chicago Law School: "It is most unlikely that any new insights or ideas, to say nothing of new legislation, will be developed as a result of" the committee's effort. But he welcomed in a resigned way "a panoramic study of the tax base" even though "the familiar briefs of the special pleaders and the tomes of the academic neutrals might easily become boring" and certainly would accomplish nothing.

The "tax base" is the total amount of gross income to which the tax rates are supposed to apply. If any of this gross income is excluded for any reason, then of course no tax applies to it—and all such exclusions along with the process of creating them are characterized by the professionals as an "erosion of the tax base." The main reason for this erosion, which is the most important fact about the tax system, is that no one is willing to live up to the grand principle embodied in the progressive schedules or to the accompanying principle that "equal incomes should bear equal tax liabilities." These principles constitute a great and necessary economic myth, quite similar to the antitrust balderdash that sustains the fantasy of a free competitive market. Both are currently required to preserve a Sunday-belief in economic justice, without which we would be left face to face with the brute facts of private economic power. Note that the last thing anyone wants to do is to "broaden" his own tax base. But erosion has progressed quite far, and is potentially a serious danger. Most of all, it is not an excrescence upon an otherwise marvelously equitable system, but its essence.

If you read the tax law perceptively as the great social document it is, you are entertained by a story with very clear outlines indeed—containing only a single under-level of transparent ambiguity. The code identifies income with magnificent Constitutional sweep, pronounces radically democratic rates of taxation thereupon, and then begins to introduce detailed exceptions to these noble principles. The exceptions constitute the overwhelming bulk of the law, and they are practically unreadable. (This is not unintended by any means: I assure you that the biggest "loophole" is a smart tax lawyer who can comprehend relevant sections of the code.) The exceptions range from generous notions as to business and personal deductions, through exclusions of income and preferential rates, to the special laws or rulings which were passed to allow Louis B. Mayer to cash in his interest in MGM feature films at the capital-gains rate, to make it more difficult for Marshall Field to continue losing money in support of the newspaper *PM*, and so on.

Most new tax law, whether by statute, ruling, or decision, ends up by introducing further exceptions, even when its ostensible purpose is otherwise, which it seldom is. (I won't bother describing the technical process, except to note that when a court or the Service finally sustains some less permissive provision, the subsequent appeal to Congress by the injured group quite frequently prevails.) The net result is a tax law so irrational, inequitable, and complicated in its sieve-like favoritism that it has become the despair of most experts, both technical and moral.

For the expert who has any breadth of interest at all,

the only engaging questions about the code still open intellectually are: 1) how in God's name did it happen? and 2) just *why* does the crazy-quilt irrationality of the tax system remain so thoroughly immovable under our political process?

Probably the best functional way of viewing our patchwork taxing disorder is as a system of subsidies. This is also useful in accenting its connection with other expressions of Federal power, since the most characteristic activity of our government has always been the dispensing of subsidy: this was always a central part of our so-called system of private property. (The second act of the First Congress in 1789 was to pass a tariff law, and the main concern of our government during the nineteenth century was to collect the continental United States and its resources and then give it away to private interests.) All that is necessary to see tax provisions this way is to take the avowed tax principles at face value; then all the preferential provisions appear as purposeful fallings away from the grace of equity and progression.

Viewing tax preferences as subsidies, the following may be noted:

1) The most important is the depreciation allowance to industry which helps to finance modernization and expansion of plant. Apart from the accounting artificiality of estimated useful lives of some assets, and the fact that other assets may appreciate in value while they are being depreciated on an original-cost basis, two points: rapid amortization of so-called "emergency" projects has been substantial—$22.5 billion were certified between 1950 and 1956; and the declining balance method of depreciation introduced by the 1954 amendments to the code is estimated to cost a cumulative total of $19 billion, assuming a constant level of invest-

ment. The great liberalizing of depreciation guidelines by the administration in 1962, along with the new investment credit legislation, is expected to cost the Treasury between 2 and 3 billion dollars in the first year alone.

2) The depletion allowance and deductibility of exploration and drilling expenses has created a superb oil industry with troublesome excess capacity, a few billionaires, hordes of multimillionaires, a well-heeled reactionary political force, and an incredible number of dry-holes (17,574 in 1960). The oil industry needs the continuation of this subsidy to produce oil about as much as Paul Getty needs another billion to feel financially secure.

3) The medical deduction has helped psychoanalysts to help make upper class life bearable in this country and in other ways (along with the charitable deduction) to support the scandalous financial structure of American medical services. This deduction can be characterized as a cross-eyed, anemic form of inadequate national health insurance, whereby the less you need the more you get (within limits): the government will pay 20 per cent of an ordinary person's $1,000 operation and up to 91 per cent of a millionaire's certified stay at Tucson, Ariz.

4) The Happy Owned Home is a favored object of beneficence. First, you don't get taxed on the rental value of the property if you live in it, which is nice compared to renting an apartment; and then you get another deduction for taxes, and for interest on your government-guaranteed mortgage. Finally, if you outfit the home with a wife you get in on the 4-billion-dollar reduction in taxes based on the split-income provision—if, that is, you are not in that basic 20 per cent bracket which doesn't split. A wife is worth nothing, taxwise, if she is accompanied by two children and

you gross no more than $4,900. But that wife, bless her, is worth $13,680 cold cash annually if you have taxable income of $100,000. (One of the objections to abandoning this subsidy of upper class marriage is that it would increase the incidence of upper class divorce. Perhaps. But on the other hand, who cares?)

5) Really good restaurants, really bad theatre, Miami Beach and Atlantic City, the Hilton hotel chain, and numerous other such things are rather fully subsidized by that Association for the Furtherance of High Living known as the expense account.

6) And so on—subsidies for various cultural and spiritual charities, insurance companies, state and local governments, old folks, the loss-carryover to turn bankruptcy into half a victory, comfortable retirement in a number of forms, and stock options for harassed executives.

7) One of the major "loopholes" not so frequently mentioned is straight-out non-compliance with the law: unreported adjusted gross income amounts to more than $26 billion. While 95 per cent of wages and salaries are reported, because of the withholding provision, it is estimated that 12.5 per cent of business and professional income and as much as 60 per cent of farm income (a benefit in addition to billions in direct subsidies to farmers) are not reported. Something close to $5 billion in dividends and interest is typically not acknowledged. Another aspect of the established non-compliance system is the deliberate understaffing of the Internal Revenue Service, which ensures selective lack of enforcement as another sizable preference eroding the tax base.

The foregoing does not touch upon bribery, influence-peddling and similar unpleasantries. They exist and not insignificantly, as any one who has been around knows; but the overridingly important point for most realists is that most practices which are questioned popularly are quite legal and in most cases even official. (In the property system generally, when a particular form of "cheating" becomes x-degree profitable it is usually expedient to make it legal, in order to reduce the overhead.) In the trade, a fine distinction is made between tax avoidance and tax evasion. Since tax counsel is supposed to tailor a transaction or organize a body of wealth so as to take fullest advantage of every applicable special provision and potential preference, and since no body of law is clear or settled around the edges, there are a whole passel of maneuvers which turn out to be avoidance or evasion only after the fact. When tax lawyers do not have a clear precedent in their favor, or find it inadvisable to obtain an advance ruling, it is called "running for luck" when they nevertheless go forward under optimum tailoring. Naturally, victories in such instances are dearer to the professional heart than the ordinary cases of pedestrian plumbing.

Thus, the essential "loophole" is a good tax attorney. (I doubt if there is a single big tax outfit in the country that does not have at least one member of its staff who was trained by apprenticeship with the IRS.) But use of this loophole requires considerable "feed" money, which in itself constitutes a very important "preference" in favor of those taxpayers who can afford the charge. Also, since the cost of tax advice is deductible, the higher the taxpayer's bracket the more and better advice in beating the government he can afford to have the government pay for. Under this system, a contest between a tax lawyer with a gross income of one or two hundred thousand and a G-11 government attorney ten-twenty years his junior, is painful to behold.

A leading scholar, Joseph A. Pechman of the Committee for Economic Development, has estimated that a restored tax base in 1957 would have been $208 billion rather than $149 billion, and at existing rates would have yielded an increased 40 per cent, about $14 billion. Or the rates could have been reduced one-third across the board. But this would have meant the neutralizing of taxation as a means of social control, as well as realizing the ostensible progressivity of the rate structure. The issues are realer and more political, and no such rationalizing is likely except as the result of major political dealings. The present campaign of business and wealth is to reduce top rates and further liberalize depreciation allowances.* Both are desirable—and both should be paid for. The lower income groups interested in this "payment" will have to grow in sophistication and wariness, however, since each tax bill since 1950 "has created a number of loopholes for everyone it closed." This is the scoop in the profession, and the bright young men follow the bills through committee and floor action so diligently that by the time of passage they are already at work revising "tax pictures" to take advantage of the new advantages. Many years ago "loopholes" resulted from Congressional ineptitude, but in more recent times canniness accounts for most of the statutory elbow-room. The duplicity involved in this shrewd bumbling has been perfected to a fine point, as for example one feature of the 1954 amendments which was supposed to stop the peddling of loss–carry-overs and, according to Representative Forand, ended up invigorating this market in red-ink companies.

We seem to have, or be headed toward, the following political technique of tax reform, if any: in arresting erosion or ameliorating irrationalities, the dollar-facts of life will be

* This latter was achieved in 1962.

recognized on a rough income-class basis, and reform will be accomplished by political packaging. For example, tax-free interest and the dividend exclusion would balance out a reduction of the top rate from 91 per cent to something close to 50 per cent. A similar low-income package worth about $800 million could be put together, perhaps out of the exclusion for sick pay and an upgrading of almost any of the personal deduction minimums, as against a modest increase in the basic exemption or a splitting of the lowest bracket. If tax reforms were to be accomplished at a time when revenue could be reduced, many of these issues might well become more manageable—but that is not likely to happen. Or if the government were allowed to finance economic expansion by borrowing, then absolute revenue could be maintained even while the so-called loopholes were being plugged. That also is not very likely, because of the prejudice against the government doing anything so business-like as borrowing to finance increased tax collections; and also because of the "real" deficits in government spending referred to in the previous chapter.

So what about tax reform? It will take some adroit, imaginative packaging based on the balance of political pressures; or it won't come about short of a war-type mobilization of the economy.

Now that we have a few characterizing facts, we are free to do some speculating. Or to put it differently: while waiting for the tax system to be neutralized and conformed to the ideal of progressivity, we might as well try to comprehend the existing tax pattern as a part of the American property system.

Take money, for example. There is now all the difference in the world between before-tax and after-tax money. Really two separate *kinds* of money. Wherever there is a strong flow of income, whether passing through the books of successful business organizations or the bejewelled hands of upper-bracket individuals, there are two kinds of money—two mediums of exchange and two measures of value. Every dollar of raw income, before it can serve as such medium or measure, must first be analyzed and identified from the tax point of view. This intellectual process is a great property-creating force in our new system. (The practitioners of this powerful intellection—top-flight tax lawyers and accountants, and tax-thinking businessmen—are among the more impressively imaginative managerial types in our increasingly complex managerial system.) For example, a tax analysis after-the-fact—the wrong time for it—may disclose that the taxpayer was remiss during the taxable year in making too much money, not losing enough, not expensing enough, failing to invest in sufficiently risky ventures, not giving away enough, missing good opportunities to overpay, or perhaps keeping records that are too easy to comprehend. One thing is perfectly clear about good tax-thinking: to be adequate it must be imaginative, and in its creative course it will necessarily transgress most of our received notions about the uses of money and the ownership of property.

Take ownership: who owns the flow of raw income—whose money is it? I can feel about after-tax money that it is "mine": I can do with it as I please. But before-tax money is never "mine" in the full possessory sense: it is only of some immediate use to me—it carries with it a potential benefit which must be availed of in specific ways and within the taxable period. I must deploy it in a way that will keep the government from getting it, and this deployment must occur before it settles down to being net taxable income—at which magical moment I must account to my partner, the government. Before-tax money is a specific rather than a general medium of exchange; similarly, the values it measures. (Big smart money never stood still, even before the Tax Age; its managers always kept it moving against inflationary loss, and since inflation is continuous there never was any rest for the wealthy.) The specific exchanges and values applicable to a particular flow of before-tax money are determined by the taxpayer's time-locked circumstance: it may be that I *ought* to eat at the Chambord again this week, but my stomach just can't handle any more rich food; or the company *ought* to put a few more millions into depreciable plant, but the market—like my stomach—can't absorb the product. Frequently the meal or the plant is purchased anyway, because the compulsion to consume is nearly irresistible.

Tax-thinking is complicated beyond bearing for some old-fashioned souls because, of course, there is a tariff in after-tax money levied on all deployment of before-tax money. That is, in order to get the available advantage out of the flow of income on its way to the government I am forced to salt it with what is conceptually some of my own real money—the $100 lunch tab actually costs me nine ownership dollars or my corporate employer forty-eight fundamental iron men. So the resurgence of primitive mine-all-mine thinking in the most unlikely places is startlingly frequent. It is almost asking too much of the older American businessman or property-owner that he adjust to and live relevantly in the modern business system. Many have to be led up to rational self-interest kicking and screaming all the way. Enter the tax expert as the manager of the flow of big income—*any* flow of big income, whether that of Alcoa or one of the individual Mellons.

The ordinary taxpayer-on-the-street is naturally enough not burdened with any of these exotic considerations—he does not have enough before-, after-, or during-tax money to occasion much concern to anyone, including himself. His relation to the Federal tax system consists mostly of smoldering hatred, bewilderment, voting Republican, and occasionally devising homemade forms of exaggeration and obtuseness in response to Form 1040's nagging inquisitiveness. His view of the big taxpayer is apt to rely heavily on the soothing reflection that if it hurts me, it must be killing him.

Although the fellows described in the preceding paragraph pay most of the income taxes, they hardly count in any effort to understand the tax system. For them the code is disarmingly simple: they pay—period. Indeed, they pay ahead of time to make certain there is no mistake about the matter. So in an actual sense most of them don't even have a before-tax dollar to bother their ordinary heads about. And their after-tax dollar is spent right away, in any event, on consumables: they don't make money, they make a living. Although they are not aware of it, the tax money they never see is the least of their daily loss; because they end up paying considerably more tax in the form of prices administered all over them by our major producing institutions, the big corporations. Incidentally, the consumer not only pays his own personal income tax, and this price tax levied at privately determined rates by corporate management, but it appears that said consumer *also* pays the 52 per cent corporate income tax which—even the First National City Bank agrees—the price administrators pass on to him.

Finally, the tax-accruals on his wages are used by employers as interim financing on a quarterly basis. The return on this money would probably go a long way toward paying for the consumer financing discussed in Chapter 6.

But for corporations and upper-bracket types, before-tax money is the realest of the real—the most important new form of public-private property. Our current economy features numerous less-than-private forms of property; but after the towering masses of alienated capital held by our big corporations, none are more significant or creative than the new property configurations resulting from tax considerations. Along with corporatism, these have literally reorganized the top layer of the entire property system. Money or property that calls for tax-tailoring may be thought of as "partnership-property." The government is a great, mostly silent partner in all its use and disposition. Although businessmen (mostly the slower ones or earlier winners) profess to hate this new thing, it has certainly added a great deal of charm, interest, and intellectual distinction to the great game of business. And like all property forms and other ways of doing business, the New Property has pervasive effects on the national style of life.

The primary tax compulsions are to convert ordinary income into income taxed at a preferential rate—capital gains, depletion, another taxpayer, etc.—and failing that, to scramble for and among deductible expenditures. As an incidental effect, the meaning of money and property in America have been decisively altered. And largely on the plus-side, I think, because over-all tax considerations have provided a great incentive to spending. Money is taken somewhat less seriously if you do not experience the abso-

lutely possessory sensation concerning it, with the consequence that, held less dearly, it is spent more freely. All to
the good. Note the similar effect of management-control of
major corporations: it's just easier to spend money if it isn't
quite yours. We were getting to the point, about 1933, where
if somebody didn't start spending it pretty soon, the whole
house of cards was going to collapse. Nowadays there are
a number of built-in spending mechanisms, which keep us
thing-oriented to a degree; and not least of these is our tax
system and its zany consumption-imperatives.

Keynes made the point very strongly: *Money is for
spending*. Although the fact may strike us peasants as quite
strange, this was a rather new proposition for the capitalist
way of handling matters, since it contradicts the most truly
basic dynamic embodied in the maxim, *Money is for making
more money*. Tax imperatives, along with general inflation,
have created billions upon billions in new paper-values—
any really important impulse in America does—but they
have also led to even more billions of honest-to-God spending which very likely would not otherwise have occurred.
All of the government's tax-receipts are spent rather than
capitalized, and private tax decisions induce even more
spending that otherwise might not take place. So all in all
the gerry-built tax system, by a series of happy accidents, is
one of our great preservative blessings; it is a more effective
economic regulator, for example, than was New Deal pump-
priming.

The spending compulsions of the tax system refer both
to productive plant and straightaway consumption. It is
enough to recall again the magnificently established oil
industry and the just as magnificent appointments of expense-account society. Examples could be multiplied end-

lessly. The point I would like to emphasize is that much of
this spending may reveal in us a certain gluttony, immaturity, pig-headed foolishness, helpless confusion, life-
hatred, phenomenal and uncalled-for coarseness in our
feelings about other people, and so on—but when we don't
spend (read: produce and consume), we are literally mad.
This country was not founded as a haven for Tibetan
monks. It was, it is, and it always will be primarily a banquet.
That some of us are more concerned with the National
Heartburn than with the next course on the menu, is a non-
economic point.

I cannot resist a couple of non-economic illustrations of
my basic economic point. It would take a little proving, but
I think the tax law is undermining modern art—as follows:
rich people can actually make money by donating paintings
which have rather arbitrarily appreciated in value over and
above the purchase price. This gimmick has been well-
publicized so I won't bother to explain it in detail. The
market for paintings has zoomed. Serious and not-so-serious
artists who were cadging drinks and working in frame-shops
a few years ago now get, in real money, four and five times
the prices they used to put on their paintings for no better
reason than that galleries required a stated price and the
artists were pleased to evaluate themselves at an impossible
figure. Since they now sell paintings, the artists are getting
used to living like real Americans. So they just naturally
tend to repeat themselves in their work in order to repeat the
sales of their work, which was no problem at all when they
hardly sold anything anyway. Modern American abstract
art, perhaps more than most other forms of expression, does
not bear repeating, even when successful. There you have
my theory, an example of what my notes refer to as "the
distant effects of the code."

Now should artists be poor? In India, perhaps; in America, no. Starving in a garret for the sake of art is one of the things we have lost by getting both feet wet in the twentieth century. Traditionalists who insist on preserving this nineteenth-century opportunity (like those esthetes who prefer hand-made dinnerware) will be disappointed by the tax law as well as other modern effects.

The problem of success is difficult, but not insoluble. Take the American theatre, for instance, the present shape and substance of which is rather fully a result of tax compulsions. To a considerable extent, we find expense-account money in front of the footlights and high-bracket losing stuff behind them. Result: lousy, lavish musicals. (The best that Brooks Atkinson could say of *The World of Suzie Wong*— "It solves the problem of the expense account trade for the winter.") Serious dramatic works, no matter how many prizes they win or what the infallible critics say, cannot achieve anything like the runs of expense-account musicals. So there has been a boom of serious theatre off-Broadway, but this soon began to suffer the effects of success, too: ticket prices went up quickly and the chance to compete with Broadway was not always successfully resisted. The way of art was never easy in the old world of scarcity; it is experiencing unique difficulties under the duress of affluence. How long did it take the so-called beatniks to become a standard theme on television and other commercial media? Just a few years. We are going to have to learn to live with prosperity: we are the transitional generation.

Money siphoned through charitable foundations (over 11,000 of them throughout the country) has radically altered academic intellectual life. The truth is that any deduction— or any tax-induced action—has its radiating social and cultural effects. Take the medical deduction: can anyone seriously doubt that the story of psychoanalysis in America would have been very different indeed if the considerable cost to the patient had not been in part a deductible expense? The stature of the movement here, its great growth since the War, even its locus on Park Avenue, are not due to the higher incidence of neurosis in this country or on that street. The high price of the analytic hour and the consequent social standing of analysts as a professional group owes something essential to the tax factor. The movement to the suburbs, the spiritual quality of being Texan, the price of tranquilizers, New York City as the corporate headquarters of the nation, and me taking a taxi instead of the subway to plead with my editor—all have been influenced and perhaps determined by considerations of tax. The smarter you are, the more you consider it—the more you are aware of the new partnership-property.

Which brings us back, although deviously, to the question of inflation. Besides their other qualities, tax imperatives are also highly inflationary. Tax reasons are new reasons, and if a paper-situation is valuable for tax reasons then new and additional paper-value will be created. Especially when there is a lot of the specific kind of "purchasing power" looking around for tax advantages. There has been since the War. The stock market boom of the fifties, which brought into being several hundreds of billions of new paper-value, resulted among other things from all the new money in the country that had no place else to go in its search for a capital gains situation. Likewise, in part, the real estate boom. Tax-compelled money is buyers' money in a hurry. Ordinary income is finally viewed as a distinct liability. Moreover, depending on what you are buying, there may be a definite willingness to overpay (of which the seller, mirror-thinking the buyer's taxes, is well aware). Take a productive asset that has been substantially depreciated by the holder, sell it to someone who can use it and who has a flow of raw income screaming for deductions, and the price of the asset will reflect not solely its real usefulness but even more the fact that it will have a stepped-up basis (depreciable all over again based on the higher sales price) in the hands of the transferee. An obvious example of this would be, say, an apartment building constructed in the twenties which has benefited from the postwar rise in real estate values. The seller takes a sweet capital gain, which the buyer is more willing to pay because he can depreciate the cost over the remaining life of the building: the price went up, but the building did not get any younger.

The value of an asset now depends on *who* holds it; its general use-value is frequently not the main thing. In the wild world of taxes, this *ad hominem* factor is all-important. An extreme example is the "tax basket" maneuver, like this: if you are doing well, it is better to be a corporation than a person. So, many people who are doing well have personal holding companies. But in order to make the game interesting, the government levies a surtax on personal holding company income unless all the proper ground rules are observed. One of the ways to avoid the surtax is to have a certain percentage of the total p-h-c income consist of gross receipts on rental property. Don't ask me why: ground rules are ground rules. So the right to receive such gross receipts is a valuable bit of property—apart from any economic benefit, any income or ownership or use value of the rental property itself. It is possible to arrange the paper covering a particular building in such a way that this distinct bit of partnership-property, no more and no less, is transferable and thus of independent value. Something from nothing: the building itself remains unchanged: paper inflation.

So the tax structure, besides inducing a great deal of good solid spending, also creates new and exotic forms of property which are paper-inflationary. How could it be otherwise when one of the more valuable pieces of such exotic property is a *loss* on the books of a corporation? The most delightful example of a tax operation built around a loss is that carried off by A. M. Sonnabend in connection with Botany Mills, beginning in 1954. (This imaginative operation was so good it received a special name, being christened the Botany or "bootstrap" formula.) In the two years following the Botany take-over, Sonnabend used the loss carry-forward to acquire twelve profitable companies, most of them not in textiles. In 1957, this potpourri based on Botany's big loss earned 59.4 per cent of its net worth—far in the lead of all listed corporations—because it did not have to pay any taxes. The "bootstrap" is so named because a business is said to "purchase itself" out of its own income— no fresh cash is used. The former owners of the acquired companies get management contracts and still run their businesses, and receive an inflated price therefor as capital gains or deferred payment which is paid out of their company's liquid assets and tax-free earnings in the period for which the loss carry-forward is effective. Botany ends up with what might be called the residual interest in profitable companies. No cash. If you understand the code and can get favorable IRS rulings, you don't need cash. And of course Botany stock went up, too.

The tax system is responsible for a great number of very powerful imperatives throughout the social complex of wealth and property, as well as a slew of miscellaneous economic and cultural effects; but it should be realized that the employment of this great force is largely unplanned. That is, the over-all system is unplanned—I don't mean that most preferences are not intended. These preferences, established by imaginative exploitation of code provisions and administrative rulings, tend very quickly to become deeply vested. Which means that tax policy, as purposeful planning of economic effect, is highly inflexible and largely at the mercy of powerful special interest groups, which "plan" for themselves but acknowledge no further responsibility. The government, more acted upon than acting, just does not have the power under our political process to take over this abandoned responsibility. So the great planning potential of the taxing authority is either unused or badly used. The effects, both good and bad, are largely random.

Corporations are much more effective planning instrumentalities, within their orbits, since they are more in control of the political processes which impinge upon their activities. But most important, their public relations is infinitely superior to that of the government. When they levy tribute it is called "price" rather than "tax." As Thurman Arnold pointed out years ago in *The Folklore of Capitalism*, taxes determined by a democratic rough-and-tumble are much more onerous than prices fixed impersonally by the automatic forces of a free market (that is, administered).

Moreover, the public which pays for both has been sold the notion that it responds to the tax collector involuntarily while it pays prices only because it wants to. When a corporation taxes an additional amount called "profit," everyone is supposed to throw his hat into the air and cheer; but if the government presumed to make a profit—say, gave a subsidy to itself rather than a private business group—we would all have to mourn the advent of tyrannous socialism. Even though *we* are the government: everybody says so, on every state occasion. And if *we*, the people and the government, do anything so intelligently businesslike, profitable and productive as build a dam as part of the TVA project, the Supreme Court finds us entitled thereto *as an exercise of the war power*. As Arnold remarked when he made this point in 1937: "Fantasy can go no further than this."

So taxes are terrible, but prices are true and beautiful. And unlike industry, the government is also rigidly limited in capitalizing its activities, although it does in fact have a lot of property and a very nice flow of income. Neither may it plan these activities with anything like the effectiveness of private industry. The public is said to be a collection of free men only in its role as victims of advertising and the authoritarian control of production and marketing; as active democratic citizenry it can only and it always does enslave itself to government, so the story goes. Money spent on schools is just naturally wasted because it is spent by the government; but money spent on advertising different brands of cigarettes, among which there are no demonstrable differences and all of which constitute a health hazard in any event, is good all around and ends up in GNP as an increase in productivity.

The foregoing are some additional "principles of taxation" which do not ordinarily appear in the textbooks on the subject.

Now we will take a look at the preferred form of government in the United States—the Big Corporation.

THE
INSTITUTIONS

8

CORPORATIONS I

THE VERY EXISTENCE of America's massive and bountiful corporations was for many years neglected, if not denied, by conventional thinking. The revolutionary issue they represent was lost somewhere between Adam Smith's ideal irrelevancies and what was most often referred to as "the monopoly problem" or, even more delicately, as "the question of imperfect competition." That the most obvious fact of economic life in this country, the central position of major corporations, could have been thus obscured is a testament both to the right-thinking energies of our official mentors and the credulity of our educated citizenry. When one reflects that Adam Smith was opposed to corporations and did not welcome them into his eighteenth-century world, this obscurantism becomes even more impressive. It is occasionally even funny that the self-exploitation of the small proprietor still lingers in our minds as a model of American enterprise, while the major corporations which supply most of our needs remain theoretical anomalies. All of this is now beginning to change, however, and a deeply significant discussion has commenced which assumes: 1) that ours is a corporate economy with each industrial or business area typically dominated by a few large organizations, which dominate no less effectively because they are not technical monopolies; and 2) that this rather obvious fact has a welter of far-reaching implications and is going to take an awful lot of explaining.

A vice president and general counsel of the Ford Motor Company has stated out loud: "It is not inaccurate to say that we live in a corporate society." This assertion is still somewhat indelicate, but we can now take it as certain that it is no longer inaccurate.

It may not be saying too much to assert also that the new thinking about collective enterprise, or managerialism, is about to be recognized as constituting a great theological crisis, on the order of the one that accompanied the introduction of Darwin's work, or even the social and political thought which followed the Reformation. We are experiencing the collapse of the economic and political pillars of the ideology which has dominated Western thought for several hundred years. A "new man" has entered onto the historical stage, and the required new explanation of him is in the making. Comprehending the corporate economy, his milieu, is central to this effort. It is, in our terms, the institutional bedrock of the Paper Economy.

"Corporation" has become one of the more important words in the language, and the people who run them, called "managers," properly count themselves among the more powerful groups to be found on this power-ridden planet. Well, what is a corporation? Technically, it is a legal entity —what is called a creature of the law—which remark, I am sure, does nothing for anyone. Reinhold Niebuhr has referred to them suggestively as "these dubious sovereignties," which I like very much but is probably too poetic for present purposes. Roger Blough's speechwriters see the big American corporation as a voluntary association of free men, which dovetails nicely with the familiar "just folks" metaphysics of our commercial culture. Writing early in this century, Veblen defined the corporation as "a conspiracy in restraint of production"; this contains an essential insight but cannot qualify as a well-rounded Aristotelian definition. To be official, the main thing about a major corporation is that it organizes and directs large masses of men and material in a more or less limited technological area. So I suggest that a corporation is a form of industrial or technological or financial government.

The two basic points about corporations were made decades ago, by Veblen and by Berle and Means. Around the turn of the century, Veblen demonstrated that large business organizations, especially financial institutions, dominated and distorted the new technological forces, and that these control-organizations used paper—that is, capitalization—primarily to make money out of making and not making goods. To his mind, profit and production were substantially opposed to each other, especially the profit derived from the issuance of paper, which is the chief kind. The second basic point about corporations was made thirty years ago by Berle and Means, who suggested that large publicly held corporations were an anomaly in the supposed system of private property. That pronouncement in *The Modern Corporation and Private Property*, published in 1932, will probably turn out to be one of the more resounding understatements in the history of social thought. Because in fact the big American corporation is engaged in a pleasant, leisurely, and continuingly decisive destruction of the previously existing system of private property. In a very neat, one-line summary, Berle and Means put it this way: "The corporate system has done to capital what the factory system did to labor."

John P. Davis, the chief American historian of corporations, wrote in 1905: "The growth of corporations in Western Europe and the United States signifies nothing less than a social revolution." That statement is more obviously true today than when it was made.

The history of corporations contains a few choice points for our purposes. The modern part of the story begins with the Dutch East India Company, which was chartered in 1602—the first *stock* corporation. (There were "bodies corporate"—that's a redundant phrase—before the modern period, such as churches, guilds, some various types in Rome, etc.) As an economic form, the stock corporation grew out of certain risk-sharing procedures in the early ship trade. The corporate form was useful, of course, where no investment was forthcoming without a guarantee of limited personal liability for the investor, and where large sums of money were required in highly speculative but potentially very profitable schemes. The early English corporations were established by royal charter for trading and colonizing, and were in effect grants of substantial monopoly power. In some instances, the power granted covered immense geographical areas, as for example, India, New York, the Massachusetts Bay Colony, Canada more or less, Virginia, and so on.*

The most important historical point about corporations is that until recently they had always been considered public agencies—in effect, specific governments. Not nation-states, even when they ruled what we would consider whole countries; but nevertheless, governments. This was nicely put by Henry C. Adams, in his presidential address to the American Economics Association in 1896:

> Corporations originally were regarded as agencies of the State. They were created for the purpose of enabling the public to realize some social or national end without involving the necessity for direct governmental administration. They were in reality arms of the State, and in order to secure efficient management, a local or private interest was created as a privilege or property of the corporation. A corporation, therefore, may be defined in the light of history as a body created by law for the purpose of obtaining public ends through an appeal to private interests.

America was founded by colonizing corporations which subsequently become state governments. A political scientist from Amherst, Earl Latham, asserts that "the basic

---

* We may note as an historical footnote that the magical paper-creating power of corporations was discovered—and violently reacted to—a bare century after the first stock corporation was set up. The occasion was the famous bursting of the famous South Sea Bubble in 1720. So many people had been hurt by their own greed and ignorance of corporate paper that prohibitive legislation was passed which, according to A. A. Berle, Jr., "practically blanked out [corporations] for a little over a hundred years in English life. The theory was that they were too dangerous." That was a fascinating early episode in the forming of the modern paper system—the emotional essence of capitalism gone wild.

form of the public government in America derived from the provenance of a commercial corporation," an ordinance of The Virginia Company in 1621. This entrancing historical circumstance might be characterized, in legal corporate language, as follows: the kings of England, in their corporate majesty, formed subsidiaries which then became greater than the parent; some time later these subsidiaries—now independent governments—formed other subsidiary corporations which have since become, again, greater than *their* parents. Moreover, if America was founded by English corporations, it seems that it was also lost to the Empire as the result of an effort to "control the market" for the benefit of one of them. The purpose of the English Tea Act which in high school led to the Boston Tea Party which in turn led to the American Revolution, was to bail out the East India Company—the same which, in someone's beautiful phrase, is said to have acquired India for the British Empire "in a moment of inadvertence." Apparently the Company lost us in a moment of ineptitude.

Royal charters were succeeded by charters granted by state legislatures. A special act of the legislature was the only way to create a corporation until the first corporate statute was enacted by New York in 1811. It remained the usual way during most of the first half of the century; but finally the statutory procedure became common among the states. They have since become a common joke, the states having competed strenuously in making their laws attractive by abandoning serious supervision of their legal creatures: Delaware gives the biggest premiums, and has an inordinate number of customers. In 1800 there were only a few score corporations in all the thirteen states. Today there are 150,000 to 200,000 new ones created each year: it costs only about $100 to start one. (It is an interesting historical sidelight that *The Federalist Papers* do not mention corporations at all; but this basic document, which contains our initial theory of government, does not mention political parties either.)

So in the beginning there was no difference between a charter for a corporation and a franchise for a public utility. Today, the right to incorporate for any purpose at all has become generally available; incorporation is now as common as contract. Corporations began as public bodies with responsibilities to the public. It was only after decades of struggle, the courts with technical problems (the Supreme Court decided in 1886 that the word "person" in the Fourteenth Amendment included corporations) and society with this great new source of private power, that they were established before the law as legal persons—with no more legal responsibility than any other person. The public relations aspect of the legal fiction established them in the pantheon of legal-economic ideology as *hard-working* persons with individual initiative and other business emotions that could be damaged as a person's feelings can be hurt. To a very substantial extent, General Motors today—with its better than 10-billion-dollar cash flow annually—stands before the government and the law as a person just as you and I do. Now isn't that silly! A cash flow of that size is equal to about a tenth of the Federal government's—the Federal government which shares with major central banks the national power to create the cash that flows. Besides, the value of General Motors stock increases rather steadily, while that of Federal Reserve Notes does not: the market value of GM's paper doubled between 1953 and 1958, while Federal currency was declining in value. But this doesn't make GM a person—it simply makes GM a more effective institution than the Federal government. Which will come as news to no one.

The briefest possible history of the beginning of corporate power in the United States would be this: Toward the middle of the nineteenth century the Federal government and the states turned over substantial amounts of their power and property to increasingly sizable corporate enterprises. Starting with the first grant to the Illinois Central in 1850, the Federal government conveyed about 130 million acres of America to the railroad companies. State and local authorities added perhaps another 25 million acres. Just to indicate what was involved here, railroad companies were *literally* given one-quarter of the states of Washington and Minnesota. Understand that this was not merely land for track, but was a means of financing the construction of the roads. The land was sold to homesteaders, and only after considerable acreage had been given away to the railroad corporations was the Homestead Act passed in 1862. Also, this land giveaway was supplemented by tax forgiveness on the part of the governmental authorities.

The railroads were the beginning of big corporate-financial enterprise in the United States. Although railroad-building required a mass community effort, the community shared in the benefit only by having a railroad running through the area: the profits went to the companies. Most of this came from selling railroad securities, rather than from building and operating the roads themselves. Moreover, the middle and late nineteenth-century railroad-paper provided the airy basis for a world of later paper, and greatly expanded paper-trading as a national pastime. As a result of all the feverish activity that accompanied the building of the railroads, we have not only the roads and the paper but also a very deep tradition of corruption in local politics, since so many legislators were bought on so many occasions.

Now it is a little easier to understand what the "free" in free enterprise stands for. It is the word "private" in private enterprise that remains obscure. All the taking was done, *in* public, *of* the public wealth, so I don't see where it was private at all.

This governmental giveaway to "private" profit-seeking enterprise has characterized American economic history from the building of the railroads to the development of atomic energy and communication by means of space satellites. In fact, it *is* our economic history. Literally and historically, governments distribute their plenary power to business corporations in order to accomplish a particular function, whether or not such government could have accomplished the purpose on its own, or by some other means, or at a lesser cost. That is our characteristic way of getting things done. That is what corporations mean.

The early corporations were all acknowledged monopolies—clear grants of governmental power—established and tolerated for acknowledged public purposes. It is both historically recent and somewhat quaintly American that such power is claimed to exist without an accompanying public responsibility. Before the railroad land-grab got underway in the nineteenth century, the prior canal system had been built by means of state enterprise. The canals worked all right, and Erie Canal bonds were one of the earliest pieces of good paper in America—but then came the railroads, by which I mean a new and superior form of travel *and* freewheeling, land-grabbing enterprise *and* reams of railroad paper.

The kind of corporate paper system we now live under is not only not provided for in the Constitution, it was not even a necessary outgrowth of our early history. Somewhere along the way a choice was made: the leading people in society decided to unleash the impulse to get rich quick by stealing—and they also decided to join in the fun. So they stole the continent, with the cooperation of most governments. (Except for the very early days, we Americans have frequently been embarrassed by the quality of our ruling classes.)

The suggestion was made earlier that our large corporations are properly defined as industrial or technological governments. Consequently, understanding the corporation is as much an exercise in political as in economic theory. As a political form, the modern corporation has assumed its present leading role for the simplest and most compelling reason: it was necessary—to administer men and things in large aggregates. In the nature of the case, the technological revolution could not proceed unorganized and unplanned. The major corporations, as stewards of the technological upheaval, have come into being in response to the imperatives of such organization and planning. Their work is political work, in any reasonable meaning of the term. This governing function—of the most important areas of activity in American life—was taken on by unofficial corporate bodies rather than by the pre-existing, legally constituted government because: 1) the corporate order grew out of the previous system of private property administered by dominant financial interests, which was itself not a duly constituted government; and 2) the alternative, to entrust this overridingly important work to the government in Washington, would have contradicted our entire political history since that weak authority had never been entrusted with anything more important than partial participation in raising and operating armies.

The corporate order is a system of *private* government. This privacy, however, is not to be comprehended in terms of private property or the private discretion of individuals. The corporate order is largely private *from*—from public accountability, whether indirectly through that other national government or directly to any of its various constituencies. The rulers of the corporate system are not elected by anybody, and they are not answerable for the exercise of their more important powers to any elected officials. The privacy of this private government serves mainly to ensure its authoritarian nature—it has nothing to do with the free action of individuals, which is what most of us usually think of when the word "private" is used. Professor Edward S. Mason, one of our leading authorities on the corporate system, has suggested that the corporation was inevitable because of the enlarged "entrepreneurial discretion" the form allows—meaning the capacity to command large groups of men and materials toward a particular purpose, much the same as in an army. And like an army, the individual corporation is (except in very rare instances) a one-party state. In other areas of government, we have no difficulty in recognizing this as a feature of dictatorship; it is only the studied absence of clear thinking that keeps us from recognizing the political fact in this area. The significance of these authoritarian centers for our otherwise somewhat democratic order is sharpened when we note, for instance, that Peter Drucker has called the few hundred business enterprises dominating the American economy "the only meaningful units of local government."

Further attesting to their essential authoritarianism, the

really important activities of private corporate governments are not governed by any constitution. Originally, the charter was intended to serve this purpose: not until the charter was cheapened to the level of contract was it seriously asserted that the lack of a constitution was a positive virtue. Without the fundamental law of a constitution, the corporation is—to put the matter succinctly—a lawless institution. A particular one may very well be a benevolent dictatorship; its benevolence may make it tolerable, or even popular—it can never make it legal. Because of the legal fiction that a corporation is a "person," the Supreme Court of the United States is unable to apply the protections of that other Constitution we all revere for the benefit of the millions of individuals making up the communities of our corporate order. Even more important, it is intellectually embarrassed in dealing with the corporation in its own terms. One perceptive theorizer (Professor Arthur S. Miller) has put the matter this way:

> Under orthodox constitutional theory, only two entities are recognized: the State and the individual person. Nothing intermediate is envisaged. The rise of groups, a development which in its present extensive form is unprecedented, has brought the need for new constitutional theories and patterns of doctrine.

This problem is of course bigger than that of the corporation alone, having to do with the relation between the individual and *all* of the large organizations which are in fact the characteristic power centers of our society.

A constitution or rule of law for the corporation (or any big organization) would deal with policy and procedure governing both individuals and groups. The latter refers to the constituencies making up the corporate community—

labor (including white-collar workers and middle-management), suppliers, dealers, stockholders, and even ultimate consumers. These should be organized for their own protection (thus mirroring the *actual* political forms in American life)—and it is perhaps a happy harbinger that the only group currently well organized, labor, has accomplished a great deal in "constitutionalizing" the place of its members in the industrial community. Indeed, from one source or another, the unions have been impelled to more progress in the internal rule of law than other typical large organizations. Walter Reuther's U.A.W. Public Review Board is an imaginative and apparently sincere departure—not copied by any major corporation or, in fact, many other unions. Another constituency, dealers, were moved a few years ago to a little political self-help. GM for a number of years had a private judiciary in which hearings were heard on complaint of an automobile franchise-holder, although (or perhaps because) these franchise contracts are not clearly enforceable in a true court of law. It was partly the poor quality of the justice dispensed in these private proceedings that led to the passage of the Automobile Franchise Dealers Act of 1956, which was lobbied through Congress by the dealers.

Reinhold Niebuhr remarks relevantly: "You must allow quasi-sovereignties, whether they are corporations, church, or educational institutions. The more quasi-sovereignties you have, the better protection you have against totalitarianism." But the gain against totalitarianism is certainly lost if the quasi-sovereignty is more authoritarian in nature than the alternative plenary national power. There is more law today running in favor of individual rights in the armed services than there is in any of our major corporate communities. I see no reason why the industrial army should not be at least as democratic as the other one. In fact, there is no good reason in the world why The People should not participate generally in the processes of our private governments. And there is every good reason to believe that our so-called democracy has a limited longevity unless it begins soon to address itself with more energy to the relevant governments in our society. Otherwise our highly organized future will overwhelm us.

The framers of the Constitution did their work too well in checking and balancing power, with the effect that, when an individualistic agricultural society was replaced by a collective industrial one, too much concentrated, illegal, and unchecked and unbalanced power grew up elsewhere than in Washington. After all, if you believe in democracy and accept the premise that a democracy need not by definition be weak, then the basic power in the society should have been centered in Washington. It was excessive rationalism at the beginning which has created our biggest continuing historical problem.

If the corporation is private property, nobody but the stockholder-owners are legitimately concerned with its government; and if the stockholder's vote ensures the property-owners control by democratic means, the managers who run the corporation are property-servants operating under a legitimate mandate. But if these related propositions are not true, then our major corporations are authoritarian private baronies legitimated by nothing more than their existence. In fact, the propositions are not true— they are simply loudly and continuously endorsed by the people who control the properties of which they are not true.

Large publicly held corporations are not private property and they are not controlled by their shareholders. Where did anybody get the idea that they were? It comes from the fact that the corporate order "grew out of" the previously existing system of private property; was facilitated by convenient, justificatory misrepresentations of *that* system, and finally buttressed by an overwhelming barrage of public relations nonsense, which by an act of rhetorical will has succeeded in assimilating the new corporate system to readily available fantasies concerning the democratic significance of voting. It is, for me at least, strangely disturbing that this conception of the magic of the vote has so much in common with the concept in Communist states, where one also votes not to make a choice, but as a ritualistic submission to unassailable power.

While shareholders are considered a continual annoyance and an occasional threat by corporate managements, it is just not true that anybody on the inside believes for one moment that they own or control anything—certainly not the corporation, and certainly not by means of the stock vote. But General Electric, pushing that low-grade Madison Avenue concoction called "People's Capitalism," is perfectly willing—to the tune of expensive full-page advertisements—to say in public that "The 376,000 owners with savings invested in General Electric are typical of America, *where nearly every citizen is a capitalist.*" (Emphasis supplied.) First of all, there are that large number of GE stockholders exactly to ensure that the GE management shall not be inconvenienced by their ownership; secondly, only about one out of ten families own any stock at all; thirdly and most importantly, it is an unfortunate illustration of the dangers of such free and illegimate corporate power that it can be used to peddle such degrading junk. The statement is a shameful lie, and whoever wrote it and whoever hired him

to write it, knew it was a lie when it was written. This kind
of national lying spree—which smells up the whole cultural
atmosphere in the country—is one of the consequences of
the irresponsible managerial power which, along with its
periodic productiveness, is the main feature of our corporate
system.

It is very difficult for the layman to grasp the fact that
no one owns a big corporation like General Motors. The
ordinary way of thinking about property and things produces a certain horror at the idea of anything so big and
so valuable striding the earth unowned. The difficulty dis-
solves easily enough, however, when we realize that we have
been assuming ownership means control. It is very hard to
conceive of something like General Motors as not being controlled, and I will not ask anyone to strain himself to do so.
But I must insist on the effort to see it as unowned.*

Paper mechanics and other managers and manipulators
of modern property forms understand quite well that ownership is frequently irrelevant—the main thing is control. And
control is often achieved exactly because ownership is
abandoned. For example, management control of a big corporation is ensured by distribution of the irrelevant ownership paper, stock certificates, among as large a public as
possible: in numbers there is weakness. (Corporate managers
typically follow the changes in the stock list on a careful
daily basis, looking for warning signs of an accumulation of
a bloc which might revive the threat of ownership-control.)

The simple fact of the matter is that the major economic institutions are too big to be owned. Too big, that is,
to be owned by any individual: Standard Oil of New Jersey

---

* The sense of ownership is so profound in us that its negation literally
feels like infinity—the wonder-state of what is "outside" of outside.

is today too much for a Rockefeller—even for a group of Rockefellers, unless that group is organized on the same principles as the institution being owned. In other words, big institutions can only be owned by other big institutions, which in turn are not effectively owned. Stop and think for a moment: how could an industrial government like AT&T be "owned"? By means of stock certificates? That's like trying to attach some significance to the notion that I own a piece of Central Park because I live in New York City. The assets of AT&T, well over $20 billion worth, are owned by the corporation itself. There are more than two million shareholders in the company. Over half of these have investments of less than $2,000. Now what is $2,000 worth of $20 billion? It is .0000001 per cent—a technical piece of Central Park. (Even when you consider the biggest institutional investors, no stockholder in AT&T holds more than a fraction of 1 per cent of the outstanding stock.)

Now how can anyone call something like this private property or private enterprise? It is owned by a disorganized impotent public, and controlled by a private self-perpetuating managerial clique. The control is important, the ownership is not. Ownership of this kind is just a very limited charge on production and, paradoxically, the means of maintaining managerial control of the corporate enterprise.

The notion that GM (or any one of the great majority of public corporations) is "owned" proceeds from the time-honored assumption that to own stock is to own the corporation. If we examine this old-fashioned "self-evident" truth empirically, we note that what the public stockholder actually has is three double-edged rights: 1) he can sell his stock at a profit or at a loss; 2) he can receive or fail to receive a variable dividend; and 3) he can vote Yes or No on certain issues affecting control of the corporation and the disposition of its properties. The first two items indicate that he owns a negotiable instrument of a certain character —consisting of an "iffy" return on capital and a lottery ticket on market appreciation. Let's look more closely at the third item, the only one of the three that even looks like ownership of the corporation itself. What does the stockholder's vote mean? To skip over several stages of a dull argument, it means that the vote can effect changes of control over "his" property, the corporation, or it means approximately nothing. Can he do this? The answer is no, not unless an ambitious, well-heeled syndicate mounts a campaign to do so, and thus gives *him* the opportunity to support *them*. This does not happen at all often.*

A mite of ownership, indeed. Especially when one considers that the essential difference between the incumbent and contending control groups is apt to be that the one has been at that particular trough for a period of time and the other has not. Moreover, in the absence of blatant mismanagement or special business reverses, it is next to impossible to unseat an in-group that is on the alert and well advised by experts. (Leopold Silberstein, who has accomplished a certain amount of unseating, has said: "It's very tough to buy control in the market if the management controls ten to

---

* A control bloc of stock, usually put at between 20 per cent and 51 per cent, affords a means of translating ownership into control; but this is a feature of the aggregate, not of individual shares—and the courts are now seeing it this way. There is a considerable body of law a-building to the effect that sale of a control bloc at a premium over the market value of individual shares is actionable on the part of other shareholders. This clearly means that the control feature is a separate element; and conversely, there is no real control quality in a single share of stock. In other words, the point is so obvious that even the courts are beginning to recognize it.

twenty percent.") Unlike a campaign for political office, the "ins" have at their disposal not only the corporate patronage but also the corporate treasury; and the voting apathy of the citizen is a form of frenzied activity compared to that of the lottery-ticket holder. Not only are most corporate "elections" carried out with only one yes-or-no slate of directors available to the electorate, but there is also no real public opinion concerning the nominees. Only in a heavily financed fight does such an opinion develop, and it is then even paler and more foolish than the usual "fantasy of issues" in our more familiar political elections. This also indicates the strained quality of democracy in our autocratic private governments.

As Bayless Manning so felicitously put it, "The modern proxy contest is at best a device for tempering autocracy by invasion." An invasion is called a "raid"—and only "bad guys" undertake them. Dean Rostow of the Yale Law School has pointed out: "Raiding is regarded as something more than uncouth; increasingly, it is treated as almost illegal." Which again reveals how far corporate authoritarianism has progressed, since a raid is the only practical means of changing a management. (A previous technique for harassing and policing autocratic management, the professional stockholder's suit, was held in such fearful disdain by the "ins" that they passed a seemingly democratic law against it: and now the great "giant-killers" of earlier decades are no more.) Following the New York Central and Montgomery Ward fights, in theory the SEC put the final kibosh on the matter by promulgating proxy-fight regulations which ensure that only nice people fighting a good clean fight may now do battle in the arena of what is charmingly called "corporate democracy."

The fundamental meaning of private property is private control over the property one owns, and all the stock-holders own is a share of stock. The corporation is not private property—only the share of stock is.

The unlegitimated power of corporate managements without basis in ownership has not gone unnoticed. It was most specifically noticed by Berle and Means in 1932, and by the early New Deal and its securities legislation. Ever since then, the moral reform of corporations has been most noticeably in the hands of what must be one of the strangest reform movements in American history. I refer to the "corporate democracy" caper—better recognized popularly by the name of its leading field captains, the Gilbert brothers.

There are a lot of entertaining anecdotes and other charming details about the Gilberts, John Campbell Heinz, and Wilma Soss, chairman of the lady's auxiliary—anybody who has had to sit through the unspeakable farce of a stock-holders' meeting can add to the lore. I will never forget the look of demonic fury on Lewis Gilbert's face when, in the midst of one of those rarely significant meetings in which control of a big corporation actually was being decided, he experienced a little difficulty in being recognized by the chair to make his usual thundering demand for a bigger and better post-meeting report. He started to charge down the aisle in order to complete his fit closer to the official steno-typist, lacking only a battle-torn tricolor in his hands to complete the picture of Democracy Outraged.

But the serious point about this weird movement is that it couldn't be more effectively misdirected if it were entirely an espionage arm of the corporate powers it presumes to attack and reform. The professional stockholder's suit was actually an effective agency for reform, so it was mostly done away with and, to be polite about the matter, partly "taken over." The corporate democracy movement has not been fought—it was first tolerated with irritation and finally welcomed.

I have come across no single detail that better characterizes the studied irrelevance of "corporate democracy" than this: it would hardly exist at all apart from the efforts of a handful of individuals. This is nicely demonstrated by the fact that out of 2,000 proxy statements filed with the SEC in 1956, only 3 per cent contained shareholder proposals—which were supposed to be one of the vital elements in the schemata of the movement. The total number of proposals was 102, *and 78 of these were sponsored by the two Gilbert brothers and John Campbell Heinz*. Other items in the "corporate democrats' " pastiche are: stockholders meetings in accessible cities rather than out-of-the-way places of incorporation, cumulative voting, public directors, post-meeting reports, independent auditors, token ownership of stock by management, and so on. None of it makes any real difference. Professor Bayless Manning* of Yale has shrewdly noted:

> The nostrums of Corporate Democracy have a vaguely familiar quality, for the prescription is largely taken from the municipal reformers of the turn of the century. . . . Nearly all of the planks in the platform of Corporate Democracy find their analogues in the reform agitations of 1900 for the long ballot, initiative and referendum, the direct primary, proportionate representation and women's suffrage.

* Manning is the author of an essay-review of J. A. Livingston's *The American Stockholder* which appeared in Volume 67, page 1477, of *The Yale Law Journal* in 1958, and quickly became a minor classic; it sets forth a completely devastating case against the illusion of corporate democracy, and is unreservedly recommended to anyone who needs further convincing.

The stock-vote of scattered, impotent stockholders cannot be relied upon to make corporate managements responsible, even to the owners. Moreover, the idea "is misconceived because the shareholders are not the governed of the corporation whose consent must be sought," as Professor Abram Chayes has correctly pointed out: the governed are *all* of the constituencies previously mentioned. "The forms and mechanisms of shareholder democracy divert attention from the real problems of holding business management to a desirable standard of responsibility," says Manning. Indeed, if we abandon the fiction that the stockholder "owns" the corporation and "controls" his property by means of the vote, we more easily notice the very rickety structure of enforcing even property-responsibility, much less institutional or public accountability, upon managements. With the façade of the vote working in their favor, managements have succeeded in escaping even the common law rigors of the personal responsibility of trustees. Livingston, in the book Manning reviewed, is rather indignant about the special deal that was made between the Ford family and the New York Stock Exchange, to overcome the Exchange's rule about not listing non-voting common stock: under the terms of the stock issue, the Fords could retain 40 per cent of the voting rights in the 3-billion-dollar company with only 5.1 per cent of the equity. Two points: 1) the public didn't care, if it noticed at all—300,000 shareholders are perfectly content if the stock goes up, and are not mollified by the vote if it does not; and 2) no one can demonstrate any actual difference at all between, say, General Motors and Ford in the quality of managerial responsibility—certainly not in favor of the "fairly" elected officials of GM.

9

CORPORATIONS II

WHAT IS THE REAL NATURE of the established corporate power? Simply, that the strength and purpose of the nation are in the hands of the few thousand men who control the few hundred bureaucracies which dominate the economy. These organizations and men are the stewards of the permanent technological revolution which *is* the economy, and which it is not too dramatic to call the hope and the despair of mankind.

There are many ways of stating or characterizing the institutional concentration of economic power which, being the heart of American power and not subject to public control, is far and away the overriding political fact of our

social order. The usual way is to state the number of corporations which own what per cent of productive assets.
For example: a study by the Federal Trade Commission in
1947-1949 disclosed that 113 corporations with assets of
over $100 million held 46 per cent of the total assets of
manufacturing firms. Or the figures which Professor Berle
frequently repeats: ". . . about two-thirds of the economically productive assets of the United States, excluding agriculture, are owned by a group of not more than 500
corporations." But I think that we should not rest with this
quick characterization of so important an aspect of our environment: to make certain that the dominating significance
of *size* is conveyed we might run through the following
miscellany.

    # Corporation income-tax returns, in a recent compi-
lation, "showed 525,000 active nonfinancial corporations reporting a total of $413 billion of assets. The 202 corporations
. . . each with assets of $250 million or more—owned 40%
of this total."

    # The minimum amount of assets required for inclu-
sion in the 100 largest nonfinancial corporations in 1950 was
$329 million; in 1960 it was $698 million. Over this same
period the number of "billion-dollar" corporations better
than doubled—increasing from 22 to 54.

    # You get down to number 405 on *Fortune*'s list of
industrial corporations before you find one that had sales in
1961 of less than $100 million; up front, you get to number
42 before you find a little item called Eastman Kodak which
had sales in that year of less than a billion dollars.

    # If you rank big corporations and governments ac-
cording to revenue, you have eight corporations after the
Federal government before you get to the first state, Cali-

fornia; then another five before arriving at New York State
and New York City; and ten more before Pennsylvania. Out
of fifty-five organizations with a billion or more annual
revenue (1958), only nine are official governmental units.

When we say that America is a corporate economy and
that the concentration of corporate power is extreme, we
must still put this fact in a proper context—that is, place it
in the general business population. At the beginning of
1960 there were about 4.6 million operating business concerns in the United States. The number has been increasing
slowly throughout the postwar period, with net gains of
about 60,000 firms a year. (These figures do not include
agriculture and professional services; but the firms so defined
account for 85 per cent of income originating in the private
economy.) *The Survey of Current Business* makes the following precise statement on the matter: "Small firms comprise the bulk of the business population—two-fifths have
no employees at all—and only one firm in 20 employs 20 or
more." In other words, a substantial amount of self-exploitation: a great number of marginal retail establishments, many
examples of a carpenter or two appearing in the statistics
under "Contract Construction," a lot of filling stations, a
bunch of "candy-stores."

There are over 4½ million "firms"; but to see the
proper context we have been thinking of, compare all of
them to, say, just one firm, the Metropolitan Life Insurance
Company, with $17 billion in assets. This company has as
many health and accident policyholders as there are firms
in the country. But here is a figure to conjure with in the
course of thinking about bigness: the Metropolitan Life
Insurance Company has 38 million life insurance policyholders.

Another approach is to look at employment. The *Survey* for November 1959 informs us:

> About 30 million full-time equivalent workers are employed by corporations, or somewhat under one-half of the total number of persons engaged in production. Proprietorships and partnerships provided work for another 21 million persons, who are about equally divided between employees and self-employed (businessmen, farmers, or professional persons). An additional 10 million workers are employees of governments—Federal, State, and local —and the other 4 million persons engaged in production are working in households, or nonprofit institutions.

And further: "In 1956 as in 1951, slightly less than one per cent of all firms had 100 or more employees; however, these larger firms accounted for nearly three-fifths of all paid employment."

All of these smaller firms still manage to survive in retail and service trades because it remains "economic" for one or two individuals to exploit themselves mercilessly. Selling television sets, once a strong trade in this area, was profitable enough to be concentrated in discount and shopping-center operations. But there is no TV repair chain: there, it is still "economic" for one technician to exploit himself—and of course part of the exploitation is the price he pays for parts.

We talk about "big" corporations and "big" business so much that the words turn flat and tend to slip by too easily. How big is big?

We try to conceive of size by referring to so many millions of this and so many billions of that, and if you make the imaginative effort, this can do the job for you. But it would be most worth while to freshen up our perception of industrial, economic and financial *size*, because size is essential to our story. It is because of size that private property is irrelevant; that major corporations can be understood only as forms of government; and it is also and finally because of size that our system has been transformed, has become the very new thing it is.

The question is important: the bigger the institution, the smaller the individual who lives in its shadow. This small individual must at least try to understand the source of the shadow.

But really, how big is big? General Motors is supposed to be the biggest industrial corporation in the world. We can begin to take its measurements by noting that the American public has decided that it is worth $12-13 billion—but that's just dollar value, and in my opinion GM is worth a lot more than that to all of us. As a matter of fact, I don't think we could get along without it at any price. If, God help us, it refused to get into the ballgame, 600,000 people around the world would have to scrape together $3.5 billion of income from some other source, and I wonder where they would find it. Some 750,000 stockholders would have to find some other paper to play with; upwards of 27,000 suppliers would lose one sweetheart of a customer; 20,000 wholesalers and 200,000 retailers would also experience great sorrow in adjusting to a GM-less world.

GM was not always so important to so many people. As a matter of fact, it celebrated its fiftieth birthday as recently as 1958, at which time it was noticed that about 68 million cars and trucks had been produced by it since the beginning. But any large corporation produces paper as well as products, so it should also be noticed that a $100 share of General Motors common purchased in 1908 was worth or had brought in more than $150,000 over the same time-span. Whether looked at from the point of view of cars or paper, that is still one hell of a lot of internal combustion.

Let's go back to those 27,000 suppliers for a minute. GM dispenses about $5 billion a year to them for materials and services. The publicity gentlemen at the Company make a rather large point of the fact that these suppliers are Small Business, and in this connection they inform us that 70 per cent of them employ fewer than 100 people: U. S. Steel, du Pont, etc., I suppose, are in the other 30 per cent. There is a great deal of power in spending that kind of money and, unlike UAW production workers, these small businesses are not organized to protect themselves. (For the time being I leave you with the thought.)

One of the things GM is supplied with is advertising, about $200 million a year. It is in fact the nation's largest advertiser—the greatest single prop for this wonderful mass culture of ours. The corporation advertises a great many things, including itself in the pure state. About thirteen advertising agencies are needed to handle the Company's business. (GM has twenty-seven publications for its employees alone.)

So there we have some aspects of big GM. I might also mention that this organization does not live by cars alone, but fabricates numerous other fabrications, and I wouldn't be surprised if it could make almost anything it wanted to make. Mostly it wants to make money, and consequently does very well at that.

General Motors is not the biggest corporation in the country—the biggest one is AT&T. But AT&T is a utility rather than a free-wheeling industrial outfit; and it is so big as to be almost indescribable.*

It has gross assets of over 30 billion dollars, and these

---

* Berle: "American Telephone and Telegraph . . . based on combined population and wealth, would be somewhere around the 13th state of the Union in terms of budget, and certainly larger than many of the countries of South America."

include the Bell Telephone Laboratories, The Western Electric Company, and most of the telephones in the country. But then there are a lot of big corporations in America. Bigness at du Pont, for example, means among other things 12,000 managerial promotions each year—about one every ten minutes of working time. There has been some new bigness, too: through both merger and regular growth, Olin Mathieson Chemical Corporation grew from a six-plant, $67 million-a-year producer of metals and guns in 1946 to a $650 million-a-year giant operating some ninety plants across the country. Monsanto Chemical went from $99 million in sales in 1946 to nearly $550 million in 1958. Just as the rich get richer, the big get bigger. (Incidentally, we have no inheritance laws to keep the major corporations from growing as big as the sky.)

Standard Oil of New Jersey, which always follows General Motors as No. 2 on the *Fortune* list, had sales of nearly $8 billion. That's a lot of gasoline, but then General Motors with its sales of $11 billion-plus produced a lot of cars, so it all figures. Standard of New Jersey is a very careful corporation: it has built a little sixty-acre "remote-control center" in New Jersey so that if in the event of a thermonuclear attack New York City should be lost, at least Standard of Jersey would be able to carry on. These apocalyptic facilities afford living and working accomodations for sixty-five executives—sort of a skeleton force. It would appear that Standard of New Jersey takes quite seriously the provision in its charter that it shall exist in perpetuity.

All this concentration of assets and general institutional size means a good deal more than it seems to mean. A big corporation is much bigger than its balance sheet, and much bigger than the percentage of industry assets that it may own. Corporate governments do not rule by ownership alone. Berle puts it this way: "The ability of the large corporation to make decisions and direct operations overflows the area of its ownership. Its power travels farther than its title. . . ." This factor can stand some elaboration.

Notice first that those business areas with the greatest number of firms—wholesale and retail trade, contract construction and the service industries—are all middlemen, that is, they are customers of heavy industry and salesmen to the public. They are therefore "controlled" insofar as heavy industry dominates the markets in which they buy. The institutional concentration of power is much more effective than any simple statistics will indicate: a small, highly disciplined military unit can always control a larger population. This has been accomplished too many times throughout history to be any longer disputable. The argument here is that the same historical factor applies in finance and industry. The fact that the operator of a small TV repair shop *owns* his tools, fixtures, etc., is merely a matter of convenience to General Electric, RCA, etc. As if GE were to force its workers to supply their own hand tools. This is another, if somewhat more obscure, virtue of non-ownership in the modern American property system.

The point is that big corporations not only dominate their own industries, but are also centers of power around which are clustered thousands upon thousands of satellite enterprises which are wholly or substantially dependent on the center. The satellites may be suppliers or dealers or customers. The dependence is not altered by the role: a manufacturer, 80 per cent of whose volume consists of supplying door handles to Ford, is as dependent on the corporation as any Ford dealer or repair agency. Logically enough, the dominating corporation as buyer may look for suppliers who are both small and tied to the one big purchaser for distribution of a substantial portion of output. (This is announced policy of Sears, Roebuck and Company.) In these circumstances, whether the satellite is an owned division or an independent contractor is a matter of indifference. To try to assimilate this situation to the image of free, competitive market dealings is about as helpful as denominating widespread stock ownership as People's Capitalism and assuming this means democratic control of corporations. The markets in which giants and satellites trade are completely structured and dominated by the giants; it is somewhat gratuitous to call them markets at all, and considerably less than candid to call these dubious markets "free." (What we have here is the primary illusion in the assumption of justice in free contract: there never was a free and just contract between non-equals because the contract must always reflect the inequality.) Professor Arthur S. Miller: "It can validly be concluded that a widespread system of satellite coercion characterizes business operations. Whether the satellite is a supplier or a dealer, he exists in a position of vastly inferior economic power." His relation to the large corporation has more of status than of contract in it.

The traditional economist sees a market as a Grand Image of All-Justifying Freedom, to be submitted to with adoration by all right-thinking people. A practicing businessman sees it as something to be organized before its dangerous potential is realized. The historical purpose of big corporations is to organize markets. In a sense that is all they are—*organized markets*. Or: the center of power around which and by means of which markets are organized.

(At one time financial power alone was sufficient for this purpose; then it was discovered that combining industrial and financial power in one organization had much to recommend it. Corporations today are as much financial as industrial centers of power; they are the newest form of banking, resulting from the fact that productive capacity, or captured technology, has replaced gold as the backing for all the paper.) Professor Mason says: "As a firm grows, transactions that could conceivably be organized through the market price mechanism are transferred to the administrative organization of the firm." In other words, with big corporations markets are "ingested" or internalized. Thus, by "owning" part of the market, much more of it can be dominated and organized.*

Once a market area is organized, the centralized power of the dominating corporation may indeed become superfluous. But it will persist—as a distorting effect of the Paper Economy. For example, the size of our major corporations today is probably based more on considerations of finance than of production. It is safer to be big and diversified— safer in terms of survival. This is recognized by the corporations, obliquely, in their present accelerated movement toward decentralization, plant autonomy, divisional responsibility, etc. Markets must be organized, and basic producing units protected, to ensure the rational and continuing flow

---

* Mason makes a helpful distinction between monopoly and concentration. He says that "the degree of general concentration depends fundamentally upon the extent of industrialization." On the other hand, a monopoly can be small—as, for example and for obvious reasons, local brick companies. If industrialism equals concentration, then the classic pattern is that of Standard Oil wherein competition—real and brutal competition—occurs in the early expanding stage of an industry, and one of the essential jobs in building productive capacity is to do away with this unwelcome and expensive phenomenon.

of goods—to ensure that productive capacity shall not, unknowingly, become a highly stylized form of hara-kiri. This technological rationalization is one thing; finance, in the Paper Economy, is another. GM needs profit instead of production only as a form of self-protection—and of course there is never enough of *that*. This requires maintenance of the price level, especially by curtailing production. Veblen called this "sabotage" (after a very precise definition). We can call it Scarcity Regained.

This is not the only size-distortion resulting from the Paper Economy: To the extent that the early liberal reformers were successful in thwarting the accumulation of great fortunes over generations, by means of the estate tax laws, they merely accelerated the growth of big and bigger corporations, the only true and lasting form of perpetuity. Decisive bigness changed its form but did not disappear.

As centers of industrial and financial power, market-organizers, and general governing bodies, big corporations are necessarily planning agencies. Planning is nothing but looking ahead—and using your head in the process. It is intelligence and knowledge applied in the administration of our complex social technology: planning and technology go together, they are common imperatives. You can, then, easily see that: 1) planning is indispensable; 2) it is in glaring contradiction to our free enterprise ideology; 3) it is something that takes both superior intelligence and training, which signifies the heightened importance of intellectual experts; and finally 4) the problem of power in the modern setting cannot be dissociated from it. Since it is so close to the real issues of power in our day, and since it involves a very significant upgrading of intellectual classes, and since to be accomplished effectively it must be carried out over large industrial areas which requires the use of national, *i.e.*, Federal, power—*therefore*, the existing private power centers necessarily oppose it when carried on by any other groups than themselves, and always obscure it no matter who does it, or why.

Big business borrows Federal power when necessary in furtherance of its planning activities—as with the Federal Reserve System: this is a fundamental pattern in the working out of dual government in American history. There are numerous examples: the planned introduction of color television and FM radio—planned by the business groups concerned, using the FCC as a medium of control; the Federal super-highway plan—something of a necessity for the oil and automotive industries; and so on. But business also plans all on its own: "There is no such thing as an unplanned corporation. . . ." Diversification programs typically involve judgments based on five and ten year perspectives. Capital investment programs, plant location, the institutionalizing of technical discovery, executive training programs, all involve present allocation of resource in response to long-range perspectives. "Du Pont often publicizes its Chart Room, where decisions are made about the rate at which the company's technological innovations are to be permitted to flow into the market." (Du Pont spent $27 million from 1928 to 1940 on nylon before it sold its first commercial unit.) All this is planning.

It is unfortunately necessary to point out that one can plan ahead without being omnipotent. That is, not all plans are perfectly relevant, not all of them are completely prescient, all must be continually modified, and every once in a while one has to be abandoned altogether. But that has always been true of thinking; and there are no new reasons to believe that thinking is useless simply because it is less than perfectly omnipotent. But if you get into a discussion about *national* planning with most businessmen, the first argument would in fact be an attack on your suggestion of omnipotence in The Plan. The most devastating argument against any form of national planning is that no goddamn bureaucrat can know everything, therefore no one should plan anything, and anybody who even thinks about it is a Communist. But behind the façade of these childish arguments, competent corporate executives are planning everything they can—strenuously, and with great effect.

An article in the *Harvard Business Review* of July-August 1956 contains a review of the limited writing by business professionals on this subject of long-range planning. The rundown reads like an elementary course in how to think effectively. For example, it is discovered that "long-range planning puts possibly a greater premium on *conceptual* skills of the manager (as opposed to technical and human relations skills) than does any other phase of top management." It is also pointed out that long-range plans should be revised frequently. (I have no objection: I revise my own long-range plans frequently. Doesn't everybody?) The writers of a book entitled *Principles of Management* suggest three types of planning—where the What being planned is not in the control of the planning enterprise, where It is partially controlled, and lastly where It is characteristically controlled. To which one can only murmur bemused assent. It seems that where the individual firm is concerned, businessmen can be cozied into thinking beyond the *carpe diem* of the next big production order.

Unfortunately, corporations plan only for themselves

—which is terribly selfish. It is difficult to understand why the executives who plan for their own firms are not more insistent about integrating these plans with over-all industry plans and even inter-industry, nationwide plans in pursuance of agreed-upon national purposes. Their individual plans are necessarily puny and failing of full effect, even for individual purposes, because not so integrated.

Also unfortunately, one of the things corporations have taken to planning is the early obsolescence of their products. Not all of them, of course: I am sure that U.S. Steel would not stand for built-in obsolescence in the new oxidizing furnaces it is buying. Nor would an electric power company go along with very much stylish product weakness when it buys big generators. At that level, technological obsolescence is about all a purchaser is willing to live with—he won't take any cleverly devised decay. But in many consumer areas of the economy, the big producers have already instituted as the law of the land what Aldous Huxley in *Brave New World* suggested would have to be the law of the future: thou shalt consume—endlessly. So industry helps the administration of this law along by making stuff that falls apart on schedule.

Superficial product obsolescence which is planned by business to stimulate sales (at a paper-creating price level: to make money rather than things) is such a widely understood and uncomfortable part of our economy that even two out of three businessmen consider it "not in the long-run interest of the United States." A few years back, the *Harvard Business Review* surveyed business opinion on this guilt-laden issue. The editors were quite surprised by the heavily emotional responses they received. It seems that businessmen had already been doing a lot of thinking about the matter, none of it comforting. The two out of three who thought that there was already too much artificial obsolescence were admitting to themselves a feeling which was in clear contradiction, in many cases, to the policies of their companies.*

We are talking about product obsolescence which is intended by the producer, but not merely as a rational response to advances in technology (what used to be called progress, until it became such a problem). We are talking about artificial obsolescence, which is effected in two basic ways: 1) you can build the thing itself so that it just won't last—inferior materials, poor inspection, etc.; and 2) you can attack the psychological utility of the item in the hands of the consumer. Madison Avenue is the moving force in this last form of uselessness. For example, you don't sell refrigerators, you sell a new design of a refrigerator. And often enough we get a rich mixture of aspects of uselessness, as where a manufacturer builds up an inventory of minor technological improvements and doles them out to the public as part of otherwise scheduled model changes. Anyway, these are details, and the main question is, Is this the ballgame we all came out here to watch? Because something else could be done with the time and effort and industrial capacity devoted to these practices. It is hardly news, but it should be mentioned again that we might instead build schools, new cities, commuter railroads, improve diet and

---

* Only 18 per cent of the respondents reported that their companies changed models less than once a year; but 25 per cent stated that there were five or more model changes in the course of a year; while the minority who defended the practice were tensely shrill in doing so—one of them in textiles went deep into history for his justification and found that "planned obsolescence . . . really started with Adam and Eve." He just blamed it on female foolishness.

health facilities, and so forth. As a result of which we could all live longer and better.

A corporation is known by its balance sheet; and the top corporate executive is first and foremost a balance-sheet tender—an impresario of the profit-and-loss statement.

Financial statements are a fundamental piece of paper in the Paper Economy. They are prepared for all public corporations periodically by accountants, lawyers, and public relations men, on the basis of internally supplied data—with the active "cooperation" of the managers who are to be judged by what the statements reveal. As previously suggested, the main thing about a corporation is its capacity to earn a profit, and just about everything outsiders know about this magical capacity is derived from the corporation's financial statements. So you can see how important they are.

But according to Leonard Spacek, one of the leading accountants in the country, writing in the *Harvard Business Review* in 1958, our corporate financial statements too often show "misleading results," too often are neither fair nor accurate reports on financial operations, and generally speaking are substantially below the level of which the accounting profession has proven itself capable. How does this happen? By the use of inconsistent principles of accounting, with the choice between contrasting principles being made by the management itself for its own purposes. The key phrase in the traditional certificate of a public auditor states that the results shown in the financial statements are fairly presented "in accordance with generally accepted accounting principles." Mr. Spacek's simple point is that there are none, and that to suggest that there are is pertinently misleading.

Mr. Spacek makes the main point very nicely when he notes that "the need for proper accounting mounts as more people become interested in an enterprise or institution." Then he ties this down by saying: "Different groups may argue as to how the profits may be distributed, but what the profits *are* should not be subject to confusion and controversy." I think we have to say that the balance sheet and operating statement, which are basic instruments of business policy, have been to a large extent assimilated to the system of distortion engineered by public relations men and other top management counsel by means of which American business presents its fuzzy public image.

If you are devoted to producing profit instead of goods, you simply cannot afford to be candid about the accounting facts of your operation—any more than if the shoe were on the other foot, a manufacturer would be apt to say: "These are lousy washing machines, but we already made 'em, so you buy 'em. OK?" Financial statements are a very delicate area in the Paper Economy because, like inventory and price-setting, they exist in a nexus where the reality and the paper meet. I repeat: if you want to understand the Paper Economy, either for esthetic reasons or in order to make it work, you must look for those areas where paper and thing meet—and avoid the magical incantations of the high priests of paper.

Prepared in this fashion, the balance sheet determines the price of the corporation's paper; the price of goods determines the balance sheet. Again, we are back to this ubiquitous question of price.

There are approximately two ideas current today about

how prices are set. One view has it that neither individuals
nor institutions exercise discretion, unless they have sinned
deeply and are "monopolies," but that prices are set and
reset every hour on the half-hour by a Great Force bigger
than any candy-store operator, including General Motors,
and this Great Force is called the Free Market. The other
idea, which is both obvious and not quite decent as yet,
is that where markets are dominated they are not "free,"
and the dominating economic institutions have, among
their other powers, the power to set prices with a certain
independent attitude. The latter have come to be called
"administered prices." The process of price administration
presumes price administrators who engage in thought prior
to decreeing their prices, who do not respond automatically
to impersonal forces. This is simply the view that "somebody" sets prices. The alternative view is that "nobody"
sets prices, and this is why all prices are exactly correct,
and need not be discussed further. When "nobody" sets
prices they are not only "right," but also "free" and even
"competitive." From the point of view of peace of mind,
you can't beat 'em.

The main thing to be understood about administered
prices is that they are not to be understood at all apart from
long-range business planning. That is, a particular price is
based on the idea that you are going to sell a particular
quantity with given fixed costs and given unit costs. In
order to figure that way you have to plan to produce and
sell x quantity of the thing. Once you decide this, the "right"
price follows. So the main thing price does, in the mind of
the price administrator, is to determine how much shall be
sold in the first place. For example, it is reported that General Motors uses a "standard volume" system for setting

prices. It wants 20 per cent profit after taxes, and figures its price in order to earn this on an "estimated average rate of planned operation." This latter has been calculated on the basis of about 55 per cent of capacity. Sales were higher than the standard volume in seven of the eight years after 1950, so GM made much more profit than it had figured itself entitled to. Which has boosted its net worth $3 billion in the decade 1947-57.

Even if the administrators of a big corporation tried their hardest to live up to the principles of automatic competitive pricing which they learned in college economics courses, it would be beyond their best capacity. International Harvester, for instance, establishes prices for 250,000 parts. It takes a large staff of people just to know *where* a price is, much less *what* it is, or whether it's "right": how could an organization of such magnitude possibly be market-sensitive concerning every price? No, big corporations know what they are even if classical theorists don't. They set prices and production quantities in tandem according to over-all and long-range objectives. Anything else would be much too dangerous for a major institution. They have the power to protect themselves, and they use it.

Perhaps, from their own point of view, the major achievement of our best industrial organizations is their low break-even points—the per cent of unused capacity they can tolerate before losing money. U.S. Steel, which must set some 50,000 prices, now has a break-even point of 32 per cent of capacity; the Company could cut its prices 10 per cent and still break even at 50 per cent of capacity, which is the national average. But I doubt if they will. Even if they moved more steel at the lower prices, the whole maneuver would be too risky; they might end up needing customers as much as the customers needed them: the terrible dangers of inventory—"real" wealth—could be realized. U.S. Steel might then find itself in a genuine "competition" between its own productive potential and the capacity of the rest of the country to consume steel.

But while the big producing units play it safe on the down-side—do not cut prices and risk the dangers of inventory—they also exercise care on the up-side, and do not charge every last dollar they could get away with. The corporation is primarily a government: its function is to rule various constituencies while satisfying certain needs, and like a government, its ultimate concern is to preserve the organization.

Our big corporations administer not only prices in our society, but also progress. By progress I mean, naturally, this great potential pool of technique for achieving everything the human race has dreamed and nightmared about for centuries—scientific technology.

Even so, private industry does not create all the technology, or even pay for most of it; but it does regularly end up controlling its development and application, generally speaking. Universities had established research laboratories before General Electric set up the first one in industry in 1900; the Navy hired inventors in 1789, and sponsored research has been substantially dependent on the military since then. In 1959, private industry spent $9.6 billion on research and development—$4 billion of their own and $5.6 billion of government money. An additional $3 billion of R&D was performed by universities and other non-profit institutions—and, again, the Federal government. Whoever pays for it, and whatever the direction given by the military, there is not much question about the technological stewardship of our business organizations.

At the level of productive capacity we have reached in the United States, and considering the current runaway force of technology, the price-and-profit system is an increasingly distorting factor in the plans of isolated (read: unarticulated) institutions. One expert says: "Intentional duplication of effort is an inevitable result of the patent system and industrial secrecy." Everybody in-business-for-himself is here quite wasteful—of exactly those energies and capacities which are most valuable: we are forced to spend an inordinate amount of time discovering what is already known. This process is much facilitated by the practice among the bigger organizations of not bothering to patent their discoveries, which requires disclosure, but of exploiting them at leisure as industrial secrets. But that is a bit understandable since the patent system is not much to be relied on—60 per cent of the patents litigated in the last two decades have been declared invalid by Federal appellate courts. It is also rather patriotic not to patent since the Russians can buy a copy of any American patent for pennies and use it throughout the appropriate industrial sector in Russia—a privilege not accorded to American companies.

Now could there be a sweeter, more poignant illustration of the inevitable imperatives of technology-wide industrial articulation? I mean, what can the most sincere belief in private property contribute toward the solution of this perfectly technical problem?

Let me state the articulation (planning) problem, for the moment, this way: Why tolerate a monstrosity like General Motors at all if you are not going to take the full tour and rationalize the whole automotive industry on the same principles which justify GM's existence in the first place? You may say that we are not politically prepared for this quantity of rational articulation. True enough. About as little prepared for that as we were for the whole technological revolution, the completion of which demands exactly the aforementioned articulation.

The big 500 corporations which dominate two-thirds of the industry of the United States are also in charge of the accumulation of approximately 60 per cent of the capital which is applied to industrial use. So the most important thing the corporations administer is the better part of our future.

We can think of this as "administered financing," and it is hardly second in significance to the great power involved in administering prices. Between 1946 and 1953, $150 billion of capital expenditures were made in the United States by non-financial corporations and other businesses. Sixty-four per cent of this money came from internal sources—retained earnings and depreciation. Eighteen per cent came from current borrowing from banks, twelve per cent by the issue of bonds (mostly privately placed), and only six per cent or $9 billion by the issue of stock. Berle describes this neatly as follows: "The capital is there; and so is capitalism. The waning factor is the capitalist." So economic initiative has been taken over by massive organizations and is no longer a function of individuals. One by one, it would seem, the classical attributes of capitalist enterprise have been institutionalized in the form of the major industrial corporation, or the major financial intermediary. These organizations, run as political units, each involve and affect the lives of tens upon tens of thousands of human beings. They are, there is no question, governments. A new society has been born.

This point about internal financing, and the consequent money-autonomy of the bigger corporations, received special emphasis from Adolf Berle in his most recent book, *Power Without Property*. For a good reason: this is one more market-force from which the corporations are freeing themselves—in this case, the capital market. They have become their own bankers. The source of these "banking" funds is not limited to profit and depreciation—in addition there is tax-accrual money and current obligations or trade accounts. The latter is "pure" corporate money, since it serves as such only between and among the corporations themselves: it has been estimated to amount to nearly $50 billion, one-tenth of the book value of all corporate assets.

Even an important critic of Berle's position such as John Lintner of the Harvard Business School grants that there has been "a marked decline in the relative importance of security issues" in manufacturing (as is well known, *not* in utilities which are regulated industries with very heavy capital requirements). But of course there remains some external financing, even in manufacturing and other unregulated industries—some bank-borrowing and security issues, both debt and equity. Professor Lintner assumes that this external financing means "dependence" on external sources, and a consequent lessening of corporate power. I wonder. I think it is inaccurate to say that General Motors is dependent on the Chase Manhattan Bank because it borrows a few hundred million dollars from it. Dependence would be a proper term if GM were borrowing up to the hilt—then, indeed, it might have to beg for a few hundred million more. But as it is, it is an honor to do business with them, and instead of being dependent on the Chase Manhattan, GM is actually doing the latter a favor when it borrows from it.

Rather than the non-financial corporations being dependent on capital markets, probably the opposite is true: the one fundamental fact underlying the whole structure of paper values is the earning capacity of the major corporations which, sustained by government purchase, credit, and other policy, sustains all else in the economy. For example, this is true not only of the $400 billion or so in stock exchange value but, more subtly, mortgages and bank financing of retail stores may be entirely dependent on the plant of a particular corporation located in the area. Real estate values in New York, since it has become the corporate headquarters of the nation, are clearly dependent on that event—and they amount to billions, with values shared between the equity of individual owners and the debt priority of large financial institutions.

As for being dependent on stockholders, we have already looked into that matter. It is also noticeable that the big corporations such as U.S. Steel prefer to get necessary expansion funds from the public by raising prices instead of selling stock. That way "dividends" are more purely discretionary, being "paid" only in reduced prices —and there haven't been any lately.

Lintner points out, properly enough, that in such industrial financing as there is, the typical situation involves trained corporate managers on one side of the table bargaining in a sophisticated fashion with trained financial managers on the other side of the table. Again, I see no compelling reason to assume that one side is more "dependent" than the other. This is financing administered in a decidedly managerial setting. When the representatives of big organizations deal with each other, I am sure that considerable dust can be raised in well-appointed board-rooms. If you call this action "competition," I don't see what has been added to the analysis. And much has been subtracted from it if that loaded term is taken to revive the image of a really dusty produce-market.

Let us at last be reasonable about things and note the substantial difference between market and institutional competition. The latter is much closer to statesmanlike collusion.

On the intellectual question of the American corporate system and the ideological issues presented by its robust existence, the thought of Adolf Berle is a great deal of the whole show. There are few intellectual areas in which the name of one man becomes and remains quite so pervasively meaningful. It all began with the publication in 1932 of *The Modern Corporation and Private Property*, which certainly marked a turning point in American social thought. The very title implies that something about the corporation calls into question something about the system of private property. This book, written with the economist Gardiner C. Means, has become the kind of unassailable historical event which it is no longer wise to discuss freshly. I am a very careful—and very indebted—reader of Berle; I find that it is not so much this book as the brilliant suggestiveness of his later (and scattered) thought that has made his current contribution to the subject so important. Berle would be the first to say that the purpose of his 1932 thesis was to stimulate speculation, and he himself has been speculating on its implications for more than a quarter-century. We would all do well to begin our own speculation by tracing his.

Berle can be placed in a general way by seeing him as a specifically American off-to-the-side variant of the capitalism/socialism argument. Bypassing this great oppositional debate is almost an American intellectual tradition—Veblen did it, too. There is an historical validity in this maneuver, which of course has been buttressed by the general population's startling lack of interest in the socialist alternative. A great deal of the force behind the socialist movement in Europe derived from egalitarian sentiments which expressed themselves in the demand for the kind of democratic forms and official rhetoric which had early become an accepted part of the American landscape. An even larger part of the force behind the movement was garden-variety class-conflict which simply fought for a bigger cut of the produce —again, less of a problem here because our system was the first to become modern-productive, in which people as consumers are recognized as a business necessity. And lastly, everything happened so quickly here on this *tabula rasa* of a continent, with an unprecedented amount of physical and social shifting, that socialism never had a chance to become a class tradition—a very important quality of the movement in European countries. On the other hand, we never lacked for anti-capitalist sentiments; but they were always crudely expressed and seldom achieved a sophisticated pattern (compare Veblen as to high quality and low influence, to Bryan and the muckrakers—or even, to be brutal about the matter, to Teddy Roosevelt). Let's face it, we have had a very strange political history, which has followed none of the traditional markers with any real faithfulness: where else, for example, could this national liberal effluvia of ours be tolerated culturally, much less taken as a political point of view?

Following Veblen, Berle largely bypassed the egalitarian issue (as also Thurman Arnold and, more recently, J. K. Galbraith) and emphasized the analytical side of the matter. He has asserted that the world revolution following World War I was "technical far more than it was social," adding, "The philosophical and scientific discoveries of the 19th century were put to work in the 20th, and whole civilizations changed as a result." The corporation was the chosen vehicle of this technical revolution. As a new form of social organization in the modern setting, the corporation is a major revolutionary force. And not least revolutionary in contradicting all of the traditional capitalist assumptions —the privacy of property, the freedom of markets, the economic importance of individualism, and the role of the government.

The last is especially significant since, as we have noted, the corporation is itself a form of government. This is the basic dramatic confrontation out of which Berle's thought and insight flows, with one added factor: observing the process of the corporation as the dominant form of economic government *in development*, it is immediately noticeable that the separate corporate governments are only primitively articulated. A more sophisticated articulation—beyond the present much too loose confederation—is the major work of the corporate system yet to be accomplished. The problem in this country is that this requires a much larger borrowing of Federal power, or more substantial amalgamation with it. Which in turn would necessarily call upon the corporations either to legalize themselves, or turn the national government itself into an illegal instrumentality. (Some years ago the latter possibility was called "fascism," and is still quite unpopular when identified by that name.) This is the context in which the discussion of planning becomes predominant: it is to this subject that Berle's thought most recently and most strongly tends.

That—and the overriding political, legal, and even spiritual problem of legitimacy.

Before we get to this final issue in our discussion of the corporation, let me point out one of the grand ironies of history—the accidental conjunction of capitalism and the scientific revolution. The revival of learning and later free intellectual inquiry was a bourgeois phenomenon as much as the trading society which accompanied it; and we tend to think of nineteenth-century industrialism, with its mechanical and chemical inventions, as capitalism proper. But there seems to have been a geometric progression in technology, not equal to the growth of capitalism nor directly caused by it. In science we have experienced, in this century at least, the most permanent of permanent revolutions. Capitalism, the price-and-paper system, has demonstrably done as much to harness as to unleash the force of science (this would be much more noticeable in the absence of the progressive effect of the military). The system of business enterprise happened to be there when science, so to speak, took off. The new dynamic factor which kept the contradictions between the two from tearing society apart more than has actually occurred was—the modern corporation, an equivocally capitalist if not non-capitalist institution. This had to be accomplished by the corporation (along with the military) in such short order that it may be excused its early illegitimacy: there wasn't time for a proper birth certificate. But the excuse is wearing thin; and modern dynamic technology cannot be contained, certainly not furthered at its own pace, without rationalizing the corporate system: *without national planning*.

The only nationally planned, fully articulated application of technology we now have, of any scale, is that of the military. Indeed, I think that may be one of the main reasons that we still have a big military—which has become exactly as much of a danger to its own domestic population as it is to the enemy population. The military provides an excuse to do what has to be done, without taking that terrible leap into the future—admitting what we're doing while we're doing it. Such admission is the very beginning of a legal order. And a legal order would not have to rely so exclusively on the military direction of the economy.

So the dominance of the corporate system finally raises two questions: 1) is it technically adequate? and 2) is the power it represents "legitimate" within the assumptions of the whole society?

The answer to both questions is No. And the answers are related.

Let us be quite clear at the outset that the legitimacy of a power system, or the lack of it, is an important issue for any society. No law governing the exercise of power ever equals perfect justice, which is like saying that law is just law. But having experienced the totalitarianisms of this century, we should not doubt that law that is just law is invaluable to us poor mortals who are just mortals. Law can never get very far in contradicting a power system (although it can express the contradictions existing in one);

but in its presumptive rationality, it *regularizes* the exercise of power and it *justifies* that exercise. Law justifies power—"gives it legitimacy"—by relating its exercise to more basic assumptions of the social order. Such justification can be, and often is, quite thin—which puts you smack in the middle of politics (the solvent and source of law), arguing for more substantial justification, or referring to some more basic or some other basic assumptions. And all the while, in law and in politics, people typically become so enthusiastic in justifying that they just naturally falsify in unconscionable quantities. But the commonly accepted need to justify gives a point to the lies. Without this need, why lie? It is in the nature of power not to rely on crude force. I am serious when I say that the discovery and wide use of fraud and deception marked a considerable advance in human history: it is so much easier and more effective to con people into doing what you want them to do, than hit all of them over the head to convince them—and you cover more social ground. Of course we have in our current century managed to carry this to a seemingly ultimate point of sophistication; but that is another matter. (Machiavelli thought so of his century, too, I would imagine.)

When we raise the question of the legitimacy of the corporate order, we are asking what basic assumptions of the society justify its power—and then asking whether they are really basic. The difficulty is immediately apparent: there are none—or they aren't.

The first defense of the system, still relied on by many ill-informed persons, is that it doesn't exist. In the course of this defense it is imagined that corporations are private property, operate in free markets, etc. In other words, *capitalism* is justified and this is thought to carry us forward with the problem of understanding and justifying the corporate order. It doesn't, really, and since this is a regular subject of most other sections of this book, I will not dwell on it here.

Frequently, the next defense is, What difference does it make? It "works." This is obviously contemptible, and beneath discussion. (See below for discussion.)

Berle has been greatly concerned with this question of legitimacy. And he has come up with something like an answer. I say "something like" because I am not sure whether he is prognosticating—describing a process whereby the corporate order *may become* legitimated—or identifying a current legitimation. In any event, his view is that corporations are developing a "conscience" because they exist in an environment of opinion that states what they ought and ought not to do. He calls this "the consensus," which consists not only of the opinion-pressures of the corporate constituencies, but (apparently even more significantly) of general intellectual opinion—university professors, independent journalists, and so on, which he calls "the forum of accountability." At times he refers to the core of the consensus as the Lord's Spiritual, as opposed to the corporate executives, the Lord's Temporal, on a medieval analogy. He has suggested that what we are looking for is a moral substitution for the Medieval Church and the nineteenth-century Free Market, now that neither is any longer adequate. He defines the corporate conscience as "a lively apprehension by the present senior instruments of production that they had better try to anticipate what is wanted and conform to it rather than wait until there is conflict." (But he later says: "The corporate conscience is merely a lively apprehension of possible state intervention of some kind.")

Berle's conscience-consensus theory is the best known and best accepted justification of the corporate order for those who recognize that there is anything to be justified in the first place. Before criticizing this idea, I should note that he will also make statements like this: "A consensus that economy-by-accident is not good enough for our complicated domestic and international society is beginning to form." And: "The corporation having won its place in the economic system must fill it." With Professor Berle available to identify consensus and specify conscience, the perspective is rhetorically useful and, as usual with him, quite interesting. In the hands of the speech-writers of leading executives, however . . .

I don't doubt that a consensus concerning proper corporate behavior exists, and that the corporate managers worry about it somewhat. I can even see that some professors have helped to create it. But one of the things that is wrong with this notion is that it can be taken to justify almost anything that both exists, and is tolerated by intelligent people. Another thing wrong with it is that the consensus which is to judge the corporations is largely created by them, as well as for their benefit. To the extent that it is not a creation of Madison Avenue's mass culture, it is as well described as the better conversation about corporations. As conversation, it is just as reasonable to say that the consensus *accompanies* the illegitimacy of corporate power in the United States as it is to say that it *legitimates* it.

I think that the consensus really is part of the quality of the power wielded by corporate managers. The organizations which give them their power are integral with the community, and so they must concern themselves with community views; but these institutions dominate the community economically, and no amount of conversation is apt to change that fact. The consensus indicates *how* to use the great concentrated power of our major corporations: it is not a functioning factor dealing with the why and the wherefore of this power. It can be seen in its more serious aspects as the *capitalization of a possible political future;* it cannot be seen as a substitute for politics, present or future. In the end, the idea of the consensus is not much more than a Happy Thought. It comes from a very idealistic view of things: "We have yet to see the time in America when ideas do not eventually establish themselves to the extent merited by their validity," Berle says. If so, then only because in our short history we have not had enough "eventually" as yet.

The consensus is inadequate as a source of legitimacy *and* as a control technique because the present powers in the country guided by the consensus they choose to be guided by have not achieved the basic existing potentiality of the people, namely, full production. Full production is not a "fancy" requirement: it is what the people want in the crudest and most direct way. To have devoted ourselves to industrialism with such single-minded fervor and then, possessing this magnificent industrial plant, not to use it to produce all the goods it is designed to produce is not only illegitimate but criminal. I would just have to include myself out of any consensus that didn't account for this point.

Very simply, the reason there is so much difficulty in legitimating the corporation is that it is an illegitimate institution. It is an authoritarian form of industrial government in a purportedly democratic society. All the talk about constitutionalizing the corporation, giving it a finer conscience by making it responsibly subject to elite opinion, and in other ways spiritually domesticating it, are all attempts to answer the unanswerable. The problem simply will not be confronted head-on by any of these conversational means. The corporation is an illegitimate form of baronial government. The fact must be stated and understood. And we should not be in a hurry to scour up some legitimation for a developing and unfinished illegitimate system. The easiest way to make the corporate order "consistent" with the basic assumptions of our society would be to ignore or downgrade the latter, especially in their democratic orientation.

The system was born in illegality: I notice nothing outstandingly legal about the way in which Vanderbilt, Gould, Morgan, *et al* went about creating it. Of course it is better behaved now: it has achieved the power for which it struggled. I should imagine that *all* new societies are born with the essential assistance of alien, illegitimate midwives. The new is not legal—it is just imperative, or irresistible, or terribly important.

The reason that the corporation, this dominant form of government in the United States, has assumed its crucial role in our world is that we wanted done what only the corporation in the first instance could do, but we were not ready enough to admit that we wanted it done and to make the doing of it legal. *The corporation is a primary American illegal instrumentality, just as the political party is, and syndicate crime is.* Indeed, I think a very good case could be made out that the real history of the United States is a history of illegal instrumentalities, or legal instrumentalities operated by illegal means.

And beyond the bruited issue of legitimacy, there is the further question of responsibility.

The power of the corporation is unavoidable, but it should exist for a particular purpose, not for its own sake. If the purpose is generally accepted, the power is in fact legitimate; if it is actually used for that purpose, it is responsible. The great power of the corporate system is both illegitimate and irresponsible because in form it has not been made coherent with other purposes in the society, and in fact it is not devoted to fulfilling the purpose for which it was created and is tolerated—production.

There is not just the question of regularizing and justifying the actions of a new power system—there is also the question of the rights of individuals who exist under it, and the duty of the power-wielders to them. Whether and to what extent individuals can experience freedom and liberty in relation to these great structures does not really depend on whether or not an acceptable theory accounting for their existence has been formulated. Note that it took some centuries to achieve what individual rights we have vis-à-vis the state; now we are faced with a similar struggle with regard to non-state organizations. Who can doubt that this is a long-term affair? And who can believe that this struggle is mainly a theoretical one? Besides, the historically immediate point is that the structure of the corporate system itself is incomplete, because modern technology requires a higher level of integration between the separate corporate empires than now exists. The individuals "involved under" these private governments can, must, should assert themselves wherever possible against the dominant and domineering bureaucratic structures. But already we, as individuals, have made great sacrifices in order to create these private industrial governments which produce the goods we so much desire, and these sacrifices will go for nothing if the industrial system is not made coherent enough to fulfill its practical purpose of the maximum production of goods. Once the system is complete, particularly with effective automation and other institutionalized science, we can then concentrate solely on individual self-assertion. As things stand now, however, our devotion to the monster is unconsummated.

To the question, Should and will the corporation be subject to the guarantys of the Fourteenth Amendment which protects individuals against governing bodies? Berle replies with an historical affirmative. If corporations are private governments, then the citizen's rights under the Fourteenth Amendment are made shallow if that constitutional provision does not govern the exercise of corporate power in relation to them. In other words, to allow the system of corporate power to exist outside of constitutional guarantys is to negate constitutional due process.

The growth of corporate power in the United States has, *pari passu*, repealed the Constitution. Veneration of the repealed document has become a perverse means of embracing the primary illegality of our social order.

10

WHAT THE BIG UNDERWRITER DOES

IN PREVIOUS CHAPTERS we have noticed, every once in a while, what is blandly known as "the role of the government" in economic affairs. Now I think we might pause and add up the score un-blandly. Indeed, it's a salty subject; there is very little economic activity which fails to be touched intimately by governmental effect. Frankly, the whole thing would fall apart if it were not for the Federal government's taxing, spending, subsidizing, guarantying, organizing, assisting-and-regulating, and generally underwriting the flow of national income. What the Big Underwriter does is to keep Big Business in business in a big way.

To state the basic American economic proposition as simply as possible—the major corporations organize and govern industry, the government ensures that the goods are actually produced and distributed. Despite all confusion and distortion, this is the true division of roles. The system does *not* run itself: the corporations are not able to run it *by* themselves. This has been clear since the Great Depression. With each advance in productivity it becomes clearer.

But there are some quite naive notions still current about this enlarged role of the Federal government. Chiefly it is thought that the use of Federal power in the economy was, in each additional instance, only "temporarily" called for and should have been abandoned as soon as the "temporary" need had been met. That Federal power has not been withdrawn to its properly limited sphere is explained, by a more rigorously consistent group of thinkers, as resulting from an eggheaded conspiracy to defile the True American Way of Life. From the far right, all eggheaded liberals are either Communists or dupes of the Communists; so in the pure simple form, all our troubles result from a Russian plot.

All of this is quite silly, since the obvious truth of the matter is that, just as the corporate form was required to organize large aggregations of men and wealth to produce goods, according to the historical terms set by nineteenth-century industrialism and twentieth-century technology, so a coherent national power was required by the same history to ensure, sustain and articulate this complicated setup. Berle characterizes it nicely: "We have a concentrated collective form of production covering about two-thirds of the American productive economy, and most of it is powerfully influenced and in some cases directed by the State."

As pointed out earlier, *somebody had to govern*. Private financial government was more or less adequate until the system matured to the point where it became too productive—of both goods and paper-values. The latter outran the former, the paper system collapsed, and with it the authority and effectiveness of private financial government in the United States. Up to the great 1929 watershed, the relation between the governing business and financial interests and the Federal government can be characterized as follows: the former took most of the land, mineral, and other wealth that the latter had; used as much Federal power as needed to accomplish their purposes, whether one is thinking of banking, the tariffs, credit, labor injunctions, or whatever; and fought a continuingly successful campaign to make certain that no Federal power existed that they did not need or could not use—that if nevertheless such power did come into existence, its effective use on behalf of other groups would be frustrated, delayed, or sabotaged as much as needed. But it is very important that this program of curtailment remained a reasonable means of governing—ethical isues aside—only so long as the private government was effective. Neither Rockefeller nor Morgan nor any of the great creators of the system believed in laissez faire or the autonomy of the impersonal market or anything of the sort; they believed in organizing and governing.

Since the 1929 collapse, there has been even more governing called for by the geometrically progressing complexity of the technological system; and, for one reason or another, a substantial amount of such governing authority has finally been relocated in Washington, D. C. which, as the history books inform us, had been the original seat of American power before the Civil War.

In its entire checkered career the United States government has spent about $1.4 trillion. It is not the result of evil *conspiracy that 90 per cent of this money has been dispensed in the last twenty years.*

Let's sum up for a moment. Traditional capitalist theory has always obscured the role of the state and all other governing authority in the economy. The keystone of this arch obscurantism has always been the image of the Free Market. If the desire had been to describe rather than ennoble, the terms employed would have been "primitive" and "mature" markets and the loaded word "free" would never have entered the vocabulary of economic discourse. We cannot stop here long enough to discuss the possible useful meanings of the word "free" but, in shorthand fashion, a primitive market is free in that it is disorganized, whereas a mature market is free in the sense that it functions satisfactorily and any un-freedom in it is not regretted by the participants. When we call a mature market "free" we are simply adding an unnecessary encomium: what we mean to say is that we like it—it's good. When we call a primitive market "free" we may be saying something verging on description, but the point is soon lost because what we mean by "free" is "disorganized," and all markets quickly tend to become organized, and properly so. These reflections apply with equal force whether the market is organized by the government, a dominant seller, a dominant buyer, craftsmen, or any of these authorities in differing combinations. An organized market is a governed market.*

---

* By "market" I do not mean to refer to a quaint plaza near the village square where farmers display their turnips and piglets. A market is not tied down or defined geographically: it is simply the form of the act of buying and selling. Even one of our wonderful supermarkets is not to be thought of as a "market" in the Real Big sense. Anyway, by the time the customer gets to the supermarket, with what's left of his money in his pocket, and by the time the goods are set out on the shelves to welcome him to a supermarket trance engineered by merchandising experts, the best part of the show is over.

In Chapter 3 we rediscovered the fact that a contract, without which there are no markets, is as good as its enforcement by state machinery and never anything much different from what a court says it is (courts being arms of the state). And we previously noted the paranoiac coloring of the business creed's view of government with which, willynilly, it has been forced to share the power involved in running America. When we swam free-style through money and credit, we certainly must have noticed that central banking and money-management, especially in its latter-day contra-cyclical Keynesian style, is a fundamental activity of government. We also observed the tax system for its powerful regulatory effect. And somewhere along in there we finally and most importantly discovered that the Federal government is the great underwriter of the Paper Economy. The extensive role of the Federal government in the functioning of the economy is as necessary and central a factor of modern existence as can well be imagined. In the present chapter we will squint with somewhat more effort at this big fact.

A few immediate facts will surely help us to appreciate the bulk and the range of Federal economic effect. Thus, one adult in five receives regular checks from the Federal government for one reason or another—25 million Americans. (On the other side, of course, the government gets checks from about twice as many of us.) For grossly revealing facts, one can dip into numberless documents almost at random—and look at governmental assets, debt, employment, annual cash flow, areas of intervention and participation, etc. Now it can only be *assumed* that all this governmental activity is essential to the functioning of the economy: an alternative view would be that governments—

Federal, state, and local—are merely additional customers, or occasionally competitive producers. But I believe that with the accumulation of the pattern of fact, moistened with a little reasonable speculation of an argumentative nature, the image of the Federal government as the great and essential underwriter—rather than the weak and semi-useless policeman—will slip properly into place. In accomplishing this, it will be helpful to keep the conclusion in mind: we have a very complicated and irrational system of dual government in the United States.

Our friend, the First National City Bank, which believes firmly in both limited government and what it persists in calling free enterprise, speaks impressively of the scope of government in its area:

> In the financial field there are over 100 federal insuring, lending, and guaranteeing agencies covering agriculture, housing, foreign trade and investment, local government organizations, commerce and industry. It is estimated that by June, 1960, existing lending programs will reach a total outstanding of $105 billion ($23 billion direct loans and $82 billion guaranteed or insured loans). In June, 1945, the total was $11 billion.

Note that this is not spending or directly regulating, but only lending and guaranteeing.

This indicates just one of the effects of the Federal signature. For another angle, let's take a look at assets. At the beginning of 1961, all real and personal assets of the Federal government were inventoried at $276 billion. These values are understated, since they are carried at acquisition cost—and some are dated a century ago. For example, the White House, including eighteen acres in the center of Washington, is carried at a value of $1,000. West Point is valued at $17 million, and could not be replaced for less than $141 million. The government holds about 779 million acres of land, including 722 million of public domain: this is one-fifth of the total area of the United States and is valued at $72 billion. This real estate is not exactly "unimproved," although it does include most of the unprofitable parks in the country. The Inventory Report on Federal real property, as of June 30, 1959, refers to 13,707 installations with an acquisition cost of $31.1 billion. At that date, the floor area of federally owned buildings amounted to 2,312,100,000 square feet. (I'll bet it's all unmortgaged.)

At anything like current market value, the government is worth considerably more than its outstanding public debt. In other words, the United States government is underfinanced; or, stated conversely, private assets are overvalued. These Federal assets are *real*—some of them even edible, as, for example, the $9 or $10 billion worth of farm surplus. Even the army tanks could probably be converted into bulldozers or tractors: if peace is ever declared, the government might consider selling them to the Hertz Corporation to be leased out all over the world in underdeveloped areas. Atom bombs are useful in creating harbors and moving mountains. I am suggesting that all these assets are inherently valuable and even productive. But of course if they were ever used as such, they would certainly knock the props out from under the inflated price and profit-making posture of the so-called private sector of the Paper Economy. And that, specifically, is what the Federal government is committed to sustaining—that is, underwriting.

As a minor part of its beneficence, the Federal government also hands it out directly to needy as well as worthy individuals. Everybody knows about Social Security, and that noble and prolix section of government, the Department of Health, Education and Welfare. But not so many people realize that the Veterans Administration, created by President Hoover in 1930, is a vast social welfare organization—for combined needy–worthy individuals. The VA operates 170 hospitals with a population of more than 115,-000 veterans (they could take a lot more). Its budget exceeds $5 billion annually. There are over 22 million veterans; with their families, veterans amount to 46 per cent of the nation's population. Disability compensation and pensions come to more than $3 billion annually; veterans' insurance has a face value of $43 billion. The redistribution of income, and provision of essential social services, which this operation represents, is obviously of great significance in sustaining the economy—for what our language forces us to call "purchasing power." To which must be added innumerable other Federal programs—not only Social Security, but also unemployment compensation, direct government employment, and indirect employment by corporations operating under government contracts. The list is long.

The Federal government is the biggest property-holder in the country—and it is not permitted to make any money on its property-holdings. Indeed, it gives money and other things away, and then creates more money to be loaned back to it—but only grudgingly, at nice rates of interest, and with much foreboding of doom.

Our men in Washington have been in the giveaway business since the beginning. It is probable, for example, that we would still be walking or riding on horseback if there had been no government subsidy of transportation in this country: apparently every form of it—from the building of the canals and turnpikes in the early part of the last century, through the construction of railroads, the development of flight, shipping, trucks and cars and buses through Federal highway programs—has been subsidized. The Merchant Marine benefits from both construction and operating subsidies—and a mortgage insurance program: more than half of the United States flagships in foreign trade are subsidized. A large part of the product of the aircraft industry is bought by the government. From the functional point of view, a particular subsidy may be an excellent investment, but again, it is that special kind of "investment" indulged exclusively by our Federal government. The chief "return" on such investment is abuse from the recipients and, once the gravy has been ladled out, large screams against interference with private enterprise. The story of Federal subsidy is literally endless—all the way from big items like $15 billion of tax-free depletion donated (1944-1953) to oil, gas, and other mineral extraction enterprises, to the 10-million-dollar postal subsidy which goes to *Life* magazine annually. Literally endless.

There would be no point in elaborating the subsidy to farmers, which we hear about so loudly every year. Looked at from a long-run perspective, what the Federal government has accomplished by supporting farm prices and otherwise underwriting the farm economy has been to contribute vitally to financing the technical revolution on the farm—maybe as much as defense spending has accomplished in, say, electronics. Which ends up defeating the purpose of the farm subsidy. For example, the acreage program has been ruined by chemical fertilizers: being paid for using less acreage, the farmers just naturally busied them-

selves growing twice as much on half the area. Which leads
to a wonderfully productive agriculture, and ever-increasing
Federal subsidy. Too much inventory—*the* curse, in the
Paper Economy. (And after paying for the food, the government is of course not permitted to lend or give it away to
those of its citizens who are still starving.)

The subject of subsidy, which we have touched on
before and will probably come across again, serves here to
introduce a discussion of regulation. Because after giving it
away in the first instance, the Federal government then sets
up commissions to ensure that the recipients employ it
successfully to their own advantage. For this purpose, we
have a slew of "independent" agencies which regulate Federal interference with the regulated industries. They also
regulate subsequent Federal donations—the when and to
whom.

The *U.S. Government Organization Manual* lists fifty-
eight "Independent Agencies," ranging from the American
Battle Monuments Commission to the Virgin Islands Corporation. These have 350,000 employees, including the
VA's 172,795—the others ranging from 743 in the FTC
to 2,358 in the ICC. The "Big Six" are the ICC, the FTC,
the FPC, the SEC, the FCC, and the CAB (along with the
new Federal Aviation Agency). The regulatory effect of
the government is not limited to these agencies—the Department of Agriculture, for example, is not included among
them—but for purposes of reasonable abstraction, the discussion of regulation usually refers to "the agencies" in a
broad, offhand manner.

In the popular mind, these agencies are identified with
the "alphabet soup" wisecracks of the early New Deal
days. Actually, the first one was the Interstate Commerce

Commission, set up in 1887 in response to strong popular pressure to counter the financial rape of the farmers by the big railroad systems—the great statutory achievement, along with the Sherman Act, of the Populist movement. After not so long, however, the ICC became an adjunct of the railroad industry designed to prevent further popular interference with the conduct of railroad affairs; and also—why waste it, since it was already established?—a borrowing of Federal power to assist the different railroad companies in dealing with certain industry problems and generally organizing things among themselves. Something like this appears to have been the fate of most of these agencies. They start out as expressions of the popular will to correct a specific large abuse or to deal with a big problem presented by an entire industry; they soon end up as something on the order of a trade association with some vague statutory power and official status. In their function of doling out air routes, radio and television channels, rate increases, and so on, they are mostly a form of organized grab. They have by no means done away with the backstairs "take," but they have limited it and more or less identified the appropriate corridors leading to the pork barrel.

It is clear that most regulation of the economy is not only of business but also for business and by business. In this sense, politics is an extension of business by other means. Even so, the kind of self-regulation for minimal motives which the agencies accomplish is a substantial advance over competitive chaos—especially the ignoble competition for the allegiance of congressmen.

As policy-formulating and policy-executing instrumentalities, they have not been worth a great deal since the early days of the New Deal. The seniors in the audience may recall the violent attacks to which they were subject during the thirties: that was before their harmlessness had been clearly formulated. This kind of attack from the rational right has almost entirely disappeared from the political scene. This suggests to me that, like the SEC, the industry being regulated has learned to live with the regulation to its own advantage; or, like the FCC or the FPC, have become positive aids to money-making in the industry. They constitute more of a threat to the dignity of government than they do to the warmed-over free enterprise of industry.

All of this is not quite so bad as I am trying to make it sound: the indignation about private enterprise feeding at the government trough and then uttering ideological screams against government interference is, I insist, excusable. But the substantial point is that the giveaway function of our government is historically established and sanctified, and provides a context for comprehending the commissions.

The best serious criticism of the regulatory agencies merely urges that besides conducting the giveaway with a little more propriety, the agencies should also exercise a larger measure of the originally intended policy and planning powers. A somewhat recent example of this kind of constructive criticism is the Landis Report, one of the first "task force" reports presented to President Kennedy after his election. We might profitably take a quick look at the point of view of the distinguished Mr. Landis, an early New Deal commissioner and former Dean of the Harvard Law School.

The ICC, according to Dean Landis, "lacks positive direction," its opinions "are presently in the poorest category of all administrative agency opinions" and are "devoid of real rationalization." (The "rationalization" he refers to is appreciated more by lawyers than by psychiatrists.) The Civil Aeronautics Board is distinguished by "the intrusion of influences off the record that appear to be determinative of pending cases" and "a failure to do forward planning." The Federal Communications Commission, characterized as "a somewhat extraordinary spectacle," is also "incapable of policy planning" and "has drifted, vacillated and stalled in almost every major area." It also appears that the FCC is even guiltier than the CAB of "*ex parte* presentations." The delays of the FCC in processing applications for channels is one of the agency's major defects. Much of this delay results from the commission's requirement that considerable evidence be adduced in proceedings to show that programming would be "in the public interest." But "the actual programming bears no reasonable similarity to the programming proposed"; and the Harris Committee hearings indicated that the commission made only the slightest effort, when any at all was made, to monitor programs of licensees, and was not known ever to have cancelled a license because programming varied substantially from that promised in the station's application. The Federal Power Commission, according to Dean Landis, "without question represents the outstanding example in the federal government of the breakdown of the administrative process." The problem of the FPC is quite simple: it has refused to accept the Natural Gas Act as being of much consequence to it. And so on.

There has in the past few years been an exceptional amount of scandal connected with the commissions. In a book based on his brief experience with the Harris Committee, Professor Bernard Schwartz of New York University stated that he had uncovered fifty cases of duplicate expense accounts among agency personnel, especially in the FCC. In one case involving an Albany TV station, he discovered that five congressmen had financial interests in the matter. He went further and said that 10 per cent of the congressmen had interests in TV stations—with large interests held by members of relevant congressional committees.

Of course most of the scandal, following the established American tradition, concerns inept raids on the petty-cash box. Few people in America ever seem to be interested in the structural aspects of a bad situation: most Americans apparently have a very shallow appreciation of impropriety. Personally, I was much more interested in the following disclosure than in any prepaid yachting adventures of a commissioner: former Chairman John C. Doerfer of the FCC claimed before the Harris Committee that his Commission knew nothing about the quiz-show rigging until receipt of a certain affidavit on July 31, 1958. The Harris Committee report goes on to note that articles alleging the fixing of quiz programs appeared in *Time* and the New York *World Telegram & Sun* in April 1957, and *Look* in August of that year. In other words, not only was the FCC not actively regulating the industry, but it claims to have been not so well informed about what was going on as millions of popular-magazine readers. Now I find that both more interesting and more chucklesome than the ordinary expense-account anecdote.

"In various areas, agency policies must be coordinated and welded into an integrated whole. Certain areas such as transportation, communication and energy are obvious areas where such coordination is essential," says Dean Landis in his Report. Which suggests the most significant and most neglected point about the regulatory commissions: they constitute our special style of inarticulate national planning.*

Our economy is not unplanned—it is just planned very badly. And the purposes served by the planning are for the short-term and short-sighted benefit of minority groups— probably less than 5 per cent of the population. Most of the private property in this country was taken from the government in the first instance and then *made* private; it *remains* private by the continual intercession of the government. That's the system. It is because of this system, not individual foolishness, that so eminently reasonable a suggestion as that made by Senator Keating of New York (an eminent representative of the system, incidentally) has not been adopted. Senator Keating proposed that licenses for television channels be auctioned off to the highest bidder. This would afford income to the Federal government, do away with wasteful proceedings in licensing contests, and would make feasible the actual use of agency power to revoke a license when actual programming failed to meet acceptable standards. It might even be provided that the government would buy the station, or at least broker it, when a license was revoked for reasons of "public convenience or necessity." But that would be in the direction of rational planning devoted to something more than orderly giveaway.**

* This point is frequently made by Berle as part of his over-all analysis of the corporate system: "We now have about thirty different planning agencies in Washington, though not called by that name. They run all the way from the Civil Aeronautics Board, to executive action under oil import quotas, to the Federal Reserve Board."
** While we are on anecdotes about Federal regulation, I would like to offer this one, which suggests some of the eternal quality of any regulation by anybody for anything. An acquaintance of mine in the legal profession went to Washington in the late thirties and worked on in-

All other governmental effect is currently dwarfed by the economic earthquake of military procurement. Apart from comprehending the quantity of production, there is one primary point to be kept in mind: this amount of Federal demand cannot possibly be viewed as "temporary." The military budget has worked profound structural changes in the economy—changes that would have had to come in any event, but which in fact were effected by this means. Changes are brought about without opposition in the name of the military which, properly identified in candid perspective, would have been resisted to the death by countless traditionalists.

Nothing is more ironic or revealing about our society than the fact that hugely destructive war is a very progressive force in it. The reason is quite clear: when military capacity is the issue, as in Korea or World War II, or when it is the excuse, as with the magnificent hospital system and other welfare programs of the Veterans Administration or the technological development underwritten by cold war expenditures, there occurs a measure of planning and proper allocation, a devotion of resources to a particular realistic

---

vestigations and prosecutions under the Public Utility Holding Company Act, which was administered by the SEC. This was one of the more effective New Deal regulatory statutes, and consequently earned the bitter hatred of utility companies and related financial interests. The statute was designed to break up utility holding company systems following public pressure to do so after the Insull debauch. This lawyer told me that in the course of plowing his way through some particular company's files, he came across a lawyer's letter to a company executive which spelled out in lucid detail a very involved transaction designed to allocate markets, fix prices, and generally defend the freedom of the company's enterprise against both its government and its customers. The transaction was well conceived, nicely worked out—my informant expressed real professional admiration for it. He told me that there was a pencilled note at the bottom of this descriptive letter from the firm's attorney. It was initialed and read simply, "O.K.—scramble the deal."

end, that is otherwise inordinately difficult to achieve in the mature Paper Economy. The production of specific goods takes precedence over the creation of paper profit. Not that the production of war material is unprofitable to our big corporations—quite the contrary. But the goods get produced: the profit is incidental.

War production is progressive because it is production that would not otherwise take place. (It is not so widely appreciated, for example, that the civilian standard of living *rose* during World War II.) The fact that what is produced is essentially useless—and much worse than useless—merely heightens the trenchancy of the circumstance. The present condition of the American industrial establishment, the modernization effected, is unthinkable without the benefit of the capacity-building expenditures of the past twenty years induced by war and preparedness measures. This is true both directly, as with plants and whole industrial sectors paid for by the Federal government, and indirectly because of the support of widespread sectors of the economy by virtue of military expenditure—the difference, say, between the military investment in atomic energy or electronics on the one hand and the purchase of military textiles or food on the other. Of course, all this expenditure is doubly useless because not only are bombs of no benefit to anyone, and not only do soldiers accomplish no productive work—although they are fed, clothed, and occasionally kept out of trouble—but the industrial capacity resulting from these expenditures is not thereafter used to the fullest in favor of civilian production. Nevertheless, the economy is kept from falling apart, the millions of men under arms are not counted among the unemployed, and the plants are there to be used productively one day—perhaps.

The worldwide scope of military expenditure is truly horrifying. Early in 1961, the Associated Press reported that the world was spending $14 million an hour on arms and armies. Almost three-quarters of this amount was accounted for by the United States and the Soviet Union. The cost of armament at that time was "about $140.00 a year for each man, woman, and child now living." That is more than the annual income of most individuals and families on earth. There are 15 million men under arms, and considering that four men work just to keep one soldier supplied, the energies of 75 million men are devoted to the waste of war.

The biggest war spender is the United States—and getting bigger all the time. There is no longer any point in fighting about the assertion that we have a war economy, or that it becomes factually more permanent year by year, and theoretically so as the terminus continually recedes, also year by year. But the matter is too important to rest the assertion on an abstraction. We had better amaze ourselves with some of the facts.

In October 1960, the Subcommittee on Defense Procurement of the Joint Economic Committee, under the chairmanship of Senator Douglas, issued a report on the economic aspects of military procurement and supply. Understandably, the subcommittee was most interested in the immense waste and continuing mismanagement involved in the military procurement programs. The report includes an exasperated history of Congressional failure in dealing with this problem. But for our purposes, the report is helpful in revealing the *range* of the procurement programs. We can accept the subcommittee's complaint about "the billions that have been wasted" and its conclusion—"It is a shame that the military bureaucracies are wasting the precious lifeblood of this country, and simultaneously stinting both the military and civilian programs of essential needs"—and go on from there.

In the nine fiscal years from 1950 on, over $228 billion was spent on supplies and weapons—this expenditure involved 38 million purchase transactions. Total military property in the supply system at June 30, 1959 (not including real estate) was $44.5 billion. Total manufacturing inventory in the whole country at July 1960, was $54.9 billion, and total retail inventory a comparatively ridiculous $25.1 billion. (So you can see what happens when you are big enough not to be frightened by inventory, that bugaboo of the Paper Economy.) As for the number of supply items, a nice comparison is that between the military system and the Sears, Roebuck catalog—the former has 3,400,000 items while our biggest mail-order house limps along with 100,000. Seventy per cent of this material is described as "common-type items"—2,310,000 of them. It costs $2 billion a year simply to contract for, store, and issue all this stuff. The General Services Administration, which buys common items for all the rest of the Federal establishment, has a stores inventory equal to about one-tenth of one per cent of the military's. What's the whole shebang worth? "The tangible assets of the Department of Defense are estimated currently to be $150 billion."

But $27 billion worth of military inventory is considered to be "surplus, excess and long supply." That is, DOD generally feels it doesn't need it.

Monthly listings of upward to 30,000 excess items of property reflect such items as screws, nuts, nails, bolts, lumber, paint, various kinds of construction material such as aluminum and titanium sheets, motors, canvas, duck, webbing, uniform material, shoes, boots, etc. etc.—almost without end from the millions of items in the many DOD supply systems.

The annual disposal of surplus inventory is now reaching a $10 billion figure—"with a net return on sales of less than 2% of cost." The government not only loses 98 per cent on these sales, but must tread very careful steps even so in order not to dislocate the different portions of the economy which can be seriously affected by these fire sales.

Just a few details to indicate the content of this massive range of military supply:

The military communications system handles 63 million messages a year. It employs 24,700 persons. The Air Force high-frequency radio traffic is fourteen times greater than that of the RCA system.

The Air Force stated in 1960 that it would spend $72 million on technical manuals, that it had spent $89 million the previous year and would spend $60 million in the next year. So the Air Force is one of our largest publishers—and we hardly hear about it.

A couple of years ago, an air base in Germany requested shipment of 300 foot-lockers from the Army Quartermaster Corps at Philadelphia. The message got bolixed up and came through as a request for 30,000 foot-lockers. Although the air base had only 4,000 men, which would have put the order at more than seven lockers a man, the Quartermaster Corps did not confirm the message but gathered together 30,000 lockers from depots around the country and shipped them to Germany (at a shipping cost of $100,000).

It is rather widely understood that numerous areas in

the nation are uncomfortably or even desperately dependent on military spending. For example, the economic condition of the state of California, in which a quarter of the procurement dollar is spent, is quite completely involved with the military as customer. It has been estimated that the industry of Southern California is "70% to 90% dependent on war plants." But there is a more serious form of concentration of military effect than merely the geographical.

The typical pattern in military procurement is the granting of a major prime contract, perhaps for an entire weapons system, to a large corporation such as General Electric, GM, etc. This big outfit then sub-contracts tens of thousands of component parts and items: in effect it acts as design, purchasing, and assembly agent for the Defense Department. It makes a profit on all this action, but even more important, the business patronage involved is obviously immense. So that these companies dispense not only their own money, but also the government's—and have the attendant power. An example of this was the report of Republic Aviation Corp. that it had disbursed $155,700,-000 in 1960 on components and supplies bought from 4,200 companies in the course of building the F-105 fighter-bomber. Seventy per cent of these suppliers were called "small business." This big corporation purchased a total of 50,000 items from outside sources—"from (fibre) washers costing $.69 a thousand to the aircraft's fire control system, which cost $50,000 each." As in *any* political system, patronage of this kind, and certainly in these magnificent quantities, is . . . much to be considered.

Many of the major corporations benefit directly from military contracts, and some substantial companies are almost completely dependent on them. General Electric, for example, received contract awards of $783 million in the fiscal year 1957-58, which was 24 per cent of company sales. Lockheed Aircraft, the next largest supplier, received $765 million, which amounted to 86 per cent of that company's sales. This picture holds generally true for other aircraft manufacturers—also for companies like Raytheon Manufacturing, Thiokol Chemical, etc. This is again one more example of strong concentration in our system: "37% of the procurement dollar goes to the ten largest suppliers: 74% goes to the one hundred largest suppliers."

From 1950 through 1959, approximately $40 billion of plant and equipment has received the special tax privilege of accelerated amortization. The Office of Civil and Defense Mobilization has said that this defense program, which does not appear in the Defense Department budget, has "brought into being privately owned facilities which in many instances never would have been built" on any other basis. The beneficiaries of this tax privilege are exactly those companies which have a high level of defense contracting in any event—aircraft, electronics, etc. In the nine-year period, the tax benefit was afforded to 22,303 projects. It is amusing that 40 per cent of these projects, by number count, fall into a category of "small business." But this 40 per cent cost only $4.5 billion.

Finally, just imagine what the effect on the economy would be if defense spending were suddenly curtailed. Southern California would become a disaster area. The bottom would fall out of our national research and development program. The greatest part of the 2½ million people in the armed services, and the additional 1 million civilian employees of the Defense Department, would be thrown upon the labor market. Not only would ordinary people become unemployed, the thousand or so top-ranking ex-military officers employed by the country's 100 leading defense contractors would be in serious trouble, along with their tens of thousands of elite colleagues still in uniform. And who would be able to rent the world's largest office building, which receives 27,000 workers every day? Who would walk through the 17½ miles of corridors in the Pentagon, drink from its 685 water fountains, or powder their noses in its 280 rest rooms? Most of all, who would watch the 4,200 clocks?

So in a thousand ways and with millions of purchases, the Federal government sustains the economy. It is the essential underwriter, conceiving "underwriting" as direct intervention as well as endorsement of paper. Which I think is the way great underwriters like Morgan conceived it. Underwriting in the Paper Economy, after all, is simply a sophisticated adjunct to the more ancient act of governing.

As a primary feature of our system of dual power in the United States, it is generally true that big public government is considered very bad, while big private government is not even noticed. So instead of discussing our two forms of government for what they are, which might result in an appraisal of how much concentrated power is necessary in each, we have the spectacle of big industrial government spending an unconscionable amount of money denying its own existence and warning the nation against big public government. This is clearly no sincere service to genuine pluralism. If the one system of power were competing with the other about which should carry out what function, we might be in pretty good shape. That would be a Good Competition. But private government has not offered to build and staff the schools which our complicated society requires: it simply keeps the public government from doing so in an adequate way. And this is no genuine service to anyone, even big industry.

Private government in the United States has some very substantial advantages over public government. For one thing, there is not all that mess about getting elected. Secondly, the private managers do not have to steal in order to provide an adequate standard of living for themselves and their families (or at least the necessary forms of theft have been legalized). But most important, the levies of private government on the underlying population are called "price" rather than "tax"; nobody's permission is needed to raise them, in most cases; and it is successfully denied that the managers of private government have any real control over them. All of which leads to something called "profit," which is a really marvelous thing. So good, in fact, that public government is not allowed to have any.

If one were to catalog a list of advantages which private government has over public government in the United States, the effort would be equally exhausting and instructive. Included in this golden list of private advantage would be: immeasurably more prestige in business (except for a few top people like the President); much more gravy (even including the Office of the President); more and better PR *and* greater secrecy and other means of authoritarian control in business; and so on. For large segments of opinion in this country, it is almost no exaggeration at all to say that everything the government does is bad, and everything private industry does is good. For an even larger group, a good job done by the government or a bad job done by industry is only grudgingly admitted.

As one rather important example of the thesis, let us just notice the difference in regard to quality of personnel.

In an article entitled "New Price Tags for Government Managers," the stately *Harvard Business Review* announced that "an acute shortage of qualified top government personnel has developed in this country." The reason: "In the race to win and hold professional and managerial talent since World War II, business has outbid government by maintaining a more realistic balance between salaries in the upper and lower bracket"—that is, they pay more.

It is also important that the kind of political system the ruling groups in this country have fostered throughout our business history favors the taking of compensation for government work in the form of graft rather than in competitive salary levels. In 1960, *Life* "exposed" the expense-account living of congressmen (*just* congressmen). The lead paragraph revealed the startling fact that Congressman Charles Buckley of New York had stayed with his wife at the Los Angeles Biltmore Hotel, the United States paying her part of the hotel bill, which came to $44.09. The implication of this big fact must have been that Congressman Buckley, one of the more important political leaders in New York City, should either "get his" in graft or live on a sufficiently reduced level so that day by day his inferiority to business leaders will be borne in upon him.

Among the many other reasons besides money, Charles Percy, the young genius of both Bell & Howell and the Republican Party, put his bright finger on this one: "It's a terrible plunge into an icy bath to jump from business, which is essentially an autocracy, into government, which is a democracy."

Under our paper system, the most valuable "property" is not property at all; it is the institutional control over profit-making enterprises and opportunities. Many of these are created directly by the government, and all are sustained by its underwriting activities. It is this institutional situation —the capacity or right or opportunity to make a profit— which is the keystone, cornerstone and top-and-bottom-stone of our national system of paper-values. I suggest that as long as we are stuck with this eccentric system, and as long as the Federal government plays so important a role in its functioning, it is really too much of a disadvantage to deny to the government the right to "own" and capitalize and so on, in order to keep its head above water in the sea of paper-values. In other words, the government should be allowed to make some profit which is not called tax.

The government is in the business of making certain that everybody else makes money. To accomplish this, the government as regulator and underwriter requires elements of control, not ownership. But beyond this, it should "own" and thus be entitled to the income from some of our national profit-making opportunities: I am for nationalization or public ownership, on occasion, for revenue purposes. There are so many ways of making money nowadays that it is no longer necessary for the government to give away absolutely *all* of them.

Doing so is the greatest form of subsidy indulged in by our national government. It is certainly a shame that the government can't make a little something on the broadcasting frequencies it gives away; or should have spent billions developing airplanes without any financial return on the paper it thus created. And then there is the Post Office, with 3,116 installations carried at a value of $1.2 billion. The Post Office runs a deficit because it subsidizes the advertising industry, takes great losses on bulk mail in order to make life easier for *Time*, or vice versa. There isn't the slightest reason in the world why the Post Office couldn't be put on the basis of a 6 per cent utility, like AT&T, and billions of dollars of money raised by selling its paper to the public. But no, the government may not take a profit—on anything. (To make this proposition somewhat palatable to the conventional mind, it may be noticed that governmental profit is very much like a sales tax. But then, so is all profit.)

The Federal government, as a matter of fact, does make a little profit here and there, almost by inadvertence. As central banker under the Federal Reserve System, in 1960 it received, for example, $897 million on the earnings of the system. That is not much compared to the earnings of the banks which could not exist without the system; and it is not very much either in comparison with the $9 billion or more the government paid out to these banks and others in interest on its paper. But the idea that the government should not make a profit is such a deep-seated article of faith that when it does make a little money, even by inadvertence, some interested party will usually step forward to suggest how it may be saved from the repetition of the sin. Early in 1960, it was making $.35 an ounce for coining silver. So a silver mining company suggested that the mint share the profits with the mining industry. One company official said: "This probably is the only profit the United States government makes on any of its transactions"—which is not as a matter of fact true, but certainly indicates the drift of things.

One of the most curious profit-making opportunities denied to governments is the "right" to supply itself with needed goods—for example, to house, feed, and clothe institutional populations. One of the greatest problems in prisons is the corrosive effect of idleness; yet the prisoners are frequently not permitted to produce goods like food, clothing, furniture, etc., for themselves and other governmental institutions such as mental hospitals, schools, and administrative agencies. The reason: this is an important market for private businessmen. The political relation between private and public power in this country is such that the unfortunate government is not even allowed to feed itself, at what would be a considerable saving to the general population.

We may note finally that what the Big Underwriter does cannot be done by state and local governments. The notion that necessary public needs should be met by state and local governments is a central feature of the Rearguarder's theory of limited government, which thus borrows a good deal of rosy feeling from the traditional American prejudice in favor of pluralism. One can get very fancy in a theoretical way in pursuit of this homely image, but the short-form description of it is buck-passing. Again and again it is proposed that the buck be passed to the more politically "manageable," less efficient, and already terribly overburdened state and local governments. (We had a foretaste of the facts relevant to this situation in Chapter 6.)

Currently, state and local expenditures amount to more than $50 billion a year. The rate of increase in the postwar period has been about $3 billion annually. The largest sources of revenue are sales taxes for the state governments and property taxes for the local ones. The chief expenditures are for schools and highways. But transfer payments are significant, too: $3 billion annually in general public assistance and an additional $1 billion for pensions of retired employees. Total employment of state and local governments comes to about 5 million persons, 40 per cent

of whom are engaged in school activities. Total payroll of
these governments in 1960 was $25 billion.

The state and local governments "entered the postwar period with a substantial accumulation of reserves,"
according to *The Survey of Current Business* for March
1961; but even though tax receipts have gone up substantially, their debt has gone up much more. The financial
picture of state and local governments would be worse than
it is if it were not for certain surpluses which they generate
annually—from utility-type enterprises, and more particularly from the pension funds held by the states, which are
substantial. Also, the sixteen states which have a liquor
monopoly and operate their own liquor stores, took in
$1,100,000,000 from liquor sales in 1959. Even so, these
governments need considerable assistance from the Federal
authority. In 1959, Federal grants to the states amounted
to $6.5 billion for such programs as highways and Social
Security. Another $3.1 billion was paid to individuals and
groups as farm subsidies, National Guard payments, etc.
About $.12 on every dollar collected by the Federal govern-
ment is returned to the states in the form of grants.*

What the Big Underwriter does is to engage in the non-
profitable but necessary activities—all and any of them—
and this includes underwriting little underwriter-govern-
ments. The Federal government keeps the show on the
road, but gets damn little thanks for doing so from the big
business that runs the show.

It is still difficult for many of us to accept, but somebody has to carry out the activities which are merely necessary or desirable even if alas! not profitable. Things are
changing, however, and more and more people resignedly

* But really much more than that—because of defense plants, etc.

come to recognize that Washington, D.C. is not "temporary." For instance, the *Harvard Business Review* has called the Federal government "the country's biggest business"—which is much too sanguine a view of the matter, but still amounts to a substantial semantic up-grading.

In all these comparisons between public and private governments, we should not overlook the frail fact that whatever else it is, the Federal government is the only institution in the country besides the Red Cross that represents *all* the people. It has at least this advantage over General Motors *et al.*

11

ANTITRUST—
ELUSIVE ARCADIA

THE ONE OVER-ALL LAW designed to regulate directly *all* trade and industry, and admitted and asserted to be such, is that which goes by the historical name of "antitrust." The antitrust laws are to be distinguished from the paper manipulation of the central banking system, which is another over-all but indirect method of state regulation serving as an accepted feature of our system. Antitrust purportedly goes to the heart of the matter and effects a direct institutional intervention: it prescribes rules for actual buyers and sellers. Very simply, it commands competitors to compete; and it assumes that, this being accomplished, no further direct intervention on any but a very limited *ad hoc* basis will thereafter be required. All of which comes to the most profound expression of faith in the efficacy of big "C" competition known to twentieth-century man.

Coercive and conspiratorial tactics tending to distort or restrain trade had been actionable under English law for centuries. The Sherman Act drew upon these common law sources. But this unique enactment was more specifically a result of the great Populist reaction against the growth of financial and industrial power following the Civil War, especially where the farmers felt it most, in high and discriminatory freight rates. Of course, railroads are to a considerable extent "natural" monopolies, and the principle has always been that if you cannot break up concentrated economic power, or it is impossible to keep it from coming about in the first place, then it must be accepted and regulated. The Interstate Commerce Act was passed three years before the Sherman Act as part of the same political impulse.

The "trust" in "antitrust" comes from the accidental circumstance that in the early period of the concentration of economic power after the Civil War a certain "trust" device was used. Perhaps the most notorious early one—and a prime object of the muckrakers—was the Standard Oil trust (set up in 1882) which controlled the entire petroleum industry before being broken up (in a later form) in 1911. As the history of American law amply attests, there are numerous ways of concentrating economic or financial power; the trust was merely an early device, and has been followed by other more sophisticated ones.

The Sherman Act was directed against monopolies, attempts to monopolize, and against combinations in restraint of trade. In its early years, under-enforcement and a hostile reception from the courts ensured its ineffectiveness.

Then Teddy Roosevelt made a personal issue out of trust-busting, won the Northern Securities and Beef Trust cases, and in general stirred up considerable dust. (This is especially remarkable since in his time less than a dozen lawyers and stenographers made up the Antitrust Division of the Department of Justice.) The practical threat involved in all this moral effort reached such proportions that the Supreme Court, in the course of ordering the dissolution of the Standard Oil Company and the American Tobacco Company in 1911, advanced a proposition which has taken a central role in the drama of the antitrust law since that time. It was called the "Rule of Reason," and it reduced substantially and complicated infinitely the majestic sweep of the Sherman Act commands. The Clayton Act, passed in 1914, was intended to supplement the Sherman Act by prohibiting combinations by new non-trust forms such as holding companies and mergers. The Federal Trade Commission was set up in the same year.

In New Deal days, it was discovered that competition can be a killer. There had always been people hurt by it, but in the Depression years when only the strongest survived, the process took on the characteristics of a massacre. It is both understandable and typical that economic groupings have preferred to enforce competition on others rather than to indulge in it on their own behalf. Pressure was built up especially by groups of independent retailers, who were faced with extinction at the hands of the chain-stores and other large, integrated distributors. One result was the passage of the Robinson-Patman Act along with provisions for resale price maintenance. These laws are simply price-control enactments; they carve out areas of price-setting which are insulated from competition. In effect, they subsidize certain less efficient forms of business organization. That does not make them "bad" laws, but it does make them substantial contradictions of the basic antitrust laws.

It must be emphasized that the whole point of antitrust is to ensure that something called "competition" occurs throughout the economy. The assumption is that if you have competition, you also have as a consequence just about everything necessary for a healthy economy, and perhaps also the Good Life. The main advantages of competition are that whatever happens in terms of allocation of resource, choice of goods to produce, and especially price, is just, is proper, and is certainly the optimum historical best that free men can attain. This being so, there is no need for the government or any other agency to interfere in the free workings of the market economy.* This is the grand theory. If you let the antitrust laws compel or reinstitute competition, you then have all the self-regulation that the economic order requires.

The thinking behind antitrust contains a fascinating contradiction: it is essentially a proposal to force people to be natural. It is easy to demonstrate that the result of historical competition in the building of an actual industry is that a time is reached when the game is over and one or more of the parties to it has won. At this stage the antitrust theorist no longer favors doing what comes naturally,

---

* Earl W. Kintner, a former chairman of the FTC, expressed the going view in a talk before a Detroit business group in 1960. He was cautioning his audience not to attack government with a spray-gun, and suggested that "one way in which we can avoid the twin perils of monopoly and statism is to reaffirm our belief in the nation's antitrust laws. They represent an undertaking by Government designed to prevent still wider undertaking by Government." Notice the language—"reaffirm our belief" —calling for strenuous mental exercise.

and in effect commands that the game be played all over again, but this time without any winners (if you have something like Robinson-Patman, without any losers, either).

The point missed by antitrust is that genuine competitors compete *for* something, and not merely for the pure pleasure of it. The something they compete for is to organize a market and stabilize an industry, to ensure that they can continue in business with the capacity to produce goods and sell them at a profit whatever the vagaries of history and the business cycle may turn out to be. In other words, they are interested in security and survival—which strikes me as eminently reasonable. They are not about to commit business suicide on the theoretical ground that endless competition is a self-evident good. They understand that the stifling atmosphere of a Byzantine order is not the only industrial danger, and that un-ideal competition, seriously engaged in, is a form of domestic warfare.

It can easily be argued that the antitrust principle was never seriously believed in and applied in our country. And it can be argued from a practical as well as a theological point of view. Not only is there a history of non-enforcement only occasionally and briefly interrupted by flurries of legal excitement, but also day-in and day-out there are 22 statutes of exceptions and exemptions, and an additional 21 acts largely putting antitrust policy and implementation in the hands of various regulatory agencies. But I don't see that this is a defense of the antitrust schemata, because it is true of many of the fundamental principles of capitalist ideology—and conservative thinkers are continually making this point. In a sense, "capitalism" has never been tried; but very simply that is because "capitalism" in this sense is a collection of moral principles rather than a description of historical realities, or a practical program to bring same about.*

Described as historical reality rather than moral principle, the fact about antitrust is this: it has not inhibited the organization of industrial markets by great economic units, but it has had an effect on the character of this organization. It has prevented monopoly and has allowed —even encouraged—a kind of organized oligopoly.

As we noted in Chapters 8 and 9, it is characteristic of American industrial sectors that they are organized around three to five major corporations. Moreover and most important, whatever the "competitive" relations between these dominant units, they do not disturb each other on matters of price. Now price is the heart of competitive theory, and conspiracy to fix prices is illegal *per se* under the Sherman Act, meaning it is incontrovertibly presumed that the effect is to restrain trade or encourage monopoly. Nevertheless, major industrial prices are identical or similar for similar products throughout many of the major areas of industry. It is accepted that the top executives of U.S. Steel and Bethlehem Steel did not sit down together to decide what the price per ton should be. What happened, instead, was that U.S. Steel decided what the price should

* A great deal of the writing on antitrust—most of it by lawyers—carries a profound aroma of unreality; the economic point, if any, is apt to be lost, or quite small when found. Despite this lack of meaty points, antitrust is one of the most overwritten fields in all of academic life. One gets the impression that these two factors are causally related. On analysis, the true economic point is always the same, in a vague way: big "C" competition as an article of faith. Which is why Thurman Arnold once referred to this literary corpus as "that massive moral philosophy known as anti-trust legislation."

be and everybody else in the industry agreed, including Bethlehem. The antitrust laws are thus not violated, but the exact effect which they were designed to prevent is in fact achieved. I am suggesting that this characteristic fact in American industry argues against the usefulness of antitrust.

"The whole body of economic principles which gives legitimacy to private enterprise and has provided a basis for public policy has been built around the concept of prices set by competition," says Dr. Gardiner C. Means with sonorous authority. So traditional theory, beginning with the competitive market image, has understood price-setting under imperfect competition only in terms of monopoly and oligopoly. But the contrary fact is that there are a whole range of price-setting powers typically exercised by large industrial outfits that are not properly understood by the use of these words. The real task of economics is to begin with a model of the typical large industrial corporation and a description of its powers, and proceed from this central institution to the exceptions and variations represented by absolute monopoly at one extreme and genuinely free competition at the other.

Administered prices are a new third thing—neither competitive nor monopolistic. Moreover, Dr. Means finds that the marginal theory of price-setting, the conventional one, is inaccurate (it assumes all impersonal market forces automatically responded to, with no executive institutional psychology whatever), and that most often the businessman actually uses a "break-even" method. With this technique, the price-setter imagines the worst, in a self-protective way, and figures the price he needs to cover costs-plus-profit at a particular quantity. In rough terms, this is simply the relation between overhead charges and unit costs. He naturally under-imagines the market quantity because of his self-protective mood. His first responsibility is to overhead, and the greatest danger is inventory you can't move: if you are going to make a mistake, over-pricing is the obvious direction in which to do it. Working in this way (the human imagination being what it is), "there is likely to be a significant range within which one price is just as good as another." Consequently, his imagination is subject to correction by an outsider and there is room for the public or social interest to be expressed in the price-setting process. In his testimony at the Kefauver hearings on administered prices, Dr. Means called this discretionary area the "zone of relative price indifference." (News of it upset the business community considerably.) Marginal theory is based on the awesome idea of Supply-and-Demand. But when you have administration rather than markets, the essence of the process changes. Infrequency of price change is typical of administered prices; it is customary to have "wide swings in production with little effect on prices." In the administered price industries, what you really have is production and pricing similar to that in regulated utilities—with the rather important difference that no public body participates in the whole complex of decisions in which prices and quantity of production are determined.

Note that in the free market for wheat, competitive supply and demand will eventuate in a single price for the grain. But administered prices, "whether identical or different," are not established in this classical manner. Because the prices are not immediately responsive to supply and demand. And the reason for this is that business must plan its operations and expenditures for a period into the future. Fortunately, they have achieved the discretionary power to do so as regards prices. The executive vice-president in charge of sales for U.S. Steel testified at the administered price hearings: "Our pricing is the product of management judgment applied to long-range commercial planning, as well as the day-to-day administration of our commercial affairs. . . . There is no place in our commercial planning for auction-type pricing of our steel products." In answer to Kefauver's inquiries, Roger Blough stated at the hearings: "My concept is that a price that matches another price is a competitive price. If you don't choose to accept that concept, then, of course, you don't accept it. In the steel industry we know it is so." Blough asserted staunchly that only when prices were equal did the customer have a real choice. However that may be, industry leaders clearly required their own kind of pricing in order to "have a real choice" about a lot of important institutional matters.

It is clear that when business leaders in administered price industries speak of "competitive price," they mean "the same price," not a price determined by supply and demand. This was the intent of the early price fixing, which was halted by antitrust enforcement in the General Electric cases in the 1920s. Even so, the one price not responsive to supply and demand is still the dominant feature of these industries. So the main intent has been achieved.

In sympathy with the managers of our big organizations, it must be noted that the supply-and-demand mythos can become quite an exasperating burden. For example, Westinghouse was accused in the summer of 1961 of having submitted an identical bid to TVA along with several other companies on a standard lightning arrester costing $836.16. The item is listed in a published catalog which is in the hands of 7,000 customers. The company wailed:

But our catalogue comes in many parts, because we have more than half a million products or variations of products in our price lists for industrial equipment alone. Physically, these price lists make up a catalogue which is more than six feet thick. . . . Based on our best estimate, we receive from 1,500 to 2,000 orders for these standard products each day; we probably quote prices 6,000 to 8,000 times a day. The sheer volume of business makes essential a standard pricing system.

I'm convinced. It's just too *complicated* to "jiggle" a price just because some ill-informed fellow somewhere started something he can't possibly finish to anyone's advantage.

It cannot fairly be maintained that the general intended effect of antitrust regarding price has been achieved. Even where monopolies have been broken up or inhibited in their formation, and some "competition" preserved or restored, the effect on price has not been compelling. It is simply that there are deeper reasons than monopoly for the general lack of submission to supply and demand as the sole arbiter of prices. An institution that is big enough can achieve considerable discretion (and not only in regard to price) by manipulating *both* supply and demand. This is accomplished by size that does not amount to monopoly. (Monopoly and competition are polar terms which are useful mainly in discussing the nineteenth century.) Technology and the resultant size of firms have greatly mollified the rigors of the law of supply and demand—and continually threaten to repeal it altogether.

Historically, the antitrust point of view has been *for* competition, not just on grounds of general health, but also because it is *against* Bigness. In this mode, especially as elaborated by Louis D. Brandeis, there is a willingness and even a demand to break up big economic units simply because they are big, and to regulate them if they cannot be broken up. This enlightened attitude, which sees enforced competition as only a single technique among a number of possible ones for domesticating Bigness, persisted in the modern day in the thinking of Senator O'Mahoney who had, for example, repeatedly introduced a Federal licensing bill in Congress (to no avail). Federal charters for corporations engaged in interstate commerce could constitute genuine "antitrust" and might well work a major economic transformation. Such realistic regulation would include an adequate arsenal of remedies adapted to the array of actual industrial situations. Instead, we have ritualistic antitrust, in which millions of dollars and tens of thousands of talented man-hours are devoted, for example, to a thorough legal determination of whether du Pont is a monopolist because it dominated the cellophane market, or whether cellophane should be viewed as only one among a number of wrapping materials not all of which are dominated by du Pont.*

---

* In legal practice, a "big" antitrust case is *sui generis*. It is apocryphal in New York, the headquarters of the corporate bar, that a bright young man can get out of law school and find himself spending the next five years working long hours on just one of these monstrous litigations. It took twenty years to terminate the antitrust proceedings against the Aluminum Company of America, and the final change in the industry was brought about not by this action alone but by the transfer of wartime aluminum plants to Kaiser and Reynolds. The typical distribution of talented manpower makes it possible to prolong these litigations almost interminably. Early in 1960, twenty-one oil companies were brought to trial in Tulsa, Oklahoma on charges of conspiring to fix prices. As the trial opened, the judge remarked on the spectacle before him—there were six government attorneys and over ninety representing the defendants, including the best in the country. The government lost the case.

Not everybody, even at the beginning, had the faith of Brandeis in the attack on Bigness, the hope of the farmers in Competition Restored, or even the charity to speak of the antitrust laws politely. In a famous remark, Justice Holmes said "the Sherman Act is a humbug based on economic ignorance and incompetence." (Many years later, Professor Mason has insisted that antitrust does not embody a respectable economic theory since, among other failings, it emphasizes restriction of competition rather than control of the market; the latter of which, as industries mature, is far more important.)

Now the problem of Bigness has been with us a long time, and is not apt to solve itself soon. From the beginning, the liberal view has been to prevent or disperse the concentration of economic power, rather than to accept it and control it. This has been the impulse behind antitrust and most other trade regulation. Whatever else may be said of this great effort to preserve capitalism in its classic image, it must at least be pointed out that it has failed. It may have slowed down or in some cases deflected the basic trend, and it certainly made a lot of lawyers rich. But after seventy years of this sort of thing our economy is more than ever dominated by big corporations. If the program is justified as a form of public subsidy to free enterprise in the form of small business, similar to our approach to the farmers, then it is perhaps acceptable if inept. But as a comprehensive program or theory, it is embarrassingly irrelevant.

And then there is the overriding question of whether Bigness itself is good, not just whether it has happened. This is known academically as the issue of "economy of size." It is assumed that the size of an enterprise has something to do with economy of production; how much, when, where, etc. is not so clear.

Proponents of antitrust assert that there is no demonstrated correlation between technological improvement and the concentration of power in large economic units. It is also not proven that small units further technological progress at a greater rate than large units. But it certainly *is* perfectly obvious that big corporations, at least in their role as financial institutions, are able to allocate the necessary quantity of resources on which a great deal of technological progress does depend. (Veblen: "The corporation . . . is a business concern, not an industrial unit.") Also, pretty obviously, the antitrust laws are not designed, nor is the Antitrust Division set up, to make technical determinations regarding economies of size and then go around the country, industry by industry, building up economic units to the required size and breaking them up when they are larger than necessary. That would be government regulation "furthering competition," if you like, but furthering a competition realistically defined. Nothing like that happens, and all the antitrust talk about it is therefore beside the point.

How efficient is size? We will never find out under the present system. Because smaller units, which might be more efficient, would still need to operate in organized markets, to ensure flow of production. The current integrated or diversified monsters are able to take on this function of organizing markets; so they are necessary, although more plant or divisional autonomy might be desirable from the point of view of administrative and productive efficiency, but only assuming the existence of organized markets. Size is an ultimate element of effective private government and you have to have government. So it is just a question of who, how, and why—and for whom.

Whatever judgments one makes about size from a

realistic viewpoint, antitrust does nothing to reduce giantism by virtue of accumulation, and very little to prevent increases in size by means of merger. Scholars consider that there have been three "waves" of mergers in our business history. The first, neatly enough, occurred shortly after the Sherman Act was passed; the other two each followed a World War. We are still swimming with the last wave, which has gathered considerable additional force because of postwar tax considerations and the related passion for diversification. With appropriate irony, the most recent merger movement has accelerated substantially since the passage of the Cellar-Kefauver Antimerger Act of 1950. In the following five years, 3000 firms went on to bigger and better things, but the FTC and the Justice Department together brought only eleven complaints.

When, rarely, a particular merger is opposed, this is always an *ad hoc* matter: such opposition is not accompanied by breaking up firms in the field which are currently as big as the proposed merged firm would be. The forbidden Youngstown-Bethlehem merger would not have produced a firm as large as U.S. Steel. So actual enforcement of the antitrust law ends up protecting the already existing giants. Since they don't compete in price anyway, what difference does it make if there are ten major steel firms or six major steel firms? And if there were a difference, it would be technological, and would relate to the efficiency of production and cost-savings, none of which considerations are dealt with by the antitrust laws in any event, certainly not in a continuing rational fashion.

Perhaps nothing so nicely illustrates the not exactly rational quality of merger policy as the recurrent dispute between the different agencies charged with formulating

it. The contradictions in approach have reached such proportions at times that "pacts" between agencies have had to
be negotiated—as between the Justice and Treasury Departments regarding bank mergers.

Or note this example: because of the depressed condition of the railroads, there has recently been a spate of actual
and proposed mergers of rail lines. The ICC has begun to
view these more favorably than it has in the past, again apparently because of the financial difficulties of the railroads.
It is asserted and generally assumed that there are considerable savings and increased efficiency in these mergers. Now
why wasn't this increased efficiency as available ten, twenty,
or thirty years ago, as it is today? I think my question is
particularly poignant in regard to railroads because they
are supposedly regulated as public utilities in any event, so
profits from a monopoly position resulting from mergers
could never have assumed runaway proportions.

Perhaps the primary fault of the antitrust laws is that
they *presume* to regulate industry. To the extent that they
demonstrably encourage competition, and this encouraged
competition is a good thing, no one can argue with them.
But they still would not constitute an adequate regulation
of industry—not by a long shot. In fact, the antitrust laws
inhibit useful cooperation as much as they encourage helpful competition. And clearly the amount of competition
they achieve in the economy is not sufficient to arrive at
that competitive state of grace envisaged by classical economists which makes any other regulation of business activity
happily unnecessary. (It has to be repeated that not all
competition is so helpful in the first place. Hillel Black
points out that the very strong competition among auto

finance companies for the business of discounting dealers' paper has increased finance charges to the auto buyer: so the dealers now sell paper as much as they do cars.)

The burden of the charge against antitrust is not simply that it does not work as intended. That has been obvious for decades. The more important point is that it makes the task of self-organization in industry more difficult; and, on a theoretical level, it obscures the obviousness of the need of government regulation for non-business or public purposes. To avail ourselves of the benefits of the new technology, markets must be organized. There are only two power centers in the nation capable of achieving the necessary measure of organization—private industrial government or the public Federal government. In different ways, the antitrust laws, and especially belief in their efficacy, inhibit both of these. (Antitrust is in reality not much more than a secondary police measure.)

If belief in the antitrust laws keeps one from being realistically concerned with the Bigness surrounding us, then something has come full circle around—there has been an ironic inversion—and belief in the antitrust laws has become a means of frustrating the intentions of those who first created them and relied on them as a basic charter for the economy. In which case, antitrust now amounts simply to a ritualistic attack on Bigness, to satisfy the desire of attack without ever harming anything real. It becomes a façade for Do-Nothingism. And its actual result has been to promote the growth of great industrial organizations by deflecting the attack on them into purely moral and ceremonial channels.

The ritualistic character of antitrust is firmly indicated by the massive extent of under-enforcement over the years.

Until 1935, appropriations for antitrust ranged from $100,-000 to $300,000 a year. The appropriations did not exceed $2 million until 1942; they were about $3.5 million in 1956. (The total appropriation from 1904 through 1956 was just a touch over $50 million.) Antitrust has been characterized not only by under-enforcement but also by selective enforcement. In the fifty-six years from 1890 to 1946, no more than 198 defendants were sentenced to prison. Only seven of these were businessmen, and all of their sentences were suspended. The minor sentences imposed in the recent electrical industry price-fixing cases involved the first prison terms ever served by important business executives. But 108 labor union members have been sentenced to prison for violations of the Sherman Act.

The belief in "competition" as solving all economic problems is a belief in magic. If we want an effect or a circumstance in the economy which does not come about naturally, then we must identify that effect and choose means appropriate to its attainment. That seems painfully obvious. But in the atmosphere of antitrust belief this idea is not obvious at all—it is heretical.

That economic regulation exclusively by virtue of competition is more an article of belief than a practical program is also indicated by this interesting fact: although the Attorney General's National Committee to Study the Antitrust Laws recommended in 1955 that the Department of Justice conduct regular studies to find out the effects of its judgments in restoring competition—a late date to get such a proposal—this has not been carried out by the Department.

The most substantial spiritual force behind the belief in antitrust enforcement is that the alternative is dangerous government regulation of the economy. But if the antitrust laws were really enforced to ensure the kind of competition desired under the theory, the Federal government would have by far a greater regulatory role in the economy than it would under any number of other systems. True enforcement would require an immense exercise of Federal power. Note that antitrust assumes business should be regulated— into being competitive. It even assumes the right, on principle, to issue a death penalty to a major economic institution. The contradiction here is both patent and thoroughgoing— and certifies antitrust finally as quite unserious. The amount of Federal power required will never be deployed to that effect. If it were, we would witness the most foolish exercise of such power imaginable. The forcible creation of spontaneous competition would literally wreck the entire economy: but that is exactly what antitrust prescribes.

It says a great deal to me that when the point is to produce a maximum quantity of goods, as during both World War I and World War II, the operation of the antitrust laws is suspended. To produce fully it is necessary to organize well, for which antitrust is a distinct negative quantity. So the ritualistic ballast is dumped overboard.

At the beginning of this chapter it was remarked that the two accepted methods of over-all regulation of the economic order by the state are antitrust, a direct intervention, and money/credit management, an indirect one. The relations between the two would make a fascinating historical study (which should be undertaken before the two are brought together to work together as a comprehensive system of governmental regulation—as is inevitable, one hopes.) The most intriguing aspect of this history is that

money management, which is essentially central banking
(rationalized by Keynes as a basis for broader social policy),
was fought bitterly throughout the nineteenth century by
the same social forces which finally triumphed at the close
of the century with the enactment of the Interstate Commerce Act and the Sherman Act. These Pyrrhic victories
were accompanied by Bryan's three defeats and the final
establishment of unassailable central banking—based on
gold, moreover, which at the time meant banking more central than otherwise. The whole century-long opposition to
central banking was ignorantly misguided; apparently the
farmers didn't know enough about the uses of banking to
be able to distinguish between the bank and the banker.
They should have fought for some political control over
central banking, rather than resisted it. As it happened, exactly the big and mostly Eastern financial interests which
the farmers were fighting ended up with more politically
insulated autonomy under the quaint Federal Reserve System than perhaps they would have had if the earlier Bank
of the United States had persisted and grown.

The early New Deal represented as much serious economic thinking in public as we have been privileged to witness in this country, at least since Hamilton. Among other
things, it greatly expanded the social uses of central banking
à la Keynes. It also ignored the antitrust laws, and tried unsuccessfully to solve everything all at once under the NRA.
The New Deal reforms were all over before Thurman
Arnold, one of the most perceptive and witty of all writers
on antitrust, became almost too witty for his own good and
began his own Vigorous Enforcement as Assistant Attorney
General in charge of the Antitrust Division. It should be
significant, at least to liberals, that the New Deal ac-

complished absolutely nothing by means of antitrust, and a great deal by numerous *ad hoc* interventions and, especially with the help of the War, by government spending. In the end, the New Deal broke the back of private financial government, thus completing the job the bankers had done on themselves; separated commercial and investment banking forcibly; picked up the pieces of the banking system, rearranged them somewhat, and then underwrote the whole structure; and introduced the basic principle of spending money in order to be generally helpful. But it did *not* manage to bring paper manipulation and direct intervention into any working coherence (except, of course, during the War).

Paper manipulation unsupported by direct intervention still has a fine future here in America—especially if accompanied by an increase of Federal debt and a continuation of the recent fright of big industry at what their own inflation was doing to the country (and what, as a consequence, the country might do to them). But only for a few years—not a full decade, I would guess.

Professor Mason informs us: "One of the assumptions of the simplified Keynesian analysis was that wages, prices, and profits were determined in purely competitive markets." So there would be an eventual although rough correlation between the absence of "competitive markets" and the ineffectiveness of Keynesian paper manipulation. Therefore, both of our over-all methods of regulation rely on big "C" competition. Too bad—there really isn't enough to go around, where it counts. If antitrust is a horse-and-buggy notion,* then the best that can be said for current fiscal

---

* This horse-and-buggy crosses oceans badly. Berle has made a special point of the fact that our antitrust laws have played a particularly neg-

policy and money management is that it is a steam-engine concept for the atomic age. The issue is institutional control of price, and the issue is not disposed of by intelligently imagined competition.

The hand will be played out with paper manipulation, whether or not accompanied by the uplift of antitrust. In judging this course of events, one should not allow his vision to be obscured by the occasional dust raised by some interested party's Vigorous Enforcement. Teddy Roosevelt set the righteous giant-killer style long ago; the antics of antitrust enforcement are about on the level of a medium-sized congressional investigation. For instance, what important effect on the structure of the American economy will the disposal of the GM stock held by du Pont have? The case took ten years, was probably at least ten years late in being started, and the disposal will take another ten years—and GM will still buy nylon and paint from du Pont; everybody else does. This minor police measure cannot significantly restructure our economy. I don't think it was ever seriously intended to.

Into what is the present paper-plus-ritual system apt to evolve? The Federal government can fulfill its underwriting

---

ative and even destructive role in the foreign relations of American corporations. Of course, through American antitrust-filled eyes, all these commercial relations inhibited by American antitrust are called by a bad name—"cartels." Other countries do not understand us at all in this regard. "To them a cartel of companies, allocating markets, regulating production more or less in accordance with presumed demands, and so forth, is the normal and intelligent way of dealing with a situation; unless, of course, the governments make the necessary arrangements by straight treaty." People who do not recognize the existence of industrial governments can hardly observe their busy foreign relations with equanimity.

function under the eccentric ground rules now existing until: 1) the limitations and other sacrifices to treasured unrealities become too expensive or foolish to be borne; 2) the demand for things increases sharply, as during wartime. Either of these imperatives would impel the government to exercise some measure of authority with respect to the source of the paper, rather than merely with its manipulation after it is created. As was pointed out earlier, gold no longer mediates between paper and thing. The New Gold (source and backing for the paper) is productive power itself—political control of the institutions which administer technology. This will have to be shared with the government. That, very simply, is the indicated direction of development. Without such further sharing, the underwriter will at last be unable to meet its commitments: too tough an underwriting contract. Since the Federal government is the only possible underwriter, the debtors will have to give in.

We may think of this notion of "shared government" as a kind of public utility concept. Which is so revolutionary that it takes us back about a hundred years to the original concept of the corporation—a chartered grant of governmental authority. National chartering of large corporations engaged in interstate commerce would restore to the Federal government the historical power of regulation which the states so shamelessly abandoned in the course of the nineteenth-century growth of corporate power. The right to incorporate would remain as common as contract under state law; but a size-and-importance line would be established, with all institutions above the line being required to submit to national licensing. The arsenal of regulatory techniques under this jurisdiction might include administrative determinations of economy of size, would hopefully include price review procedures, and so on. It would certainly bring the constituencies of our major economic institutions once again under the protection of the Federal Constitution. Mergers would be freely allowed under the line, and realistically dealt with above it. Under this regulatory scheme, a basic jurisdiction would exist within which the welter of current governmental effects might be made coherent—all with the purpose, hopefully, of ensuring full use of our productive machine.

Sounds awfully radical, doesn't it? Well, Federal charters for large corporations were termed a "must" by Henry C. Simons, a leading theorist in this country on competitive theory. A bill to this effect was often introduced by Senator O'Mahoney; and under his chairmanship, the proposal was put forward by the famous TNEC. It was recommended by the Commission on Industrial Inquiry in 1899, by Presidents Theodore Roosevelt, Taft, and Wilson, by the Brookings Institution and the Twentieth Century Fund, and by a number of important scholars. There are many differences of opinion as to the content of the proposed regulation, and that is properly a matter for political dispute. (Undoubtedly these political differences would persist and work their way into the actions of the chartering agency; and there is always the chance that the corporations being regulated, as has happened before, would pull the teeth of the agency "regulating" them and then assist it to gum itself into mumbling futility. But that's political life in America, which offers numerous occasions for irony and other fun, and none, in my opinion, for pained withdrawal.) National chartering provides a structural basis for recognizing the differences between our major corporations and other economic units, viewed darkly or otherwise through the glass of *any* economic theory. After seventy entertaining years, that cannot any longer be said for our pious antitrust laws.

However, the faith in Competition dies slowly, if at all. The reason is very clear. *Without supply-and-demand competition, there is no such thing in our society as a legitimate price.* Belief in antitrust is needed to make competitive theory respectable; and competitive theory is needed to make society itself respectable. That is the hard chain of spiritual need. It can lead Dean Rostow of the Yale Law School, for example, to admit at one moment that competitive markets do not exist in large areas of the economy, and immediately thereafter to protest the unfeasibility of abandoning the classical models. He rejects non-competitive theory as follows:

> The literature of "managerialism" from Commons and Veblen to Drucker, Burnham and Berle suggests no criteria to replace the standards for judging the propriety of wages and prices which the economists have painfully developed during the last century or so.

When old theory takes precedence over new fact to this extent, there is nothing to do with the resulting sentiment except to use it as a lead-in to the next chapter—on "managerialism."

THE
PEOPLE

12

MANAGERS
AND
MANAGERIALISM

THE PAPER ECONOMY, based on concentrated corporate pricing-power and underwritten by the Federal government, is tended by people. That is, somebody runs the American property system. We have been looking at it from a structural point of view. But even though we understand power to be little more than a function of social position, we must finally look to the inhabitants themselves. The people who *manage* things.

The classical capitalist view assumes that all power is distributed according to the ownership of property, and all power not so distributed is bad, should be kept at a minimum, or its existence denied. The classical view is quite decidedly wrong in describing our current circumstance because, for us, ownership is no longer decisive. What is most important now is the *control* of property. Ownership remains significant in the final distribution of product, but less and less important in its manufacture. Recognition of the prior importance of control and its dissociation from ownership is what, in a general way, is meant by the term "managerialism." Ours is a managerial system, not a traditional capitalist one. This big change has been characterized as "the managerial revolution."

The happily descriptive phrase is James Burnham's. In 1941 he published a book with that title in which he advanced the thesis that Stalin's soviet bureaucracy, Nazi rule in Germany, and a combination of the New Deal and corporate control of the economy in the United States, were all variants of this managerial revolution. Burnham had been an important American follower of Leon Trotsky and his book was bitter tears flowing out of a deep disappointment in the failure of the ideals of the socialist revolution. It was written in a white heat following a terrible intra-party conflict with Trotsky, which led to Burnham's final withdrawal from socialist politics. The ideas are mostly Marxist, but they are used to demonstrate that the socialist revolution as envisaged traditionally was an illusion, and that the actual historical revolution occurring in our century is a Machiavellian monstrosity.*

---

* In his very witty book, *A Skeptic's Political Dictionary*, Max Nomad has the following relevant entry: "MANAGERIALSM—The theory that the office-holder and manager, and not the worker, is going to take over the inheritance of the doomed capitalist. First briefly hinted at by Michael Bakunin, later developed by the Polish revolutionist Waclaw Machajski, subsequently presented to the American public by this writer, it became the subject of a best-selling book by an author who gave no credit to his predecessors. He was a teacher of ethics." James Burnham, that is.

Not much more of Burnham's approach than the phrase has survived in the current discussion of managerialism in America. It is understandable that his sour socialism is not a matter of much concern to the advanced economists, businessmen, and publicists who are dealing with managerialism in its immediate contour—as for example, *Fortune*, in distinguishing the current corporate elite from the historical robber barons, or the *Harvard Business Review*, in pushing the professionalization of managerial strata. In more or less candid manner, the current discussion assumes control of the primary productive capacity of the nation by a self-perpetuating oligarchy of non-owners. It recognizes, again with more or less clarity, that this is quite a different situation from that formerly existing or still envisaged by classical theory. The discussion then becomes downright relevant when it is further assumed that most of the important activities in our society require large organizations, all large organizations must be managed, and there are some fundamental similarities between all the managers of any and all large organizations. On these assumptions, managers emerge as a class—a new class. (Which proposition becomes even more startlingly significant when it is noted that something similar seems to be happening throughout the advanced world.)

The homegrown class-analysis of the man on the street is that rich people run things—and that this state of affairs has been going on for a long time. Despite all the fearful newspaper talk about big government, I doubt that the ordinary American really feels that the Federal government runs anything important besides the Army; local governments, whose regulations impinge more directly on the citizen, are generally felt to be corrupt irritants which do in fact attempt to run some things and more or less consistently fail to do so properly. Of late, however, there has been a rapid growth of interest in corporate executives and their style of life. The public is beginning to construct an image of corporate men which differs from the images of other elite figures. Evidence for this is found in the spate of business novels and movies and television dramas, and a rather general awareness of expense-account society. But this is a bare beginning of a change in popular national consciousness, and it probably cannot be said that the essential distinction between control and ownership has penetrated the mass mind. Moreover, our consumption-minded populace is more entranced by the standard of living of the corporate elite than by its social and economic power.

My point is that rich people are no longer running things in America, except insofar as the managers care to listen to them. And because of the complexity of managing any paper fund or agglomeration of actual things, most of the listening is done by the rich owners, most of the talking by their managers. Moreover, the bigger funds and organizations do not have dominant or even important owners. And again moreover, if an owner does his own managerial work effectively he will in fact be operating as a manager rather than an owner; his ownership will be incidental. It takes distinctly managerial effort and talent to make ownership effectively controlling. (Many noblemen used their feudal wealth to become effective capitalists in the early days of the last big changeover; there is a quality of survival among the members of any ruling group: the ubiquitous Talleyrand.)

The position here is that a managerial revolution is, in fact, under way; that, as Burnham stated, it is worldwide;

that it more and more requires the participation of the state; and it is probably as inevitable as any major historical movement—by which I mean it is not a conspiracy but the response to widely understood necessities. But aspects of its character and especially some of its important contradictions have not been properly set forth.

There are *two* types of managers. The distinction is not black and white, but it is very real.

The larger group consists of people who are technically trained to do a specific kind of work, and actually do it. This would include engineers, scientists of various kinds, lawyers, accountants, advertising and PR specialists, merchandising experts, personnel people—a very long and varied list of specialized activities. The smaller group is made up of the ruling strata of executives; in every organization there are a few people at the top who direct the work of everyone hierarchically lower in the organization, who control the organization and make its policy and direct its course, who represent it officially in its external relations, and so on. These latter are group-politicians; their work is to adjust conflicts among individuals and sub-groups. In a major corporation there will of course be political leaders and factions all the way down the line in every department and section. But the top corporate executives are the full-time, leading politicians of the organization.

Perhaps the most distinctive facts about each of these managerial groups today are these: 1) the increasing independence of the top organizational managers from wealthy owners, bankers, and indeed all outside influences (although their operating environment is structured for them by these and by government, labor unions, and even the desires of their customer-public); and 2) the enhanced importance, prestige and income of the technically trained group which actually accomplishes productive work. The picture can also be presented this way: in order to administer the technological revolution, so many organizations must be created, and these organizations become so important, that we can say that society is essentially made up of them; next, we cannot do without them unless we abandon our commitment to the technological revolution; they clearly require large numbers of trained people to do the work and administer the work which is the purpose of the organization; these people are key members of the new society.

Organizations have replaced individuals in the system of wealth and property. And the income-producing capacity of the trained individual is becoming the dominant form of "property."

Veblen described this process a long time ago as a conflict between the engineers and the financial managers of the price system. In the hands of misguided enthusiasts, his ideas became the basis of the technocracy movement which had a certain play in the late twenties and early thirties. What was wrong with Veblen's view was the lack of political content. He did not see that industrial institutions, like all human organizations, are essentially political creations and require political activity for their continued existence. It was terribly naive to think that the solution of the problem was merely to turn over the productive system to the engineers. They cannot dispense with the politics of institutions, and they are not necessarily the best institutional politicians.

Managerialism will be observed here as if the existing essence of the matter were the two types of managers. In order that this should not create too much of a distortion, the context of prior assumptions should be kept clearly in mind: under the duress of modern technology and the population based on it, the increased complexity of society is exactly on the order of a major historical mutation. Both the technology and the complexity accompanying it are administered by increasingly comprehensive organizations. Organizations are patterns of individual connection—organizations of people, primarily, not property. So we want to get some notion of the new types or classes of people created by these organizations. We call this managerialism, and to make the discussion manageable we might even, for further convenience, name the two groups—the Politicians and the Intellectuals.

But this distinction is a matter of convenience. Everybody does some expert work in his organizational career, no matter how talented and quick-rising a Politician he may be. And an expert has to be quite an expert to get along without being something of an organizational politician as well. Despite blurred lines, however, the distinction remains basic: most Intellectuals have to work, and many prefer it; others respond to the call to politics devotedly—and early. The distinction is useful in many ways (for those living out their lives in organizations it is difficult to get through a day safely without it), but more than this, it is profoundly important because it contains in kernel the chief contradiction now apparent in the new managerial society.

The relation between the top political leaders of an industrial organization and the staff of experts who get things done was nicely stated by Henry J. Kaiser in an interview early in 1960. Mr. Kaiser, who benefited from World War II as much as any single individual in the country, was attending a Madison Square Garden dog show. The reporter noted a number of Mr. Kaiser's current projects—a major housing development in Honolulu, steel plants in South America and India, and so on—and suggested that all this activity "seemed a lot of enterprise for one man." "The secret is to find people who know more than you do and then get the work done," Mr. Kaiser said. "There is no other way." A president of Shell was even more (and almost unpleasantly) outspoken: "Take care of those who work for you and you'll float to greatness on their achievements."

Since we are talking about hierarchies, we can assume that some managers are more important than others and that straight quantity cannot be too significant. And since we are talking mostly about authoritarian business hierarchies, we can further assume that power is concentrated at the top. (A recent edition of *Poor's Register of Directors and Executives* contained 75,000 names—almost all men, incidentally.) As for the educated masses, the other aspect of managerialism, a rough indication of size would be the number of college graduates—edging now toward a half-million annually. Another rough size-indication of the whole process is contained in income figures: in 1959 there were about 3 million families and unattached individuals with income before taxes of $15,000 and over.

In November 1959, *Fortune* published the results of a survey of 1700 (probably *the* 1700) top executives in American industry and finance. Eight hundred and thirty-four companies were covered: these men managed $500 billion of assets. Their median straight salary was $73,585 yearly, ranging from $92,647 in metals manufacturing to $50,658 in insurance. It was clearly established that "the bigger the company the better the pay." That is not surprising—and neither is the fact that 80 per cent of them are

Republicans. Their background is "typically Middle Western or Eastern" and most of their fathers were businessmen: 17 per cent of the fathers were corporate executives, and this trend is increasing yearly. Two-thirds of the executives were college graduates (a large percentage of the chief executive officers have Ivy League degrees) and 85 per cent of these "majored in law, business, economics, engineering, or science." Most significantly, the majority of the top executives "were employed in specialized activities" when they began their work careers; but only one in three of the engineers stayed in his field and "40 per cent of the lawyers gave up legal work."

If we can imagine a "first generation" of managers, it is fairly persuasive that they were selected by the big owners; they were heirs of the robber barons. But even if we allow for some continuing influence of the rich, it is also pretty clear that the second-generation managers were chosen by the first generation. This has been characterized as a "self-perpetuating oligarchy," which is also fairly clear and persuasive. After the image of the fast-moving luxury of the executive life, the popular mind is most entranced by this question of how and why one person rather than another is chosen to live it: one of the most popular pieces of business fiction in the fifties, *Executive Suite*, was a novel about corporate succession.

C. Wright Mills has suggested that "qualification" amounts to nothing more than "conformity with the criteria of those who have already succeeded." That would appear to be an unexceptionable statement. Professor Mason quotes Chester I. Barnard, who stresses "compatibility of personnel": "Those are chosen who fit, and fitness includes 'education, experience, sex, personal distinctions, prestige, race, nationality, faith, politics, sectional antecedents,' and 'manners, speech, personal appearance.' " So just about everything is relevant, down to tone of voice and the way you part your hair. But since this seems to be a matter of the relation of generations, something of a father-son thing, we may note that generations are never really the same, no matter how strong the command to conform: the subsequent one simply "acts like" the prior one (which must make for a richly overheated atmosphere up top in our big organizations). And there is the further complication that some few people have to be selected, even in and around the top, who are qualified only to do the fragments of non-political—or "real"—work that must be done.

The qualifying process includes the wives of aspiring executives. William H. Whyte, Jr. says in *The Organization Man* that in one company, 20 per cent of the trainees were turned down because of their wives. Elsewhere, an executive was side-tracked because the president of the company believed his wife had "absolutely no sense of public relations." The ladies in general do not "qualify" as excellently as their husbands—their "personalities and behavior patterns are far more varied," according to Warner and Abegglen. That the women should be less conformist than the men is an intriguing little fact which suggests the enormous pressures toward conformity emanating from the organization. The wives are socially more mobile in an upward direction than their husbands. These circumstances, and the fact that the busy executive is frequently absent from the home, may account for the considerable alcoholism among upper-echelon wives (reported by Whyte and others). But also, Warner tells us: "A psychological testing of executives shows that many, probably most, regard sexual relations as frivolous and diverting from the main objective of life." From, that is, *managing*.

Once qualified, an enviable style of life awaits the political executive. The qualified wife gets a good home containing all the recent trinkets, and that's it. But the man gets much more. He has the power and prestige, which is only reflected on her; he has a life of action and command, while she must be satisfied to "wait" in luxury; and even the material part of his style of living transcends hers. He lives in the limitlessly prepaid society of the organization, which she is only permitted to visit on occasion. She and her brood are "taken care of," including an adequately insured future, and neither the husband nor the corporation expect any trouble from her thereafter.

The texture of prepaid living is the most obvious quality of the executive life. But it is not the most important. This consumption, including its conspicuousness, merely adorns and sustains a life of command. The top managers are top dogs in an exceptionally vital political order; they are not ward-heelers hanging around for the graft alone. The primary commitment to consumption is left to the women, the rentier paper-holders who own the system, and indeed to a whole nation of customers. The Politician does not own the system—he is much more interested in running it. Which he does.

Well-upholstered living so entrances the populace, however, that we may not safely ignore it. No possible advantages are missed by way of standard of living, comfort and luxury, in carrying on the business style of life. It seems clear that one of the reasons New York City is becoming the corporate headquarters of the country is that the entertainment facilities of that city are so far superior to those of any other. Most of the gross receipts of most of the best restaurants, hotel and resort accommodations, and entertainment emporia in the country end up as deductible entries on somebody's P & L.

Expense account life is one of the bigger industries subsidized by the government. But again, whether expense account society draws on $5 or $10 billion of produce annually, or twice that amount, is not a very important issue in terms of structure and control of the economy. It is just another chapter in the long story of the unequal distribution of income. Even this situation has changed in a fundamental way, and an elaborate meal at Voisin does not take food out of the mouth of a Southern millhand. What takes the food out of his mouth is the inability of the system to distribute sufficient income to him to allow purchase of his portion of our farm surplus. The entire upper class in this country could continue exactly the standard of living it enjoyed last year and still, if the system were capable of full production, the charge upon total product would probably not be intolerable. It is not the ownership of paper or managerial status, and the consequent unequal distribution of income, which is decisive; it is the unwillingness to produce by those who control the means of production.

As an example of high living, it would appear that the airplane (apart from war use) was invented for the benefit of executives. I would imagine that a great proportion, perhaps a majority, of passenger miles flown on American commercial airlines are paid for on expense accounts. In any event, aircraft owned by business concerns flew 6 million hours in 1959, while commercial airlines flew less than 4 million hours.

And where do the businessmen fly? As another minor

example, they fly to conventions and other business gather-
ings. Monroe Fry estimates that 10 million people spend $1
billion annually at and on conventions. In New York City
alone there were 782 conventions and expositions held in
1959, at which 3,089,550 delegates spent about $222,900,-
000 on accommodations, restaurants, theatres, etc. As part
of the payola scandal, it was revealed that in the course of
a disc-jockey convention held at the Americana Hotel in
Florida, May 29 to 31, 1959, eighteen record companies and
a radio corporation picked up a tab of $117,664.95: over
2,000 people attended.*

In 1959 there were 1,100,000 Diner's Club members,
700,000 American Express card-holders, and 100,000 Carte
Blanche subscribers. Since the credit card is largely an
expense account device, this would indicate that as many as
2 million people have enough expense account action to
make it useful or necessary to hold a credit card. Diner's
Club members are almost all businessmen of one kind or
another.

Nor is it all a matter of restaurant meals, theatre
tickets, and so on. There are executive diningrooms, company hunting lodges, yachts, limousines, and more, more,
more. A good bit of the paraphernalia of the earlier modish
life of the extraordinarily rich, such as yachts, has been
taken over by corporations and their top executives. The
late Robert R. Young of New York Central proxy fame
paid $38,000 for a 40-room house in Newport which had
been built in 1905 at a cost of a quarter of a million dollars
by one of the Philadelphia Drexels.

And then there is the Office—the command center

---

* A Congressional witness characterized conventions of this sort by saying, "This seems to be the American way of life, which is a wonderful
way of life." Which is a wonderful kind of statement.

away from home. The *New York Times* for July 16, 1961, reported on recent developments:

> Among the marks of prestige named by half a dozen designers last week were executive washrooms, bigger offices, windows with views. . . .
>
> "The rule of thumb is that the size of one's office depends on one's position in the hierarchy," Godfrey Dallek, president of Dallek Design Associates, said.

Another designer felt things were changing, however:

> "The status thing has gone out," [he] said. "I know of four or five executives who gave up the idea of private conference rooms because they cost too much."

Not everything "has gone out"—certainly not the executive washroom, called "the No. 1" symbol. (In law offices, the traditional euphemism for a partnership is being given "a key to the partners' toilet.")

> Among the appointments to be found in today's executive washroom . . . are massage tables, barber chairs, showers, bookshelves, carpets, telephones, and exercise machines. . . .

But another designer denied that the search for prestige caused the installation of washrooms.

> ". . . an executive washroom is a necessity. . . . I'll admit that for one corporation with ten top vice-presidents we installed a washroom for every one of them. But with the exception of the advertising agencies and motion picture business, it's not a matter of individual prestige—more a matter of the corporate image."

Expense account charges are entered on the books of a business under the heading of "selling expenses," or "ordinary and necessary business expenses" for tax purposes. The range and variety of these are to be noted. One recalls

Edward R. Murrow's broadcast of January 19, 1959, about girls subject to call for business purposes. Both executive and female participants in the program stated that many major corporations conceive of a complete expense account evening as involving something more than liquor, food, the theatre and night-clubbing. The New York *Post* reported Murrow as saying that New York City had "as many as 30,000 high-priced prostitutes." The exact figure is certainly open to question, but the existence of the practice came as shocking news only to the New York City Police Department and the District Attorney's office. These particular services were of such a necessary nature, according to the traditions of salesmanship, that some of the girls were on monthly payrolls—as secretaries, of course—and some of the madams received monthly payments somewhat on the style of a requirements contract. Other girls were said to make as much as $25,000 a year, on which they paid no taxes. The most delightful observation to come out of this startling exposé of well-known facts was the explanation by one girl of why she didn't pay any taxes. She said: "I don't feel as though the government's entitled to anything, because these men are all legitimate businessmen. They deduct you at the end of the year." They sure do; indeed, there is no telling what a really legitimate businessman can deduct.

There is no question that the top executives take care of themselves, very nicely. Anyone who needs further proof of this may take a look at the annual reports on executive compensation published by the unassailable *Harvard Business Review*. These make it quite clear that salary levels are tied to corporate profits, and pleasantly tied in the sense

that they rise with an increase in profits much more decisively than they decline, if at all, with a decrease. The
reports also note top management's fringe benefits: for example, three out of five companies have stock option plans
and nine out of ten have pension plans.

The unquestioned power to take care of themselves is
too often used with a clear sense that they have no one,
really, to whom they must account. From the *New York
Times* of April 10, 1960:

> As rumors began to increase that the Alleghany Corp-
> oration, which controls the New York Central Railroad,
> was headed for a proxy fight the president of the railroad
> signed a seven-year contract. Alfred E. Perlman, the presi-
> dent, signed an agreement that would give him $100,000 a
> year against his present salary of $125,000. Previously he
> had no contract.
>
> After Mr. Perlman retires at age 65, seven years hence,
> he will receive $50,000 a year for services as a consultant,
> according to the contract.

This is standard procedure (with or without threatened
proxy fights).

Despite this sort of thing, we should not confuse a
secure standard of living with accumulation. Mr. J. A.
Livingston, a perceptive financial writer for the Philadelphia *Bulletin*, thinks that the "tax-sheltered managerial
elite" is "an over-privileged class in a democratic society."
But they are workers and spenders, not accumulators. They
don't build family financial empires any longer; the estate
and income-tax laws, and the corporate bureaucratic organization of wealth, have seen to that. Somebody could doubt-
less still build a temporary empire by merchandising a
frozen daiquiri that can be drunk under water, but such
events no longer characterize the system. "Free enterprise"

has become a minority sector of the economy; still noisy and exhilarating, but no longer the big show.

Perhaps this point that the important managers are mostly not important accumulators can best be made by recalling what the old days were like—before the Pecora investigation and New Deal securities legislation, for instance. Describing the business system in the heyday of American capitalist accumulation in *The Theory of Business Enterprise,* Veblen devotes several choice pages to the "accumulation of wealth" by corporate executives. His point was that the corporation men made their fortunes by trading in the stock of the corporations they managed. To this end, their purpose was served by a "discrepancy . . . between the actual and the putative earning capacity of the corporation's capital." So the directorate gave out "partial information, as well as misinformation" to create such discrepancies. If this was not sufficient, some actual mismanagement could be indulged in, if desired, to depress the stock. In those days, great fortunes could be and were accumulated.

Today, we have stock options, one of the few "fringe benefits" which, it is true, do carry the privileged executive beyond the usual standard-of-living benefits. The expense account, company airplane and Miami office, along with the executive's high salary which is taxed at ordinary rates—all of these are consumption benefits which must be taken on the wing, so to speak. But with certain types of pension benefits, and especially with the stock option scheme (and, let's come out and say it, with certain types of "patronage"), the executive is in a position to accumulate some capital—to build an estate.

Stock options are valuable only if the market goes up, but it mostly has risen throughout the fifties, so that has not been a problem. Also, there is no problem about financing the purchase of the stock under option, if it is worth anything. Finally, the gain is taxed at the 25 per cent rate rather than the steeper one. It should be realized, however, that the big fortunes in stock options are made only by the leading executives. The amount of options generally made available to lower-level men is not enough to make them independently wealthy—it just comes to a little added sweetening.

Some nice fortunes have been made in stock options—and on negligible risk. E. J. Thomas, president of Goodyear Tire and Rubber Company, made an actual or paper profit after taxes of nearly $4 million in the fifties. Ernest Breech, a leading executive of the Ford Motor Company, made a similar gain over a shorter period. Indeed, all of the Ford executives did quite well: about 200 of them have an actual or potential gain of over $100 million based on early 1959 prices. General Electric executives made or stood to make over $160 million on options exercised or outstanding between 1953 and early 1959. Ralph Cordiner, president of the company, was in for about $2 million. U. S. Steel executives had a gain of about $135 million over a similar period. If the stock goes down, and the free ride does not proceed according to schedule, all is not necessarily lost: the market value of Aluminum Company of America stock declined after the granting of options in 1956, so in 1958 the stock option committee cancelled outstanding options at a price of $117.25 a share and reissued options at the more reasonable figure of $68.50 a share.*

* This is about the outer limit of daring, since the whole rationale for the issuance of stock options to top executives is to give them an incentive to make the company's operations profitable and thus boost the price of the stock.

The estates thus created for some of the top executives by milking the corporation's paper-value undoubtedly serve to bless their declining years and leave their families secure after their demise; but the corporate elite will not end up owning any important piece of American industry by virtue of this paper graft. However, managerial control of corporate assets can still be used, as it was in the old days, to a very considerable advantage. Insider knowledge is still, one way and another and despite SEC regulation, a big edge in making money out of the company's stock. And business patronage is even more (much more) significant: it strikes me as very reasonable to assume that the case of William C. Newburg, president of Chrysler Corporation, who resigned after disclosure that he had made $450,000 in profit derived from ownership of interests in Chrysler's suppliers (in effect, a form of kickback), was not an isolated example. A great deal of money can be made and other advantage had from the power to let contracts to suppliers.

Moreover, executives own other stock—44.8 per cent of all of them, over 300,000, as long ago as the early fifties (according to Kimmel). It may even be that something like Morgan's "Peerage"—his famous preferred list of business leaders, bankers, and major politicians—is in existence here and there for the even further benefit of our handsomely cared-for executives. (Who knows?—it's a *private* government.)

Executive man does not live by pâté alone. It would be both vulgar and misleading to leave the reader with the impression that he does. This airbrush job on the big executive just would not be well-rounded without a word about the consequences of fulfillment.

The dominant institution in America is not Private Property, the Beautiful Woman, or even the Push-Button Nexus of Existential Reality—it is Success. The category of Success-and-Failure is so completely a fundament in this country that it is not more widely noticed and discussed because it is so frequently confounded with Life Itself. Failure is defined as acceptance of what you have—whatever that may be. Success is indefinable—in essence, a mystery: which is appropriate for the whirlwind-core of any great religion. The American devotion to Success, we all know, grew out of the hysterical mood generated by the opportunity to rape a virgin continent of great beauty and potentiality. It was, then, initially identified with and formed by *the perspective of infinity* regarding the accumulation of wealth. And *there* was the tragic flaw in the national character. Because it was not possible to maintain the infinite perspective in the personal accumulation of wealth.

The crisis today in our basic character-forming institution of Success derives exactly from this little bit of history, and from the brief story told here of managers and managerialism: *it is no longer enough just to make money, and nobody is quite sure what the What-Besides is.* One way of stating the big difference between the Politicians and the Intellectuals is in connection with this crisis. The latter are satisfied with a style of life built around their work and their current notion of an adequate standard of living; the Politicians dream bigger. But they are no longer permitted the one grand old dream of infinite personal accumulation. (The true dream of power is political, and both types of managers—each in their own way—are discovering this truth, now that the money-dream is in eclipse and the standard-of-living dream is fulfilled.)

Interestingly enough, it is the entrepreneurial successes rather than the triumphant bureaucrats who suffer most from this crisis in the meaning of success. The managers are better trained for the modern world: the pure money-dream is disciplined out of them by the long bureaucratic crawl to the top. The entrepreneurs are survivals of an earlier age. Having dreamed the dream pure, they expect much more from the achievement of money-making. But it is really very crowded on top—in terms of the promises of the dream. You are very bright and energetic or you get stinking lucky and make ten or a hundred million and then —surprise of a lifetime!—you don't end up owning the world. Worse, you find yourself being sucked into the vortex of consumption, with nothing to do with the money except spend it. Moreover, there are so many ways of making money nowadays that too often it is made early in life. Add to this the fact that people live longer (especially if you have the money to buy the best in medical care) and you can see the seriousness of the problem.

After a while, all the man has left to him—unless he gives in pretty completely to the consuming woman—is the fact that he Made It. So, in elaborate fashion, many businessmen become modern-type philanthropists (meaning fund-raisers): all these societies for the prevention or cure of cancer, heart trouble, backache, and athlete's foot exist not merely because these maladies exist—they are the aging successful man's non-sexual "outlet," as Kinsey might have said. Which proves something rather nice about the affluent section of the human race: there seems to be some hidden seriousness in all of us. It comes out as a kind of "return of the repressed"—the Whatever-It-Was that we repressed in order to get organized to devote ourselves to making money, long ago. It is, of course, no problem for most

people because they never make enough money or become
burdened with so much success that these painful considerations intrude on their medium middle-class idyll. But the
point about the American experience is that enough people
have made it and have become thus burdened, so that the
problems thereby generated are, at least, sub-mass in nature,
for the first time in history.

One further word about the personal problems of awful affluence. Really successful people, deprived after a
while of the opportunity to work for money in any meaningful way, have had to go deeper into themselves, often
with destructive consequences, to find any "reason" to
work at all. Or, most destructively of all, to work without
reason, and to hate it. They are in effect deprived under
modern capitalism of working with the true and beautiful
idea of capital in view. They can only enjoy, and this dis-
orients them considerably. Enjoyment has damn little to do
with the Protestant ethic. That is the point, say, of the conservative attack on the income tax: the deep unrealism of
the conservative position in America derives from being a
defense of a character-formation (not merely ideas) which
is so profoundly needful and old-fashioned that it dares
even to ignore, in its flight from affluence, the more obvious
structural aspects of the modern reality.

But with all the marvelous *fin du mondisme* of the old
entrepreneurial order, let us not confuse matters regarding
the new world of the managers. They have their problems
of fulfillment, too. Galbraith has expressed this so well that
I will not bother resisting a rather lengthy quotation:

> The rise of the public relations industry, which draws its
> clientele overwhelmingly from among business executives,
> shows that business achievement is no longer of itself a

source of acclaim. At a minimum the achievement must be advertised. But the first task of the public relations man, on taking over a business client, is to "re-engineer" his image to include something besides the production of goods. His subject must be a statesman, a patron of education, or a civic force. Increasingly some artistic or intellectual facet must be found. A businessman who reads *Business Week* is lost to fame. One who reads Proust is marked for greatness.

On this very intriguing point, permit me an anecdote. I discussed this very issue with a substantial PR man at one time, and fortunately caught him in an intelligently loquacious mood. He said his clients were very successful men who come to him at that age when they have lost interest in sex. They have money, a great deal of it (or they couldn't afford him), but in his interpretation what they lack and want is "a style of life." "The men who come to me want something they worked for and didn't get. I make up for the deficiencies in the American institution of success. You might say—but don't say it—that I'm in the business of building big pedestals for small statues." (*Laughter* —but somewhat embarrassed, because the pedestals aren't that big, and after all in the American mode the statues aren't that small, either.) "For instance, not long ago a man came to me who had built a great chain of, let's say, retail stores over a lifetime of hard work, which he thought and truly believed—at the time he built it—would lead directly to Valhalla. I suggested to him that he had no real problem" —the hell he did—"that he had struggled hard to get to the top of the hill, and that in fact he had arrived there. He said 'Yes, but not *this* hill—*that* hill over there is the one I want.' So he spent money and I made money: we're now changing hills. But of course it's never the real thing."

"These men have power and they like power and they no more want to give it up than any politician wants to be voted out of office," says Berle. That's what the story leads to—away from money to politics: individual moves to Washington by the highly trained top fellows (Messrs. McElroy and McNamara are good examples), local committee and group stuff for the juniors. Which in personal terms mirrors the coming amalgam of our dual government here in the United States.

13

MORE ON THE MANAGERIAL REVOLUTION

THE SECOND, less widely discussed aspect of the Revolution of Non-Ownership is even more intriguing. What we are witnessing, it seems to me, is a rather quiet and mostly polite "revolt of the intellectuals." Many of the people concerned would be horrified to think that they were parties to anything so dangerously improper as a social revolution (most of them don't even think of themselves as "intellectuals"). But if you asked them did they want to increase their prestige, standard of living, and scope of discretion in work? they would answer affirmatively. If you went on to inquire, Were they going to do this by accumulating capital? they would say, No. It is these motives which create a revolution-in-fact, whether or not the participants are aware of it or desire it. (As a writer in *Esquire*, Edward A. McCreary, put it: "Rather than create empires, graduates [of business schools] want to join them." That gets the sense of it.)

When I speak of "intellectuals," I am not thinking of Greenwich Village or the Left Bank. The Intellectuals in issue are avant garde only in spearheading a social revolution; they are not avant garde in the usual sense, meaning culturally advanced, highbrow, or disaffected. They are intellectuals in that they are intellectually trained to do, and actually do, intellectual work: They use systematized concepts in their productive, earning-a-living work, and it is necessary that they be trained to do this, which distinguishes them from those who have not received such training. The training, or education, is a new form of income-producing status which replaces and serves the same function as the older bourgeois ownership of income-producing property. These new people, moreover, can use their education with as much entrepreneurial aplomb and daring as previous generations used their bits of property. They are making out very nicely, both by steady accretion *and* entrepreneurial leaps.

The new class of Intellectuals has increased enormously in size over the last few decades: we are creating a *mass* of educated people to staff the bureaucracies of the organized society. Galbraith leisurely identifies the members of the new class as those people who do more or less pleasant, interesting work, who don't work too hard, that is, at really unpleasant tasks. I don't appreciate this view as much as I do his wit in expounding it:

The economist of impeccable credentials in the conventional wisdom, who believes that there is no goal in life of comparable urgency with the maximization of total and individual real income, would never think of applying such a standard to himself. In his own life, he is an exponent of all the aspirations of the New Class.

All the pleasant jobs are included, but not all the jobs included are so frightfully pleasant as that of a university professor. Seen in gross perspective, the new-class phenomenon is an aspect of the widely-noted burgeoning of white collar jobs. C. Wright Mills referred to this in terms of what he calls the new and the old middle class, the old being proprietors and the new being dependent white collar employees. He stated: "Roughly, in the last two generations, as proportions of the middle classes as a whole, the old middle class has declined from 85 to 44 per cent; the new middle class has risen from 15 to 56 per cent."

Daniel Bell offers the following basic figures: "From 1947 to 1957, the number of non-production workers in manufacturing increased by 60% (from 2,400,000 to 3,900,000), while the blue-collar force remained almost stationary (a little under 13 million)." Steel, as an example: when the union got a 19.4 cents an hour increase in 1957, the white collar non-union employees were given a 26.6 cents an hour increase—37 per cent higher. This is excellent divide-and-rule technique. Bell, an expert labor analyst, very shrewdly suggests that all that remains to collective bargaining is to press for a true annual wage for production workers which would raise their status to a point similar enough to that of the white collar worker so that the unions could organize the latter. To overcome the color of the collar would put us in a position to judge work officially the way it has mostly been judged by the people doing it all along—by its inherent distastefulness.

What we are getting is not a nicely new democratic society, but rather substantial additions to the ruling class of the old one. But that's an advance, certainly. It is exactly the kind of advance we can expect from the managerial revolution.

William H. Whyte, Jr. was describing the New Class —under the heading of "middle management," a favored *Fortune* and Harvard Business School term—in *The Organization Man*. The point of his book was that the modern middle-class individual has a deep longing to collectivize himself. He has seized the opportunity offered by organizational life to do this, rather than taking it for the threat to his individuality that it really is. For example, Whyte is made quite unhappy by the fact that in gaining his education, the organization man-to-be is not in revolt against anything; he is passively interested in techniques, and getting in there and doing his job. But isn't this because *his* revolution has already been effected, and that getting his income-producing education is his way of participating in it? His existence, his education, and the job he will get and carry out during his life, is in itself the revolutionary managerial fact. What's to rebel against? The "revolt of the intellectual" consists in making a living—a good living, as those things go—out of being one. And this revolt is achieving its object: it is making what the new man has—education— as much or even more important than what he doesn't have —property.

Absolute democracy is a great unrealized dream, but we may be approaching something for a large minority of the population which could be called "educational Jeffersonianism." (We should begin about now to get very clear about the terribly obvious fact that members of a democratic order must be actively qualified therefor, or the "membership" becomes merely formal. A no-contest fight is no fight at all.) I mean, the fulfillment in part of Jefferson's ideal of a democracy based on a large number of similarly situated individuals—but with the similarity in situation consisting not of land tenure, as Jefferson saw and imagined it, but of education/status as we are beginning to experience it. At least this allows us to re-imagine a democratic society, which is becoming increasingly urgent in the modern world. This is not an exciting prospect to some of us big dreamers, but it is democratically entertaining. And it is real.

The story of managerialism is left hanging without a word about the "professionalization" of the managers. In any occupation, workers like to think of themselves as professionals—as being specially trained and uniquely qualified to do what they happen to be doing. If we think of scientists, engineers, doctors, lawyers, and so on, the idea of professionalism seems simple enough—deceptively so. Because a plumber may have as much special skill as a lawyer, so there is a prestige factor involved. Indeed, it is the main factor: the difference between a "trade" and a "profession" is entirely a matter of prestige—and not only the ancient prestige accompanying brain-work as compared to hand-work. (During the War, naval officers from good colleges called Annapolis men "trade school boys.") Any day now, public relations will become a profession rather than merely a trade or occupation: it has already happened in advertising. One of the best ways to qualify an occupation as a "profession"—besides just plain insisting on the point frequently—is to learn something about it in a school somewhere, that is, gain some impractical knowledge about it as an adornment. A certificate to this effect is especially useful. Which gives us an insight into much American education: it is a means of affording professional status to an increasing number of occupations.

I am not suggesting that one cannot learn anything useful for practicing a particular trade in one of our professional schools or courses of study. For example, in the traditional three years it takes to get a law degree, about three to six months is quite profitably spent in learning how to read a case and a statute. These are the tools of the trade and must be mastered before practicing it. But the remaining two-and-a-half years is mostly adornment; all of it can be learned on the job—most of it has to be re-learned there.

In business, this process of professionalization is in the hands of the business schools, with Harvard in the lead. It has proceeded to the point where graduate business schools, a minor matter twenty years ago, now turn out 3,000 candidates annually for elite occupations. Also, there is a growing amount of professional education afterwards. The American Management Association offers 1,100 management courses to 70,000 executives each year. The president of AMA stated that ten years ago there were no more than 10,000 executives "enrolled in formal training courses either in their own companies or in universities." There are now 500,000 such student executives.

Whatever the means to professionalism or the content thereof, once achieved it has a marvelously mellowing effect. "The methods, morals, and social education of the leaders of big business actually seem to have improved substantially in a generation," says Adolf Berle. He partly credits this new maturity to the professionalization encouraged by the graduate school of business administration at Harvard. I think the point here is that, in an environment where status-education plays the security role formerly provided by property, one can't have too much of it, whether it is true training or real ritual.

Apart from trade-knowledge like accounting and so on, what the studious executives are learning is something that they have decided to call "human relations." I believe this is the business word for inside organizational politics. It has become an elaborate subject of study. Whyte maintains that all the human relations stuff in industry growing out of Elton Mayo's work amounts in fact to an ideology—an ideology of the organization man, and consequently of middle-level managerialism. I am willing to believe that people-management is the central managerial problem in organizational life. "The biggest trouble with industry is that it is full of human beings," says a former president of International Harvester.

These people-management problems are gone at "scientifically" in the big organizations. Which requires more expert Intellectuals. (One day soon we will have a social scientist elected president of a major corporation, instead of the more usual lawyer, engineer, accountant or salesman.) There is also some scientific-type thinking utilized in advertising and merchandising. It would seem that this approach is favored where people are involved. But I find it instructive that in financial matters top management relies on intelligence, savvy, and shrewd insight, and gets along without much "scientific" flavoring. Whyte makes the point that the scientism of human relations is ubiquitous in organizational life. It certainly serves: 1) to give the people-managers a professional status; 2) to obscure the raw political nature of the organization; and 3) to defend the managers from the creative anxieties of managing the humanity of others, by rationalizing the techniques thereof. All of which is a rough beginning.

(This question of scientism is much too big to be gone into here fairly or effectively. Just one moral word in passing: The main decisions in life are not made with scientific precision, and when they are nevertheless made with the *idea* of scientific precision in mind, they are made badly —worse than would otherwise be the case.)

It is interesting that wherever we turn for impressions of the new managerial order (in our look at the institutions *under* the paper), we always at last come up with something very much like politics, broadly conceived. If to some of us this is surprising, or seems forced, that is only a sign of how far we have strayed from reality in following the ideology of the former system of private property, so-called. Any property system is political, and this previous one only *seemed* to be self-executing for a while, by virtue of effective self-advertisement. In any event, as Berle says: "It is a fair question now whether sound academic distinction can be made between political science and economics." It is clearly a political project to organize great numbers of people for technological and productive tasks. The relations among such groups are even more obviously political. Both of these political projects, whether or not officially undertaken by the official state, are in the hands of the New Class.

One of the key words for politics inside the group, we have noted, is human relations: the important terms with which to comprehend the full range of political activity among organizations are finance, price, money—i.e., paper. Profit-making—the creation and management of paper— is a survival of the older system, but in the new order its function has subtly and profoundly altered. Paper is now a primary means of governing the relations between organizations; it has been the means of pensioning off the owning class and thus effecting the managerial revolution bloodlessly; and it is a necessary form of self-defense of the separate organizations. So paper is now serving as the politics of the transition. (The beauty of it has always been that it is such a malleable instrument.)

Under this transitional system, the paper-manager manages the managers of production. He is, in effect, the manager of the purpose of production. The purpose is the paper-position resulting from production. If we were talking about the Soviet Union, the distinction here would be easier to describe: in that special society all the managers who manage the managers are hierarchically organized in the Communist Party; their roles are more easily identified. The production superintendent of a factory in Russia may or may not be a member of the Communist Party, but one way or another he is still under the direction of someone above him in the Party who is charged with managing the purpose of production. (Besides, the purpose of production is more nearly actual production there than here, it would seem.) The role here closest to that of the party under the Communist system would be an amalgam of paper-managers and the more readily recognizable politician-managers of various official governments.

Berle has taken the position that the financial managers of large funds—he emphasizes the growing billions held in

pension funds—could end up controlling our major corporations. There are a number of existing and potential
conflicts between different groups of managers, but this
does not strike me as among the more significant ones. If
the dominance of the pension fund managers became ob-
noxious to the corporate managers, they simply would
appeal to the government to intervene on their behalf. The
present situation already involves a considerable degree of
power participation by the financial people. They are typically represented on the boards of the major corporations,
their ideas and policies are certainly taken into consideration by the corporate men. If you look at the matter realistically, you discover that either there is no cause for alarm
or we should have been alarmed a long time ago.

The pension-fund managers are simply a modern form
of banker. The conflict between bankers and production
men (described a long time ago by Veblen) is the deeper
contradiction. But note that it occurs *within* the corporation. Indeed, the typical structure of our big corporations
recognizes the distinction: in the widespread U.S. Steel
pattern, a production man is president and the superior
financial man is chairman of the board.

A new character and a new vitality have been given to
this traditional struggle by the rise of that group of managers we have called the Intellectuals. The Intellectuals and
the Politicians are increasingly engaged in an intra-class
struggle. The former want, simply, to be managed less by
the latter; or they want a fuller expression of the new managerial order, which is their work and their status, and they
want it sooner. The Politicians—at least in the West—have
reason, however, to go more slowly: 1) they are the brokers
of the big changeover, especially the leading financial fac-

tion, since they are charged with mediating between the New Class and the paper-rentiers; and 2) they are variously over-cautious, inept, frightened, and occasionally down-right suicidal in approaching the inevitable amalgam (or at least further meshing) of public and private governments. They hanker after the old days inordinately.

The new Intellectual class will eventually be as great a danger to the top ruling strata of the managerial order as the dispossessed workers were to the earlier age of capital-ists. I would even suggest that the ideological rigidity, along with extra-legal police measures, which characterize Com-munist society, are necessary to control the rising class of specialists even more than the workers. The regime is en-tirely dependent on this group of people, just as the under-lying population is dependent on them, for the benefits of the new technology. The pressures that Khrushchev has responded to by way of increasing consumption in the Soviet Union undoubtedly have come largely from this group, and any increase in consumption goods will redound primarily to their benefit, not to the peasants or basic fac-tory labor. The exceptionally high status and comparative freedom and standard of living of scientists in the Soviet Union indicate the potency of these considerations.

The Intellectuals are coming on. They are increasingly strong, confident, and assertive. They know they are needed—and they are in fact needed more and more every day. Notice the fabulous extent of the mass flow of tech-nical personnel from East Germany, certainly a dramatic "new class" maneuver. But even under Communism they take care of themselves nicely, as to standard of living. For example, the following report from Bucharest published in the *New York Times* of March 2, 1960:

A fancy new night club called Continental Bar opened in downtown Bucharest last night. . . . The only night club in the city, the Continental is the most forthright acknowledgement to-date of a blossoming of the new moneyed class in Rumania.

Members of this class are the technicians of the new industrial society. . . .

In America, the new elite does not have to fight for night clubs. All they have to fight for is a bigger and ever bigger place in the sun. A growing segment of the Intellectuals here know that they are exemplars of a social revolution—know it not just intellectually but in the most profound way, as a sense of their distinct identity and the difference of others.

Among these self-conscious ones, the self-styled eggheads, are to be numbered the liberals who were so startlingly catalyzed by Mr. Stevenson's candidacies. (It is a question, but I believe they created him rather than the other way around: they needed him, they were ready for him, and they more or less insisted on him.) As is well known, they failed to elect their candidate—but that may well have been one of the most penetratingly successful failures in the history of our peculiar nation. Out of pique or whatever, thus galvanized, these people are carrying out a political revolution within the Democratic Party. Along with the Negro struggle, they are busily at work changing our political system in the most practical way imaginable. They will be successful in their efforts, too, because it is not all in the head—it is an expression of social/status/money changes. They are new people—the first of the managerial corps, having arrived, to take the broad view. Their stale New Deal rhetoric is only frosting on the essential managerial cake.

The so-called eggheads are administrative intellectuals (and, in the traditional American style, with lawyers in the lead). They are what used to be called the "middlebrows," although you never hear them called that any more, they've become so important. The liberal middlebrows are the vanguard of the managerial revolution in this country. They are very strong in teaching, which has had and will have a greatly enhanced status now that so many people feel it is necessary, and possibly even useful. They are well placed in all intellectual activities—foundations, mass culture in all forms, governmental bureaus—and are making out, although more slowly (and by hiding their advanced ideology), in the corporate bureaucracies as well. They are a considerable self-conscious leavening. Whether their particular self-consciousness will survive in a later, more mature ideology of managerialism is another question. To the extent that it is based on scientism and the administrative view of man, I am afraid so—that grows out of their training and circumstance rather than the heritage of liberal rhetoric. As for the latter, that is nearly official and accompanies almost everything that happens in public in the United States, so presumably also managerialism. Its improvement must wait on long-term cultural advance (and, hopefully, the corrosive effect of boredom).

The political effect of managerialism does not depend on the self-conscious Intellectual or, for that matter, on the rear-guard determination of the leading Politicians. Much more important is the kind of politics that always takes place everywhere, even in the Soviet Union where it is forbidden—the kind of politics involved in the everyday events of an individual's life. That is why the *real* politics is always the politics of social revolution and class movements. It is the factory worker's irritation with the foreman which, however finally expressed, is the important event—not his vote for a Democratic or Republican congressman. Of course this kind of fundamental politics takes a long time to mature, historically. That hardly makes it less important. But just as Marx hoped to speed up the socialist revolution by urging class consciousness upon the proletariat, so *any* consciousness of circumstance can help to speed up the resolution of the contradictions inherent in that circumstance. When the Intellectual experts, the essential working staff of our new technological society, become aware of their numbers, their positions, their prestige accomplishments and their enhanced status, they will undoubtedly be emboldened to assert themselves more and more forcefully.

For instructive contrast, notice the role of "The Party" in bringing about the managerial revolution. The essence of the Party is ideological unity, professional devotion, dynamic activism. It is in effect a rationalized continuing conspiracy—a group of such intricate, superb organization that it probably should be seen as a human historical invention on the level of the Greek phalanx, or the Roman legion. At its best, it is a more effective power-instrument than an army, because the Party can accomplish socially what an army, with guns alone, can not. Besides, it is in the nature of the Party to transform itself into an armed group whenever necessary; and one of the social institutions it is designed to take over is the armed force of the state under attack.

I imagine there were always cliques and other more or less coherent groupings around the throne—the seat of power—throughout history. But certainly in the modern period these have developed remarkably in the direction of cohesion, self-consciousness, continuity—and importance.

It would seem that the rationalistic constitutional state which replaced monarchies in the West cannot exist without them. The United States clearly could not.

Now the question of conspiracy: Lenin did not invent the conspiratorial Party, he simply brought it to its highest point of perfection. Moreover, conspiracy—the use of illegal means to attain an objective—is at least as old as poisoning. Compare Lenin's kind of Party to, say, Tammany Hall: if you accept as a fact the alliance of the political machine with organized crime, the moral difference will run in favor of the Leninist Party, which after all has revolutionary purpose. And of course the Leninist Party is much more self-conscious and publicly outspoken about its particular notion of the Higher Legality which justifies conspiracy. The realer difference between the two lies in the limited objectives of the one as compared to the other's perspective of social revolution. If Tweed was more successful than Lenin, it is only because he achieved what he intended, which was low and limited enough. Lenin did not achieve what he intended— unfortunately, he achieved a great deal more.

The key to the problem of the Party in its connection with the managerial revolution is provided by Milovan Djilas, the remarkable Yugoslavian theorist. Djilas, with his exceptional credentials of experience (he was Number Two man to Tito until he ruined himself theorizing in public), is a brilliant expositor of the nature of managerialism in the Communist world. In his book, *The New Class*, he says:

> The party makes the class, but the class grows as a result and uses the party as a basis. The class grows stronger, while the party grows weaker; this is the inescapable fate of every Communist party in power.

That statement bears re-reading and further rumina-
tion, because it offers an essential insight into the Communist
system and also poses an exceptionally intriguing question
for non-Communist managerialism: Since there was no
Party in most of the West, who or what created the class?

The American "conspirators" were the financial men
who created the corporate-paper system, because that is the
non-property base of managerialism in the United States.
The big symbolic names would be J.P. Morgan and Franklin
D. Roosevelt—the one for starting it going, the other for
saving it and then reconstituting it on a firmer basis. (Remember, the purpose of the New Deal was to save the
corporations, with or without their connivance.) Morgan
did not, nor did anyone like him, create the technology
which made the corporation useful, profitable, and inevitable (nor did Roosevelt, for that matter). But Morgan and
people like him did put the modern Paper Economy in
working order, despite the existing commitment to private
property, capitalism, free markets, and that sort of thing.

It is to these practical-minded heroes that we owe the
peaceful course of the managerial revolution in the United
States.

Conceiving managerialism as an extended historical
movement, we should notice that in its non-Communist form
it has not yet accomplished, on its own and as itself, that
fine, rigid level of self-awareness which we call ideology: it
is not yet ready to convince all comers that it has arrived
and is prepared to live forever. In the past few decades it
has, however, begun tentatively to distinguish itself from
its intellectual forebear, the traditional capitalist view of the
economy and the universe we noticed in earlier chapters.

But quite tentatively: because on the one hand, managerialism is afraid to abandon its reliance on the justificatory free market; and on the other, it is not fully prepared to deal with the essential problem of the legitimation of industrial government, especially in its relation with elected governments. What managerialism has achieved to date is an awareness that corporations are major social institutions and that they have effects on society and responsibilities toward it which go beyond the simple principles of profit-making—but only on self-chosen occasions.

About the best official position developed to date is that of the *Fortune* intellectuals with their inept theoretical construction of "limited government." This is a patent retreat from managerial premises to the old laissez-faire notions (on half-pay pension). The First National City Bank in this mode typically calls for less government interference, less labor interference, and generally less interference of all kinds, so that business can "grow" and spread the blessings it was designed to bring to mankind. This is transparently unacceptable thinking and indicates the present impasse of managerial thought. The problem of managerialism in this country is not to be left alone, but to integrate itself in a democratic order.

By general repute, the highest level of applied managerialism is the kind achieved by the executive staff of the International Business Machines Corporation. This company was one of the first to set up an annual wage for production workers; in 1958 it put 20,000 of them on a weekly salaried basis. IBM was in a position to undertake such forward planning because it has an immense backlog of orders and is operating in a growth area in which the achievement of full use of capacity suffers no contradiction with the profit motive. Moreover, the company is so completely in the business of advanced technology that it cannot and apparently does not even want to try to sidestep awareness that its main capital is trained personnel. But all of these conditions do lead to significant ideological advance. Thomas J. Watson, Jr., the chief executive of the company and son of the founder, addressed the NAM in late 1959 and called for greater sacrifices from the nation in order to compete adequately with the Soviet Union (a year before candidate Kennedy sounded this theme). He called for higher taxes to achieve this purpose and stated straightforwardly that the necessities of the struggle with the Soviets cannot be achieved on "a 'business-as-usual' basis." He suggested that "to spend everything necessary to strengthen America" *and* balance the budget *and* lower taxes, were incompatible goals. All in all, this company represents very advanced thinking along managerial lines. It is also reputed to be in all ways a very excellent organization (and thoroughly capitalist, if by that is meant paper-worthy, in that it has for some years been valued at 50-100 times earnings on the stock market—about $13 billion until recently.)

It is heartwarming to see what the managers can do when they accept their true roles, give up on the old rationalizations, etc. Because there is no question that we need them—the society won't work without them. In the long perspective, I prefer them to the owner-capitalists. I find myself nodding in sympathy with Hilferding who believed that the non-owning manager of a big corporation acted "more vigorously, more boldly, more rationally, than an individual owner-entrepreneur" because the latter had his judgment obscured by personal anxieties and similar considerations. The analogy would be that of a lawyer acting as his own client. I find this not only convincing but also amusing, since it exactly contradicts the classic notions of overblown individualism.

They are the essential part of what lies behind the paper. Bayless Manning points out that rather than work for the shareholder, the managers actually just hire his money. "In competition with other managements seeking capital, they sell, for what the market will bear, the opportunity to share in the economic results of their managerial efforts." Manning refers to the new postwar diversified corporations very acutely as "operating mutual funds." He notes that "the buyer of stock does not know even what business the company may be in tomorrow. He is betting on management. . . ." In a very real sense, we are all betting on them.

They are the leaders.

14

PAPER RICH
AND
REAL POOR

WHO OWNS THE PAPER in the Paper Economy? What does paper-holding still mean in this society undergoing transition from capitalism in pure plutocratic form to the new and still somewhat unknown managerialism?

The subject of wealth is almost as interesting as the subject of sin—and they are not unconnected, the one often being the means to the other (at least in the popular mind). But the meaning of wealth has changed in the full rich society of consumers. It is fast becoming reduced to a spectacle of consumption, in competition with many other spectacles. Like the royal family in Britain: monarchy as ritual, wealth as ritual. The substance has been sloughed off elsewhere.

Wealth once meant power—and nobody found much occasion to distinguish the two. Today the world can only be misunderstood in such terms. Not that powerful people are ordinarily poor, but that wealthy people are not necessarily powerful. Why? They decided it that way. They didn't have to, but they did. The rich we have always with us, but never so irrelevantly as today.

There was never such a time in history when men pursued wealth so ferociously as a road to power as they did in America through the nineteenth century and up to the Great Depression. Our history to that date is an amazingly simple story: the rape of a continent, the amassing of fortune, the creation of enduring paper. Wealth can mean two things: power and privilege. This paper in the hands of its owners created Newport, Southampton, Tuxedo Park—and, at the same time, it might have organized and ruled these United States in an enduring fashion. But that was not the choice that the too-quickly rich ruling class in this country made for itself. It chose rather to live high. It has. But it has not ruled the country the way it might—certainly not since the first real difficulties occurred in our special plutocratic form of government. It has, finally, taken the privilege and abandoned the power, with immense consequences for the nature of our society in all ways, including cultural. Ours is one of the only ruling classes in history which has a built-in system of self-abdication. The rich have taken the privilege; their brilliant servants have taken the power; and the managerial servants have finally taken the rich, leaving the privilege—along with its lack of consequence—to their victims. The American rich have not trained their sons to rule.

One cannot get very far in understanding American society without making this distinction between power and privilege. Privileged people take advantage of this society of ours, sometimes extreme advantage; but the power is for serious people, who run things and are not misled by the dream-like perspective of life conceived as an endless movement from pleasure to super-pleasure to final pleasure, and home again. That is childishness, and our society is not run by childish people. No society ever has been. Misguided, perhaps; inadequate, certainly; on rare occasions, mad; but not childish.

Discussing the withdrawal from economic activity of the wealthy classes, which is a feature of the advance of managerialism, Burnham remarks that "to rule society . . . is a full-time job." I think that is very obviously true—and the obviousness of it should not be allowed to obscure its significance. To reach a little broadly and dramatically, it might even be said that managerialism derives from the necessity of servants, their consequent proliferation and final elevation to the point where their masters become formal, official, and unimportant. As the Prime Minister of England is said to serve the Queen.

For purposes of illustration, we might compare property controlled fully by its ownership to political power exercised under the divine right of kings. Just as the absolute discretion of the king became such a burden to his servants that it was circumscribed and finally dispensed with altogether, because the servants realized they were more important than their master, so the servants of property in its modern aggregations have had to take over so much of the owners' discretion as to make ownership relative rather than absolute, formal rather than operative, and generally less than divine. This is facilitated greatly when ownership occurs as scattered, impotent shareholding; but it is not limited to this. A lot of wealth, even if title is in one person, can only be a lot of complicated modern technological property—and this is the golden entree of the manager. The divine right of property is disappearing historically because the property concerned has so changed that it cannot be managed or operated by divine right. It can only be managed by technicians (for the things), and full-time organizational operators or "politicians" (for the people).

The seeds of every new society are to be discerned, after the fact, in the precedent order. There was a kernel of managerialism—servants-more-important-than-masters—in capitalist society from the beginning. The first managerialists, on the thing side, were the independent intellectuals, the inventors and other creators of modern technology; and the lawyers, on the people side, accompanied and followed by the bankers and other financial people. When a new order forms itself within the old, the process will be obscured by the fact, among others, that certain people identified as Leading Citizens of the old order will fill roles defined by and devoted to the new order. (This may be done unconsciously: it is not less effective thereby.) Describing an earlier transition, Burnham emphasized that "in some, not a few, cases the capitalists came from the ranks of the old ruling class, from among the feudal lords themselves."

It is much clearer today that a big owner must be a competent manager to avoid being reduced to the role of a passive rentier. The latter is the role of his class, and he can avoid it only by joining the ranks of the new class. Owning and managing property are two separate roles: having the one, he of course gets first crack at the other. But he has to seize the opportunity, or resign himself to a life of philanthropy and elaborate consumption. The women, who own more and more of the rentier property in this country, do not fight the issue very strenuously.

In the last hundred years, too many people have made too much money too quickly in the United States. This fact has had some very serious consequences. For one thing, the cheapening of wealth has made the problem of consolidating class rule based on it almost insurmountable. Coherent class rule may be founded on wealth, but must consist of more than wealth—for instance, educational and cultural continuity, traditions of ruling, broad class purpose, etc. (*vide*, England). For another thing, so much money in crude hands has facilitated the growth of managerialism.

"Money—sheer, naked, vulgar money—has with few exceptions won its possessors entrance anywhere and everywhere in American society," says C. Wright Mills in *The Power Elite*. The historical picture one gets from Mills is of waves of new wealth washing up against hastily fixed status structures, and periodically overwhelming them. In each backwash, the ruling classes have been increased numerically and also made increasingly heterogeneous. This may make the class more representative, but it drastically reduces its effectiveness as a ruling group. There never was time to housebreak the newcomers and integrate them in a continuing class-cultural pattern. The Ivy League gentleman, for instance, is as often an adornment as he is a leading figure in our genuine centers of power: he will be a manager more often than an owner when he is important. And he is as much of a class-type as we have managed to produce in America. (Our common "style" is nothing so deep as that which identifies, say, the members of the English Establishment; the American style is not much more than the glossiness accompanying privileged consumption and involvement in the celebrity system, which exists as much by virtue of its representation in the newspapers and other mass media as by the actual activities—dining, nightclubbing, sporting, resorting, etc. It simply expresses the sweet brassy surface of American life.)

One gets the impression that the case was different before the Civil War. There seems to have been a ruling class, based on wealth but consisting of something more, in both the North and the South—symbolized by Boston and Virginia. After all, the American Revolution was made and the early Republic established by cultured gentlemen, albeit colonials. These two groups were never able to coalesce—the continent was too big and too rich—and so the Civil War was allowed to happen. It is worth noting that until this inevitable mistake was made, the American ruling classes did not disdain Federal power—did not depend so heavily on weak, weaker and utterly weakened central government—but took it as their class responsibility to run it, as far as possible. Having failed to coalesce, the Virginian was destroyed and the Bostonian was swallowed up by the fabulous new wealth created by the conflict and the industrial surge following it. The demise of cultured ruling groups is accompanied historically by the rise of private financial government: dual government in the United States dates from the Civil War. A Pulitzer Prize winner in history, Roy F. Nichols, writes of this post-bellum situation: "The fact of the matter was that a large degree of power was in process of transfer from the government to the leaders of the growing business world." He suggests that in the course of this transfer, the basic conflict in the country shifted from a North-South axis to an East-West one. The major story then became the successful exploitation of the chief natural resources of the country, namely, the farmers and immigrant labor.

After the Civil War, the rule of raw wealth was so free and ferocious that what ruled can hardly be called a class at all. In Washington, non-government was enthroned; necessary law and order were supplied eventually by Wall Street. But the result was a set of traffic regulations for making money, not a coherent class for ruling the nation. The idea that there is a nation to be ruled, and that this requires a large group of people prepared and willing to do so for reasons beyond crass personal profit, has only recently been revived in the United States. Its revival is one of the outstanding achievements of managerialism to date. And it is appropriately ironic that, after so long an hiatus, our wealthy patricians have at last taken the lead again in this late act of survival.

The relation between wealth and its managers is a complicated subject. It is also a subject that is not apt to be solved once and for all, since it is a dynamic and evolving relation. How profoundly evolving is beautifully illustrated in an essay by Norton E. Long, a professor of political science at Northwestern University, concerning the effect of the corporation branch office in local communities, which in the past had mostly been organized around wealthy or at least the most well-to-do families. Mills had pointed out that the power elite, comprising a national system of power and prestige, had reduced the formerly prevailing importance of local power-clusters. Long's essay indicates that the national system, based primarily on the big corporations, has reacted back on the provinces most significantly.

The corporation has profoundly changed the role structure of the local community. Increasingly, it replaces the old families as owner and operator of the most profitable local business. In all except the largest communities the growing number of enterprises are branch plants run by *bureaucratic birds of passage,* with career lines stretching onward and upward to the magic haven of the head office. [My appreciative italics.]

The corporate managers have been impelled to take over more and more of the functions of the local wealthy elite—charitable, cultural, welfare, etc. This may even become a matter of company policy; but however done, it is a very different matter from the old way. Long even suggests that union people, being less mobile than their corporate fellows, develop a more important personal influence in the community. Of the corporate people he says: "Careers are made in the company rather than in the community." And he adds: "The phenomenon of absentee ownership, on which Veblen lavished his irony, has developed into the practice of absentee management by nonowners." Which certainly makes for a lot of organizational distance.

Economic dominants who are not, and do not become, part of the local social structure may be as foreign within local communities in the United States as the United Fruit Company in Latin America. The upward-mobile branch executive and his associated corporate birds of passage may be as alien as the white plantation manager in the tropics. . . . The passing of the regime of the old families has created a gap between positions in the economic and social tables of organization.

I feel certain that, in time, the New Class will fill the gap. And if they happen to include union people—*well,* that wouldn't be the end of the world, either.

If all the wealth of America had been divided equally a few years ago, each citizen—man, woman, and child—would have held $6,000. The opportunity for this thrilling egalitarianism was not taken at the time, and most of us, oldsters as well as kids, hold nothing like $6,000—and I don't suppose I have to prove the fact. If I did, I would refer to Victor Perlo's estimate that working-class families hold about "o.3 per cent of the marketable supply of stock in the United States"—a mere $750 million worth. (When poor people hold stock, its value hovers around $1,000.) As Galbraith has suggested: "Few things have been more productive of controversy over the ages than the suggestion that the rich should, by one device or another, share their wealth with those who are not." Since we have enough controversy to occupy us without indulging this classical one, we will forego it (for the time being).

As we enter upon a statistical reprise—suggesting answers to our original question, Who owns the paper?—we must mention at least the following factor impinging on this classical issue. It is one thing to accept a society characterized by elaborately unequal distribution of assets and income—but something else and more to have as poor a notion as we do of how much there is and who owns it. Speculate for a moment on the possible uses of a really adequate national balance sheet. We could see each year where the effort went, and who ended up with what advantage. We would know who if anyone "owned" our major institutions; we might find out if the estate and gift tax was working to its ostensible purpose of forestalling financial dynasty. There would be dozens of excellent uses. Not least of all would be a new tone of honest candor in the atmosphere which would do more for our culture than a

billion man-hours of freshman English. Eventually, more
than bankers would be interested in certified net worth
statements. For example, if an individual has to file one to
get a loan of money, why shouldn't he be called on similarly
when applying for a loan of the public trust—when he runs
for office, or is appointed to one?

Today we have only guesses concerning these fundamental matters—a great many of them fairly airy. The
National Industrial Conference Board, using SEC figures,
suggests financial assets of individuals (presumably excluding equities in homes and other material objects) at $959.1
billion in 1960, as follows: insurance and pension reserves,
$219.7; securities, both debt and equity, $558.0; and currency and deposits of $181.3. W.H. Ferry of the Fund for
the Republic states the over-all percentages concisely this
way:

> As of mid-1959 the poorest one-third of Americans own
> 1% of the wealth of the United States. The next 23% up
> the scale owns 5%. Thus, well over half the population
> owns 6% of the wealth of the United States. The richest
> 1.6% own nearly one-third of the country's material assets.

That appears to be the general picture. (But please
keep in mind that I am presenting a rather carefree potpourri of data: preparation of these figures is an extremely
complicated matter, and methodological refinements are of
recent date.)*

* One of the leading workers in this field, Raymond W. Goldsmith of
the National Bureau of Economic Research, published a major study late
in 1962 entitled *The National Wealth of the United States in the Postwar Period*. His summary conclusion is as follows:

> The national wealth of the United States (i.e., the aggregate value
> of all tangible nonmilitary assets located in the United States plus net
> foreign balance), measured so far as possible by the market value of
> the assets or the nearest approximation to it, has increased in the post-

Robert J. Lampman of the National Bureau of Economic Research published a study in 1960 which it will profit us to look at less cavalierly. Called *Changes in the Share of Wealth Held by Top Wealth-Holders, 1922-1956*, it is based on the estate-multiplier method, under which a top wealth-holder is defined as anyone having more than $60,000, which is the estate tax exemption. The technique is to use the number of top wealth-holders who die each year, the stated value of their estates, and relevant mortality rates, to arrive at an estimate of the number of living top wealth-holders and the value of their property. (Incidentally, special mortality rates have to be used because one of the advantages of being rich is that you live longer.) Without going into the further refinements of the study, let's look at the results:

In 1953, 1,658,795 top wealth-holders held $309.2 billion—30 per cent of total personal wealth held by 1.04 per cent of the total population. Comparing 1922 and 1953, the top wealth-holders held about the same percentage of total wealth—but there were twice as many of them in the later year. This is partly accounted for by tax considerations which make it smart to spread property around among members of the family. The top 1 per cent of adults owned 31.6 per cent of everything in 1922, 36.3 per cent in 1929, and only 23.6 per cent in 1953 (happily, this was back up to 26 per cent in 1956). A previous study, concluded in the last century, estimated that 1 per cent of the families in the country owned 51 per cent of the wealth in 1890.

---

war period from about $575 billion at the end of 1945 to just over $1,700 billion at the end of 1958. . . . Wealth per inhabitant thus has more than doubled from $4,100 to $9,800. . . . In constant prices of 1947-49, aggregate national wealth has increased from almost $790 billion to nearly $1,250 billion, while wealth per head has risen by one-fourth from about $5,600 to $7,100.

Of special interest for us paper-fanciers are the figures on the concentration of ownership of specific kinds of property. Here is the author's impressive summary for 1953:

> The top group owned at least 80 per cent of the corporate stock held in the personal sector, virtually all of the state and local government bonds, nearly 90 per cent of corporate bonds, and between 10 and 35 per cent of each other type of property. . . .

By inversion, the "other types of property" reveal the kind of holdings spread out among the population existing under the top wealth-holders. For example, the 1 per cent on top holds only 12.5 per cent of the real estate and only 5 per cent of the country's pension and retirement funds, and 11.5 per cent of the insurance equity. This is to be expected —though in fact the real estate figure surprises me, and indicates a high level of upper class investment in the postwar boom. The figure on state and local bonds reflects the tax-exemption of this kind of security; it was more or less created for individuals with high ordinary income. The figure on the extreme concentration of stock ownership, which is the one item that has been increasing in recent years, will come as a surprise only to the NYSE publicists who have a professional interest in peddling the "People's Capitalism" line—the Who-owns-America?–You-do view of things.

The *Federal Reserve Bulletin* reported in 1952 that two-thirds of the total value of stock was held by the 1 per cent of the country's spending units (a special economic definition of family) that owned $10,000 or more. (In 1957 the Board reported that only 11 per cent of the 56.1 million spending units in the United States owned any publicly held stock.) In 1952, the NYSE commissioned the Brookings Institution to do a study on share ownership. Widely known as the Kimmel Report, the study revealed that there were 6,490,000 people who owned stock on March 1, 1952. When the Exchange updated the study in 1956, it found that there were 8,630,000 stockholders. It is probably fair to say that the number of individual stockholders has doubled in the fifties: stock ownership goes up as the market does. Pointedly unlike the later Exchange studies, the Kimmel Report had something to say about the concentration of stock ownership. It found what we already know from the Lampman study—high concentration: 2.1 per cent of shareholdings were 1,000 shares or over, and these accounted for 58 per cent of total shares held; 67 per cent of the stockholders held less than 100 shares.

All these statistics bear out what everyone knows anyway, that the distribution of the ownership of income paper is something like the distribution of income itself, only more so; and there is almost none of this paper at and below the median level of income (except insurance, life-and-death savings, etc.), where the imperatives of consumption are absolute. (Kimmel reported 560,000 stockholders as "Retired, Dependents.")

Lest we become too bedazzled by the statistical astronomy of upper-class paper-holdings, we should recall that all paper is gold-tomorrow. Today is real, tomorrow is a speculation—and paper-wealth is all tomorrow. The shrewd Thurman Arnold says, "Wealth . . . is nothing more than a present-day guess as to what goods and services an individual or an organization can control in the future."

This comforting bit of philosophy duly digested, we can now proceed further with the almost incredible story of concentrated wealth in this unique country of ours. It will be very clever of us to take a quick look at personal trust funds, because this form of wealth-holding is seriously concentrated among people who are seriously well-to-do in the first place. Anybody can buy a share of stock or two, but somebody in your family has to be burdened with truly big money before an expert gets around to suggesting a trust. It is a fundamental spray-technique used in facing up to the imperatives of both the income and estate tax facts of life. When you look at state and local bonds, which are tax-exempt, there is not much to say: *all* of them are owned by the very rich, the whole $60 billion-plus, because the bonds are typically overpriced unless you are in such a high tax bracket that the tax-free interest is an important feature for you. (Mrs. Horace Dodge, Sr., apparently in a fit of right-wing pique, put her entire legacy of $56 million into this kind of snobbish paper.) With personal trust funds, which come to another $60 billion-plus (less duplication), we at least have a subject for conversation, although the figures on trust funds suggest rather than state the size of the fortunes behind them. Trust funds are icing on the cake: they represent the dispersion of great fortunes—part of what rich people give away to members of the family while they are alive, or necessarily leave behind them as they depart.

The bank-administered personal trust fund is the biggest single form of institutional stockholding. It has been estimated by Victor Perlo that "personal trust departments of banks hold close to one-fourth of all corporation stocks." The magazine *Trust and Estates* estimated that bank trust departments held $62.6 billion at the end of 1954. "In 1954 trust departments of national banks administered 289,000 personal trust accounts with $43.4 billion of assets," Perlo informs us. If the figures are based on all banks, including state banks, it is much higher. (It is higher still if non-bank-administered trusts are counted in.) "The Federal Reserve Bank of New York reported that in 1954, 83 banks in the Second Federal Reserve District handled 115,000 personal trust accounts with $48 billion of assets," evidencing considerable concentration in the New York area. Moreover, the wealthier you are, the greater the likelihood that you will have a trust account as well as individual stockholdings. Forty-eight per cent of those with assets of over a million dollars were beneficiaries of trusts as well as active investors on their own. Dividends from stocks came to 71 per cent of the total income of bank-administered trusts in 1958; total income of all trusts was over $3 billion in that year, plus over $800 million in net capital gains. There is as much concentration among personal trusts as in other property; 1 per cent of the trust returns received 28 per cent of the trust income reported to the IRS.

For perspective, let's look at the not-so-rich investors. Mutual funds are supposed to be the common man's special area—about $20 billion-plus. A few years ago, representatives of one of the funds offered this financial portrait of the average mutual fund investor: besides his $4,100 in mutual funds, he had $8,200 in other securities and $3,300 in a savings bank. Merrill, Lynch, Pierce, Fenner & Smith reported that in 1959 its "typical" customer had an account of over $10,000. (That lets most of us out.)

One of the main things about the rich, we noted in an earlier chapter, is that they get richer—just by being there. R. H. Tawney, that impressive Englishman whose righteousness never really succeeded in obscuring his perception, expressed the proposition very well:

Wealth in modern societies is distributed according to opportunity; and while opportunity depends partly upon talent and energy, it depends still more upon birth, social position, access to education and inherited wealth; in a word, upon property. For talent and energy can create opportunity. But property need only wait for it.

Wherever money is being made, the people who already have it are there; that is, their money is there even if they are not. The most convincingly exciting example of this phenomenon would be the stock market boom of the fifties: the top wealth-holders' 70 per cent plus interest in stocks better than doubled in value. A research outfit has figured out what would have happened to an "average" $1 million in stock between 1913 and 1958. If a man bought about $10,000 of every stock listed on the NYSE in 1913, the price would have been $1,014,855. He would have received $38,842 in dividends that year. In 1958, the stock was worth $20,391,806, and the dividends would have come to $741,729. The exotic beauty of this picture of passive enterprise is somewhat marred by inflation and taxes, but I for one can still respond to it through these cracks in the pigment.

Looking at the richest of the rich, Victor Perlo guesses as follows:

The TNEC compiled, as of 1937, the main stockholdings of some wealthy families. For example, the du Pont family was estimated to have $574 million in stock; the Rockefeller family $397 million; and the Mellon family $391 million. Allowing only for publicly reported changes in these family holdings—and there is no evidence of their significant dispersal (*sic*)—by 1956 the value of holdings of the Rockefeller and Mellon families exceeded $3 billion each and of the du Pont family $4 billion.

(*Fortune* asserted that incomes of $1 million increased 39 per cent in one year from 1953 to 1954.)

The point of these figures is—Can the nation afford all this paper-frenzy in perpetuity? I would answer, Certainly—if both the membership of our class of paper-rentiers were limited and also their take, at something like recent levels. But if their numbers and their take continue to grow, the country might well become dangerously top-heavy, with unforeseen but nerve-wracking consequences. We would then be firmed up as a nation of 200 million well-fed house-servants to a few million professional super-consumers. It would then have to be said of us by future (and foreign) historians that the people of the United States, having been the first to arrive at a consumer's society, showed themselves to be unequal to the historical task of overcoming its least desirable potentialities. Our epitaph would be, "The vanguard of poor starving humanity, having arrived in the scientific paradise of milk and honey, soon thereafter expired of overeating and the worship of overeaters."

The charge upon national production of all this old paper is substantial—an old-age pension with a vengeance (and one, moreover, for old and young alike). Also, this privileged consumption is in addition to that of the managers—because there is no question that we will have to pay off in higher standards of living to the growing class of managers, expert and otherwise.

Whatever our reason for envying the rich, we must not misunderstand them. They are important and influential —wherever they go, and whatever they do. But they are not, in a great dark conspiracy, running the country—as if there were no other sources and kinds of power in the nation. Indeed, they are less important than they have ever been, and increasingly so year by year. Their power is the power of owners, and that kind of power is no longer adequate to run our big institutions, which are everything.

More and more, the big rich are just big consumers.

A lot of paper in one package is still a means of control, of course. What I want to suggest now is that the title to it in one person is almost an adventitious circumstance. If what the title-paper controls is big enough, it has to be managed in the same way as a publicly owned corporation or fund. Like monarchy, title is becoming a formality even when it is a genuine control-feature.

It would be at least one separate book to discuss in a factual way the great family fortunes which were created so quickly in America, and have been such an important and exotic part of our history. The list of names tells as much as I can manage in this space—Girard, Goelet, Astor, then railroad money like Vanderbilt, Harriman, and so on, and Rockefeller, Carnegie, Mellon, du Pont, and another fifty or a hundred names. And a few hundred beyond these. (There are 38,000 conjugal family units now listed in the twelve volumes of the Social Registers.) And today there are dozens of major representatives of each of these several hundred (or several thousand?) major fortunes. (Add in recent oil money, some of it personally aggregated in bunches in excess of ½ billion; and events like Reynolds with his ballpoint pens and the government's aluminum factories; and so on.) Also, all the unsung real estate and retail merchant fortunes spread out comfortably from Bangor through Biloxi by Butte and all the way to San Diego or Honolulu. Whatever it is we the people made, they have it.

Until recently, that is, when the institutions became so big that the people running them day-by-day become more important than the people owning them quarter-by-quarter.

We could hunt up a thousand facts like how much the first Astor left when he died ($20 million), what Rockefeller's dividends were in 1905 ($72 million), the details of the Marshall Field trusts for his sons (complicated), and more. That's what Gustavus Myers did in his remarkable work, *History of the Great American Fortunes*, published in 1907 (and again in 1936 by the Modern Library in 732 close pages). Of course, he leaves out fifty years and more of fortune—and there has been some. Paul Getty and a few others are currently habited in the neighborhood of $1 billion-plus; there are hundreds of other almost as lovely stories to tell. Myers' book, a really awe-inspiring bit of scholarship, is still worth reading for fact-mongers. With this warning: it is a period-piece—grandiose scholarship dwarfed by rolling waves of indignation. The price of participation is two lines of morality for one of fact.

Inheritance taxes and antitrust were companion articles of faith in the progressivistic attack on Bigness in the early part of this century. They have worked out, over half a century, with remarkable similarity: giantism has been inhibited, Bigness preserved in whitewashed form. *Fortune* reported in 1957 that "the president of one of the biggest trust companies in the United States" said the big accounts were getting bigger and that there were 60 per cent more of them. "Uncle Sam *isn't* taking the big estates," he assured the reporter. We don't have time for details, but there are simply too many effective ways of avoiding the doom of the steeply graduated estate taxes. Collections on these taxes did not top $1 billion until 1956 (it runs about at the level of customs duties), although it is estimated that more than $25 billion passes through estates annually. Just as antitrust has restrained outright lordly monopoly, the estate tax laws have made imperial primogeniture impossible here. The main effects have been to spray portions of the great fortunes among a larger group of relatives, to upgrade substantially the financial power of women, and to create our major foundations.

Notice also that no income tax is ever paid on the appreciation in value of securities held for a lifetime. In a long-rising market, it is distinctly possible to leave more than you started with, *after* estate taxes. But it must be spread around. You can lose some, too, of course: Richard Mellon sustained a $28 million loss in Gulf Oil over the summer of 1957; he held $242 million of it, about a half or a third of his total fortune. But he probably made it back by late winter. (As you may have surmised, everything is different Up There.)

For the purposes of our property-managerialism theme, note that the great paper fortunes which in fact remain are substantially in the hands of the managers. I am thinking of more than the big funds that are professionally managed, the trust officers of banks, the lawyers, accountants, investment specialists, foundation managers, and so on. I am referring to the fact that a Rockefeller is a corporation. The circumstance that a Mr. Rockefeller may more or less consistently and competently occupy the position of chairman of the board of directors (or even ambitiously start in the shop and work his way up to the top job), is not so all-important as it appears on the surface. Anybody with title to that much property is necessarily institutionalized. Like great movie actresses, they are soon thingified: "their" property, like a movie queen's appearance and personality, is managed professionally as the productive or control asset that it in fact is. Title to a great fortune, whether it means control of a factory or a bank, cannot long endure as a truly *personal* thing. The best that the individual can hope for is to function effectively, and perhaps even enjoyably, *as chief executive of himself.*

Title to such an aggregate of property is just another way, like the institutional control of a managerial clique, of ensuring perpetual re-election as the top executive. (If we have difficulty understanding this, it is only because the underlying proto-idea we have of what it is to "own" is essentially what it is to "use"—applicable to farmers, consumers, and other thing-tyrants.)

Moreover, in order to be big enough to compete with the biggest public funds, the biggest title-holders are required to join forces, on a natural or acquired family basis. The simplest example would be the retention of ownership-control of a previously closely held corporation through one generation or more by spreading the necessary amount of stock among a necessary number of descendants. But the descendants, in the second if not the first generation, would have to organize themselves, and work together sufficiently well to maintain the integrity of the control-bloc. They would in effect become a membership holding company. Something like this seems to have been accomplished on a grand scale by the du Pont dynasty, which as far as I know is an anomaly in this country, considering the size and importance of the assets held. (The first du Pont in America set up shop in 1802; they were in munitions before they became the biggest chemical company in the United States.) Christiana Securities Company holds nearly 30 per cent of

E. I. du Pont de Nemours & Co., Inc. Christiana is controlled by members of the du Pont family. But now or soon, the shares of Christiana will come under the dispersal-effect of the estate tax laws. The problem can be handled by spreading the paper among more and more individuals named du Pont. But all these du Ponts have to act together to preserve the dynasty. And eventually they will have to do so willingly, rather than under any legal compulsion.

The du Ponts are an old family, with established dynastic traditions. Undoubtedly, this was the factor that led them to lead their lawyers to try to hold the situation together through such extreme reliance on personal title. One of these generations, they will have to give in and establish a foundation, like Rockefeller and Ford. And one day the foundations and other big public funds will have everything the government didn't get. That, and a great deal of paper to live-on-and-control-nothing sprayed over an ever-widening class of paper-rentiers all distinguished by shrewd birth certificates—another important piece of paper in the Paper Economy. But still not the main one, at least not for running things.

Charles F. Kettering, with a very substantial General Motors fortune, turned it all over to the management of the Winters Trust Co. several decades ago. R. A. Smith of *Fortune* tells us that only a quarter of the $50-million-and-over people handle their own money. With surprising candor for that magazine, he says, ". . . a substantial section of the American rich . . . have become rentiers in the most passive sense."

I believe the corporations are getting bigger, despite the antitrust laws, at a greater rate than the paper fortunes, in part because of the estate tax laws. Corporations are the only vital and accepted form of dynastic perpetuity. They have replaced the family as the basic unit of power.

L'état, c'est moi. (Mais moi, je suis une corporation.)

Ignoring for the moment who and what runs things, let us at last pay momentary homage to the substantial pleasures of truly big money. Only God knows what images of grandeur filled the heated atmosphere of Hearst's mind as he planned and half-built his La Casa Grande on the top of La Cuesta Encantada in San Simeon, California (at a cost of $50 million) and then turned it into a warehouse for millions of dollars of artistic bric-a-brac. Or indulge yourself for a moment with speculation regarding assorted soirées aboard the 325-foot, 3-million-dollar yacht of Mr. Aristotle Socrates Onassis, with its El Grecos, crew of forty-six, movable swimming pool, seaplane and automobile, the Italian mirrors in the master bedroom, etc., etc. Take a look, sometime, at the cities built for the occasional habitation of the very rich—Newport, Palm Springs, Tuxedo Park, Santa Barbara, and so on. And some *nouveau* nonsense: a Los Angeles builder has taps in his kitchen which release scotch, bourbon, champagne and beer in his $250,000 home. But this fellow seems to believe in gadgets in a general way because he has a typewriter (as well as a bar) built into his Cadillac so that his secretary can type (and he can drink?) on the way to the office.

We could have a lot of fun with this sort of thing for page after page—there is no lack at all of purple fact and cerise anecdote. When you have so much money that it takes an effort of imagination to figure out how to spend it . . . well, the quality of imagination is revealed: Tiffany &

Co., a novelty store for the rich in New York, offered for sale one Christmas season a 14-carat gold putter for $1,475, and advertised same in *The Wall Street Journal* as a proper gift for the man who has everything. (Vico said: "Men first feel necessity, then look for utility, next attend to comfort, still later amuse themselves with pleasure, thence grow dissolute in luxury, and, finally, go mad and waste their substance.") But on to more serious matters, namely, poverty.

The American income-picture that has been developed here consists roughly of three panels: 1) several million high-fliers; 2) a growing stratum of consumption-minded middle-level managers, primary beneficiaries of the postwar "income revolution"; and 3) the rest of us. The income curve for #3 begins with a moderate, mannerly decline and ends with an abysmal collapse. Over 32 million people live on less than $50 a week for a family of four and these families include one-fifth of the children and 8 million men and women over 65 years. Everyone can think of that as he pleases, or ignore it: I find it disgusting.

Out of about 56 million family units in the United States in 1960, half made more than $5,600. Let's look at the half who didn't. At the bottom, we have 7.2 million units with incomes of less than $2,000, which is 13 per cent of all families and unattached individuals. In 1947, there were 7.4 million such units surviving on the same $40 a week or less (in 1960 dollars). In uncorrected dollars, GNP better than doubled in those thirteen years: in 1945 dollars, it went from $314 billion in 1945 to $426 billion in 1959. Conclusion? *Over seven million families have benefited not at all from the entire immense postwar boom!* (Or each one that did was replaced by one that didn't.)

This boom indicates more than anything could the

lopsided affluence of American society. Between 1947 and 1959, production of air-conditioners, television sets, clothes driers, and boats increased beyond 400 per cent; more than forty types of goods showed an average production increase of 58 per cent, which was double the population growth. Residential electricity, to make the gadgets run, increased 272 per cent over the period. The residences in which to use the electricity represent a major part of the postwar boom, as we all know. The decade of the fifties witnessed a 78 per cent growth in owner-occupied dwellings: 29 million in 1960, with 90 per cent of them (compared to 70 per cent in 1950) in sound condition with all plumbing facilities. But still there was enough junk around to keep God's rain off the very poor: one in six dwellings were dilapidated or lacked complete plumbing, 8,800,000 lacked private toilets or bath or hot water. (Half of the lousy housing is located in the South, but in 1956 there were 484,000 units in New York City suitable for the current victims of the Paper Economy.) Meanwhile, one million people owned a *second* vacation/retirement home.

In 1959, Michael Harrington estimated in an article in *Commentary* that "50 million Americans continue to live below those standards which we have been taught to regard as the decent minimums for food, housing, clothing, and health." He took a figure of $3,000 annual income as his minimum, which is quite a bit under most official estimates. Only 18 per cent of the families in his total were living on farms. He catalogued the poorest groups as the old people, unskilled workers, migratory farm workers, and minorities like Negroes, Puerto Ricans, etc. (the non-white earns on the average about half of what the financially superior races earn). "A large section of the poor inherits its poverty," he notes. One *learns* how to be poor—and does not forget the early lessons easily.

It is very important that under the New Deal and early War years, we experienced a genuine decline in poverty. But not during the postwar boom. The reason is partly that in the thirties the decrease in poverty was *intended*, and since the War there has not been any concerted attack on it. The poor have been left behind while the organized workers and the new middle class continue their climb up the ladder of consumption.

I think we must pause now for a moment of pure disgust. In a country of such opulence, it is a morally revolting spectacle to behold the low and even dangerous standards of life of the big minority of citizens at the economic bottom. After the Negro rights issue, this is the great shame of our exceptional nation. Both of these configurations are derived from prejudice and stupidity—there is no real hard necessity of any kind involved in their continuance. They are that rare thing—stupidly willed evil. Gross poverty in this country is perfectly unnecessary. Two people fighting over one loaf of bread is a kind of human situation —even if one of them already has a few loaves stashed away somewhere. But that is not our circumstance. Our wheat surplus is large enough to produce twenty-five loaves of bread for each man, woman, and child on the whole planet.

In his essay on American affluence, Galbraith noted accurately that economic inequality is no longer the high moral issue it once was in our history. But as the issue ceases to be moral in the old sense, with the old urgency, it becomes an immediate esthetic issue on the crest of the fading moral point. Just about everything the poor need is in surplus supply either as existing inventory or productive capacity. This is, then, a *new* form of inhumanity—not any longer the old rich-against-the-poor dichotomy. There are many new events in America, and among the most startling is the fundamentally altered nature of the struggle between the older classes. Both the very rich and the very poor have become somewhat irrelevant, outside the mainstream in a power sense. The relevant historical issue is the inhibition of paper-madness and the distribution of the readily available product.

American families each owned $131.89 of surplus food in 1958—14 bushels of wheat, 21 of corn, 300 pounds of sorghum, a peck of soybeans, a bushel of barley. The government spends over one billion a year just taking care of it for them. *Much of it was harvested by our migrant labor families who desperately need their share of it.*

For contrast, note that the 26 million dogs in the United States consumed 2 billion pounds of specially prepared dog food in 1958. Space does not permit going into a class-analysis of this animal society, or the breakdown of the $150 million spent on accessories. That would have something of the quality of the infinite recession of mirror-images in a mirror.

THE
ISSUES

15

THE OVERRIDING ISSUE OF ORGANIZATION

OUR IMPRESSIONISTIC DESCRIPTION of the Paper Economy is completed. What remains is summary and argument—and a quick comparison with the Soviet Union.

The argument of this book is simply this: Technology creates organization; organization is power; power is the substance of politics; politics is the whole point. Notice that Private Property, competitive markets, and similar eighteenth-century baggage have been lost in this fast shuffle. They are no longer key concepts for understanding the economy, and are used today only to obscure what simple perception will disclose. The categories of appropriate comprehension are—technology, organization, power, politics.

I did not say they *should* be, that the world would be nicer or better if they were—I said they *are*.

Veblen noted (nearly forty years ago) that "any established order of law and custom is always out of date, in some degree." Ours is now terribly out of date. Our world is almost totally different from the ideas being used to describe it. This is partly because things have changed so quickly; partly because of our cultural immaturity; partly because, to too many of us for too long, life without the money-passion has seemed not exactly worth living; and finally, an undetermined responsibility for our predicament must be ascribed to the perennial cussedness of the human race. We're just never as smart or as candid or as fair-minded as we might be—even if the result is self-destructiveness.

We simply have to try to get over the idea here in America that all activities other than making money are merely hobbies. Our leaders, the people who have already made it, especially have to get over this idea.

An economy based on paper in the devoted way that ours is, cannot keep up with the rest of the world. All our natural power, all our magnificent industrial head start, even the exceptional qualities of our melting-pot population, will not be enough to preserve the preeminence which the accidents of history have forced upon us. To date, our triumphs have been rough-and-ready and relatively easy. But the future, all of it, looks much harder: the task from here on in is establishing a dynamic order for the whole planet, not just exploiting a rich continent swarming with ravenous immigrants (at a very fortunate juncture, moreover, in the development of technology). No, from now on we are going to have to use our heads a little.

The basis of the economy is the new technology, and that is all headwork. The whole set-up has become dangerously lopsided with all that high-class thinking at one end, and all this glaring mindlessness at the other. Technology is initially in the hands of devoted, talented and innocent scientists whose whole technique of discourse and action guarantees their political irrelevance (despite their considerable leverage); organization is accompanied by a very primitive state of awareness, dominated by scientism in which human beings are rediscovered only on an IBM card; power is discussed as if foreigners were frequently guilty of it; and politics is partly a form of ideological ancestor worship, partly a way for cigar-smokers to make a living. All of these—technology, organization, power, politics—require, instead, the best thinking of which the best of us are capable (and the rest of us had better listen carefully). The remainder of what goes on in our minds besides thinking is just spiritual homemaking. These are usually the ideas and images provided by one ancestor or another. That would be all right, as it has been in the past, if tradition were able to help us. But tied as we are to a technological maelstrom, adherence to tradition is likely to get us blown off the planet.

Paper covers the economy, directing and distorting its performance. If not for paper, we would be discussing the technological or the organized economy, something like that—and somebody else would be leading the discussion. But it is a Paper Economy—paper, meaning the symbols of Private Property on top of all the real events, the thing-property and all the educated effort of the population. We have got to see through the paper wall—past all the engraved and certified symbols, to the realities beyond.

Or, to be fair about it, there are always two realities in human life. One is physical, the other social: the first consisting of perceived events, the other of the richer meanings we give to these events. The Paper Economy is, finally, a humanly inadequate form of social reality. Taken in unsophisticated form, it is increasingly absurd as a purported description of the course of events, or as a reasonable means of dealing with them. Appearance-and-reality—that is what we have been discussing—by means of the metaphor of Paper-and-Things.

Or put another way: *money isn't real.*

From the early English colonial corporations through the period of railroad building and the growth of Standard Oil *et al* to the present era of immense corporate enterprise, business activity has always tended to be a form of government. Business is the politics of production. The "government" created by business activity can be compared with the better understood forms of historical government as to productiveness, rapacity, authoritarianism, progressivity, and so on. In this comparative effort, business governments will appear in a better light in some instances, and in a more shadowed guise in others. But these comparisons do not disturb the central term, namely, that business is a form of governing.

In a sense, business is a fairly irresponsible form of government since ostensibly it makes a commitment only to its own self-interest. In the early days of capitalist ideology, the self-interested businessman was understood to be doing God's work: he was justified thereby, as much as a king's lordly prerogative was justified, as a matter of divine right. In the simplest terms, what capitalism has meant to the West has been a broader sharing of the power, previously monopolized by the nation-state (or at least groups of ruling families), to steal from and exploit the underlying population. Where the usual political body used its booty thus derived not only to entertain itself lavishly but beyond that to wage war, and thus supposedly to add to the wealth of the body politic, the businessman from the beginning has been a more progressive factor in that he accumulated productive assets. It turned out that business activity was a much more profitable and therefore progressive form of acquisition than warfare (although, of course, the two frequently went together).

It has been a central term of the argument here that the supposed basic conflict between government and business is decidedly unreal in that business and government are decidedly similar and decidedly necessary to each other. If the human struggle for freedom can be conceived only in the anti-state terms of the seventeenth and eighteenth centuries, then it does not have very bright prospects in the twentieth and twenty-first centuries. The heart of human history has been and will continue to be politics; and politics is concerned with power. In a democratic society, defined for modern purposes, *all* power centers would be subject to political questioning, review and action, under certain minimal rules of procedure. Yet we now have two governments in the United States, only one of which is subject to political action on the part of the electorate.

Granted our commitment to technology, this second non-democratic government is necessary. And it is not such a bad government, in the sense that it still works fairly well, and without undue reliance on police power. But from the point of view of the development of a viable democratic culture, it is a disaster. The second government governs mostly by denying its own existence, which requires immense ideological distortion, and by additional domination and perversion of the entire national culture, which it finances. It attacks directly and covertly undermines its weak sister, the official government, on a continuing basis. It lives not by the sword, but by perfidy. If the traditional state exists by virtue of a domestic monopoly of armed force, then our second form of government exists by exercising a national monopoly of effective fabrication.

Organization is power. We are as powerful as we are because by one means or another our productive system has achieved a certain measure of organization. Moreover, it is puerile to view this intricately developed system of organization as "free enterprise." It is, simply, *ad hoc* organized—to produce certain desired goods. If any of us want the system to produce more goods or other goods, then such of us ought to try to alter or augment the organization for such purposes. This is feasible, consistent with the historical nature of the system, and is not a sin against God. Doing so is called "politics." The only thing that stands in the way of politics is ideological nonsense utilized as an instrument of power to defend a status quo, for no better reason than that it is a status quo, and often enough against the interests of those favored under this particular status quo—which last can only be called a form of social madness.

Organization is the heart of the problem of building the modern world and making it habitable. When science is applied in the world, as technology, it requires drastically new forms of social organization. The effective technology then leads to more people living longer—what the news-papers call the "population explosion"—which again calls for a heightening of organization. "As the body grows in aggregate size, the organization must be more complex," notes Berle. The organization is more important than the paper representing it legally; the term for understanding an organization is hierarchical power, not ownership; exit the sway of property, insofar as it remains private. All modern roads lead to organization. The modern population, despite or because of the technology, can neither survive nor prosper without it.

"Organization" according to Berle "is essentially the mechanism by which the decisions and instructions of a central individual or group can be made causative at distant points of application." Another way of putting it is that an organization, being the complicated pattern of individual habits by which large numbers of people live and work together, is in each case a society-for-a-special-purpose. The immediately noticeable factors about such complicated patternings are: 1) that they exist at all; 2) the high order of cerebration required to create and sustain these *ad hoc* societies; 3) the new and special powers resulting there-from; and 4) the morale, or spiritual effluvia, which is an essential aspect of the continuity given to the organization by mortal men and women.

The essence of organization is the new power it cre-ates—power to accomplish the task which led to its estab-lishment, and power over the individuals who make up the organization. It is the latter which presents itself as the great problem of the age. Organizational power is not simple and does not rely much on direct physical force. Berle: "Power other than that derived from immediate capacity to apply brute force can be exercised only through organization." (In effect, you implicate the individual and mobilize his cooperation in a system designed to control his own behavior.) Physical action is the most primitive form of power, and not very important in our time. If the world is blown up on purpose, the act will be accomplished by some conferences, some cerebration, and the nod of a head. The rest will be mechanical.

If not force, then what *is* the power of organizations? It is, simply and magically, the power of shared weakness. In organized life, *nobody* does anything or controls anything which by itself would keep him alive. It is, literally, by making the individual weaker and ever weaker that the power thus abdicated individually is agglomerated into the centralized and overwhelming power of the organization. Thus the problem becomes to avoid making the individual so weak that he cannot manage any longer to accomplish his iota of organizational work; indeed, that he won't cease being a viable individual altogether. To forestall this is the function of morale or ideology: having been destroyed as a physical unit capable of self-accomplished survival, the individual must be resuscitated, born again, made whole, on the spiritual plane—and by symbolic means. And without much assistance from traditional religion—because the deeply felt belief in God belongs to the simpler, more natural man. The God-fearing man takes care of his own life, while the God he fears takes care of the death he fears. But the man lost in organization does not have the opportunity to fear death actively enough to create something like a belief in God out of that natural fear: he needs a god minute-by-minute just to remain whole enough to stay alive. That god is ideology, the deeply felt belief that the Organization will keep him alive.

Thurman Arnold's *The Folklore of Capitalism* is an original and indigenous work, one of the most richly suggestive political treatises in the American repertoire. Written in 1937, and being hotly of that New Deal moment, it is perhaps a better book today than when it was written.

For our purposes, his two key subjects are the relation of ideals (ideology) and practices in sustaining institutional morale, and the theory of the *sub rosa* accounting for the creation of necessary organizations. Arnold's theory is that in order to have a successful organization of human beings, a creed is required, the creed must afford security, it must sustain institutional habits, and all this must be held together by a mythology. Without these elements, "organization can be maintained only by force, and force cannot continue long because it is too exhausting." Perhaps the essence of his view is that existing orders create a mythology which can be summed up with the one word, "principles." These are typically in conflict with needs. New forces cracking through the old order require practical power solutions, not principles. But the tendency to sacrifice effectiveness in favor of principles—also to formulate new problems in terms of old principles—is the source of the basic difficulty of the human race in its organized form.

Organizations need "principles" to exist; but the principles keep the organization from taking on new and necessary tasks, or disqualify the principled people from creating new and necessary organizations. ("It may be asserted as a principle of human organization that when new types of social organization are required, respectable, well-thought-of, and conservative people are unable to take part in them.") As a consequence, the new-and-necessary is frequently, in the first instance, illegal. This is Arnold's theory of the inevitable law of political dynamics: "Given a situation where the ideals are in contradiction to the needs, a *sub rosa* organization must develop." And he adds: "The growth of the new organization, however, will be due to the opportunity created when the older one was unable to act."

Organization is necessary—and also, therefore, everything that demonstrably goes along with it. It must be remembered that Arnold was an important administrative participant—and leading intellectual adornment—of the New Deal, which involved as much new organization, as fiercely resisted by principled people, as anything in our whole history. He witnessed at closest range the grand comic spectacle of principled people trying to frustrate a practical-minded government's efforts to save the country. Out of this experience, he fashioned his special (and early) view of dual government in the United States:

> Thus we develop two coordinate governing classes: The one, called "business," building cities, manufacturing and distributing goods, and holding complete and autocratic control over the livelihood of millions; the other, called "government", concerned with the preaching and exemplification of spiritual ideals, so caught in a mass of feeling that when it wished to move in a practical world it had to do so by means of a *sub rosa* political machine.

Also, like everyone else in his generation, he had lived through the eccentric phenomenon of Prohibition—surely the classic illustration (along with the corporation itself) of the creation of a necessary *sub rosa* organization. There are numerous other examples, including prostitution, gambling, political parties, etc. These are all old ones that official society has never officially accepted; often enough, a necessary organization beginning *sub rosa* is ultimately accepted in the community of organizations and accorded official status. But this apposition of official and illegal is complicated: it is typical of Arnold's intellectual charm that, using the gangster and his rackets as an illustration of his theory, he will nevertheless add, "It was Insull, not Capone who wrecked the financial structure of Chicago." And that's certainly true.

Organizations exist by virtue of planning. Their power is the power to plan—to project the interrelated activities of tens of thousands of men, and the uses and movement of almost unlimited material objects: limited only by the uses technology can devise for matter. Planning is the essence of technology, if indeed there is any real difference between the two. Acts of planning as exemplified by General Motors, AT&T, du Pont, IBM, the Department of Defense, the Soviet scientific establishment, the Manhattan Project, the creation and maintenance of the State of Israel, and dozens of other major examples are *the* most significant power-achievements of the human race: they make the building of the pyramids look like amateurish fumbling. And all of them put together are as nothing compared to their meaning as witnesses of the future. Planning is simply effective thought and appropriate implementation on a grand scale—a grand and ever grander scale. It is the final transcendance of the historical (Christian) dissociation of thought and action.

But "planning" is a dirty word in the United States

of America. A "planned economy" is a standard term of abuse in our newspapers and other cultural institutions. It is used not to refer to General Motors, the Department of Defense, the AEC, NASA, or indeed the FRB or any of our major planning agencies. It is used to refer to any change in our system, any recognition of what our system is, and foreigners. This weird use of the term is anti-intel· lectual down to its shoe-tops—and is a continuing insult to the tens of thousands of highly intelligent and highly skilled managers of this and that, without whose planning efforts (as an example) the presses, the newsprint, and the whole logistics supporting the dissemination of this abuse would be impossible. Why? Why this nastiness?

In our technological and organizational set-up, planning is thinking. Proposing one plan or another, differing as to objectives and techniques—all this will be recognized as part of thinking by all who have indulged. The anti-planners are anti-thinkers, or vice versa, because and to the extent that planning involves central, official, legal authority. For them, planning by non-Federal financial, industrial and even governmental units is either all right or it doesn't exist, depending on the mood. But the slightest increase in Federal planning activity is, each time, the beginning of the end. Mere mention of existing Federal planning powers—especially in a conversational tone—is nerve-wracking, in bad taste, and may ruin the whole day. This, and fiscal irresponsibility, have replaced Roosevelt-hating for those who would rather not be bothered with the major portion of the twentieth century.

The serious impulse of the anti-planners is that planning should be carried out by and largely for the benefit of "private" financial and industrial institutions, not by the

Federal government or for the benefit of the general democratic citizenry. But their problem is that separate institutional plans need to be integrated on a national level. They
have no solution to this problem beyond military spending
(neither had the Kennedy administration, for that matter,
during the first year or so in power). I guess they are bothered by this very dangerous deficiency in the system they
run, but they are not willing to reveal their concern in
public. Also, they apparently believe they can survive a
while longer without facing up. Perhaps.

On the less serious ideological side, the opposite of
planning—the pedestal of the anti-planners—is our old
palsied friend, The Free Market, *requiescat in pace*. The
difference between the ideal of the Free Market in the nineteenth and in the twentieth centuries is the difference between being unable to think effectively about something
and being unwilling to do so. If by "market" one always
meant to refer to an area of activity not subject to central
control of any kind (including that of a dominant buyer
or seller), or one that did not require articulation, by means
of conscious control, with some other area of activity—
then we could all live with it, planners and anti-planners
alike. Reinhold Niebuhr, who is not an anti-planner, has
cautioned that "we must not plan too far down the line." In
a discussion sponsored by the Fund for the Republic, another theologian, Father John Courtney Murray, said:
"What I am against is some dream or image of the world
or the country as it ought to be which we will now fulfill
by appropriate steps." I think we can all agree. That is bad
thinking, bad planning, and it is unnecessary. What we
need is good thinking, good planning—and to face up to the
necessities (and opportunities) of the organized society.

It is not a question, in the modern world, of planning or not planning. It is only a question of who does it, and how well. And for whom. And how soon.

One final note on planning—and the maladroit ideology of the anti-planners. It is a disturbing sign of the intellectual bankruptcy of business leadership in America that it has now deviously reversed its historical allegiance and has raised Jefferson above Hamilton in its affections. What mainly recommends Jefferson to the leaders of American business is his certified irrelevance to modern conditions. Hamilton, however, "was a convinced and active economic planner," says George Soule. Since in his day it made little difference whether the secure class or the government of the secure class did the planning, he was not a government-hater. No need to be. It is another revealing irony of American history that Hamilton, the conservative, is the more "liberal" of the two and is in fact a prophet of modern economic measures, whereas Jefferson, the revolutionary, is currently used to justify reactionary policies as he was formerly used to buttress the Communist line.

This book is not "about" technology, but it does centrally concern itself with the effects of technology on the property-and-power system. "The advance of science has for many years been undermining the two pillars of our economy—property and work," says Gerard Piel, publisher of the *Scientific American,* in his pamphlet, "Consumers of Abundance." Technical training is becoming the primary productive asset, not things of any kind; and if you think of "work" in its historical meaning from right after the Garden of Eden until yesterday, it is disappearing in this country. "Compared with the day's work that confronts most of mankind every morning, most American citizens are not engaged in work at all." Most of us have to go to a job in the morning—but that is not the same thing as work, although it may well be worse than work in many ways.

What is technology? It is just brains. We have reached a point in history where the noodle has finally come into its own. It now counts for more than force—indeed, effective force is now entirely dependent upon it. But it is not one man's brains. Veblen defined it this way: "It is a joint stock of technical knowledge and workmanlike habits, without the use of which the existing material wealth of the civilised nations would not be wealth." Technology is a social effort, the institutionalized consciousness of the observable and experienced world. It has rationalized and organized the life-process of learning: thinking and acting in conjunction, to a purpose. I find it very gratifying that this should turn out to be one of the greatest forces in the world—one that the most powerful organizations struggle to contain, and cannot contain at their discretion. It is easier for a governing force to control a body it needs than a mind it needs.

The more recent wonders of technology are discussed currently under the heading of "automation." This word has taken on a newspaper-meaning of the push-button factory and consequent unemployment. In fact, if the term is taken even to stand for no more than a part of the promise-and-threat of modern know-how and can-do, it portends a great deal more than that.

Peter F. Drucker, one of our leading managerialists, is very penetrating on this question in his 1957 book, *America's Next Twenty Years*. In his conception, automation is not just "the use of machines to run machines." It is a "methodology," more social than mechanical, and of greatest concern to the managers: "increase both in the numbers of managers and the demands made on them may well be the largest of all the social impacts of Automation." Because unless the managers can figure out how to move the huge quantities of goods that automation will create, it will turn out to be as great a threat to them—and their system—as to the production workers. Automation is a non-stoppable process from raw material to consumer. The commitment to automation makes it immeasurably more difficult to curtail production for the standard price-and-profit reasons. So there must be assured markets—otherwise the investment is unwarranted. It is being made anyway, in part, because the savings in direct labor-cost and consequent independence from the unions is all but irresistible. This builds a terrible problem for the future, however—what to do with the goods?

Automation strikes at the most vulnerable aspect of the Paper Economy—the preference for paper over things. And it also reveals another great structural weakness, the lack of organization among firms and sectors of industry on any but a primitive buy-sell basis, which makes price more important than product, and inventory the greatest danger to businesslike behavior.

> Automation is not technocracy under another name and . . . the push-button factory is not its symbol. Automation is not gadgeteering, it is not even engineering; it is a concept of the structure and order of economic life, the design of its basic patterns integrated into a harmonious, balanced, and organic whole.

Now some people may object to the quantum of managerial mystique in this prose-poem by Mr. Drucker, but I like it because it indicates the underlying audacity of automation. It will not spend itself until society is nicely organized into one well-meshed, producing-consuming unit. It is *not* a new way of making money—quite the contrary, it is the *best* way of making goods. And I just will not bother to suppress my glee at the pain and difficulty this will occasion our dominant production-curtailers and other pro-price saboteurs.

It also carries forward irresistibly the managerial revolution and its instrument, the New Class. "Automation requires trained and educated people in unprecedented numbers." This is another basic problem presented to our society by the opportunities of automation. Noting that a college education is becoming, post–World War II, the kind of usual or necessary thing that a high school education became after World War I, Mr. Drucker reviews the dreary story of higher education in the United States. The salary level must be raised—"doubling it will barely be adequate." Besides, "large companies in particular will have to become educational institutions. . . ." The basis of the financial crisis in higher education, one could have guessed, is "lack of planning."

A word about Russia. *Automation is the Soviet Union's secret weapon.* Whatever is wrong with that society, it does not have our problem of being unable to accept technology and its imperatives. It is willing both to produce goods to its capacity and to train its people to carry out this production. That is power—the primary power of the modern age. The Communist Party is not in business to make money.

In this book I have repeatedly referred to our unused industrial capacity, the great scandal of the Paper Economy.

I never got over the New Deal's curtailment of farm production at a time when there were hungry people in the country. I will never forgive Henry Wallace, who will remain in my mind as a pig-murderer, harsh as that may seem.

Early in 1961 around the Inaugural period (a quarter-century after the pig-murders) I had a chat with one of the incoming officials of the new administration, an experienced businessman. In the course of complaining about unused capacity, I made some reference to the lack of candor of the steel industry leaders, who had just announced that capacity figures would no longer be published. This gentleman asked me what I meant by unused capacity and I told him—*un*used capacity. He then said that if he understood me, that was not very important—the important figures were comparative production of the current and most recent years. This view had the virtue of being simple, if indefensible. At his press conference of July 6, 1960, President Eisenhower abandoned this particular virtue in presenting his own indefensible ideas on unused steel capacity:

> Now, the one thing on which they must be predicting this recession is the fact that steel is operating on the order of 50 per cent.

> Now, there are two things to remember. One, that such a tremendous capacity was—productive capacity of steel—was built in the few years in the past that now the 50 per cent activity is something on the order of 75 (per cent) some very few years back. And possibly there is a reserve capacity that is a very good thing.

> And you would not expect it to operate at 100 per cent all the time, because then you would have to build some more and then you would still have a low percentage or a lower percentage.

If our leaders insist on competing with an earlier, friendlier portion of the twentieth century, rather than the current chapter which includes an admittedly unfortunate amount of Communist growth, then we are finished—it is the same thing as surrender and should be called by its proper name.

The rear-guarding refusal to face up to this biggest of all our problems is not at all new, although it does have a terribly new and frightening aspect in the current Soviet-American conjunction. On October 25, 1929, the day after Black Thursday, President Hoover stated: "The fundamental business of the country—that is, the production and distribution of goods and services—is on a sound and prosperous basis." If that had been the fundamental business of the country, he would have been correct. But the business of America is to make a profit, not to produce and distribute goods and services.

Just how much under-production we typically experience is arguable and, when argued, quickly degenerates into a technical discussion. During the 1960 campaign, for instance, the Democratic Advisory Council and Leon Keyserling insisted on a short-fall during 1953-59 of $175-200 billion of production, and the Republicans countered with statistical juggling and undignified arguments about "growthmanship." I am not a research team and so cannot contribute fresh statistics to the contention. But note the following considerations, which do not rely on fresh statistics: 1) the immense promise of unleashed technology is not in dispute; 2) we know what we did during the War; 3) the meaning of our frequent recessions is only too obvious; and 4) the discrete examples of unemployment of men and machines are too numerous and too definite either to be ignored or to be taken as exceptions.

The most obvious and widely discussed example is steel. Operations at 75 per cent are considered "normal," and the steel industry would have been pleased most of the last few years to rise to this low level. But the steel executives fight with great determination to "raise productivity" —they literally lust after all technical innovations. For example, the use of oxygen, which has increased output of open-hearth furnaces 20 per cent to 100 per cent; and in 1961, the steel-makers got excited about using fuel oil and natural gas to increase the production of their blast furnaces. And on and on. But to what avail? *They replace existing facilities which have never been used to full capacity with new and better installations which also will never be used fully to make steel.* Having taken care of their standards of living, the steel executives no longer even care primarily about "profit" as such. Of course, they want a nice-looking balance sheet. Who doesn't? But what really motivates them is that *their* company—with which their lives are identified—possess the best up-to-date factories and be a well-run organization. They are not motivated to produce steel: that is inventory, and it can ruin you. They want to *own* the best facilities; but to *use* them is to court disaster. They cannot use them fully without assurances of institutional survival forthcoming from the outside world— meaning, in the absence of a seller's market, the government. To produce steel fully they would have to surrender power to the government (or to buyers) just as the individuals making up the organization surrendered *their* power of survival to create the organization in the first place. They are not about to do this voluntarily: it feels too much like suicide. (Notice, moreover, that as the pace of technology quickens, this whole insane game of building factories which will never be used is also played at a heightened pace.)

What is true of steel is true of many other industries. Also, steel is too "pure" an example—because you don't reach the question of the *purpose* of the product. The steel that could be and is not produced could be and is not used by a lot of people, without getting into the-what-for-which it might be used. A good "un-pure" example would be the automotive industry, which produces more cars than we need, and makes them to last not so long as we need them. For me, the following is a truly breathtaking statistic: in 1960 the American people *junked* 4,340,873 automobiles. Meanwhile, the air becomes more and more unbreathable; and traffic in a major American city seems to have been devised mostly to test the credulity of the inhabitants. The automotive industry doesn't *have* to do this to us—it is capable of other things. (GM could make a great deal of almost anything we decided we needed or wanted—it has the *capacity*, roundly considered: it could, for example, make enough decent buses to carry our migrant farm workers to and from their various enslavements—and enough trucks to deliver our farm surplus to their dinner tables.) Notice the following from the *New York Times* obituary of Charles E. Wilson, former head of General Motors:

> Mobilizing G.M. for war, Mr. Wilson supervised the production of about one-fourth of all the tanks, armored cars and airplane engines built in the United States; almost half the machine guns and carbines, two-thirds of the heavy trucks and thousands of carrier aircraft as well as three-fourths of the Diesel horsepower used by the Navy.

The wonders of war—what Veblen called "this diligent pursuit of disaster." World War II was our most important national experience—indeed, I would nominate it for the most creative mass act in the history of the human race. That was when industrial technology came into its own: immense purposive production, organized on a mass scale—and superbly, from the initial meeting of man and machine with matter, to delivery of the product to the ultimate consumer. And no paper stood in the way, at any stage of the process, including the free delivery. Magnificent. And utterly mad. (Of course, all wars are eminently reasonable—even clearly necessary—the day before the fighting begins. Looked at in this realistic fashion, there isn't much to discuss except the details of the fighting. So we won't look at it that way.)

Referring back to Thurman Arnold's theory of the *sub rosa*, we may say that war is the most important illegal institution in our society. Now by "illegal" I don't mean it should be put in jail: I mean it contradicts our premises and professions, and we don't like to admit it exists or that we need it. But in fact we couldn't possibly get along without it. It is so essential that, not having a real war to fight, we have invented a make-believe one so that we do not have to attempt the impossible and forego the benefit of it. Why? Because war is artificial demand, within the terms of the Paper Economy, and the only such that does not raise any political issues. The essential aspect of this artificial demand is that the *product* does nobody any good —only the *process* is beneficial: *war, and only war, solves the problem of inventory.* In the past, it was expected that resource devoted to war would be recouped by plunder in the event of victory. It was a speculative business venture, financed by daring entrepreneurs, with the price of the goods to be collected after effective delivery. Modern war is no such rational thing. The goods are given away. Payment for them would ruin the recipient: *vide*, German reparations after World War I. Further, one of the substantial but less noticed advantages of war is the opportunity after "victory" to give away more goods in order to rehabilitate the customer.

If instead of war production an equivalent quantity of useful goods were produced and distributed to any living human being who could use them, what would happen? First, the government, which would have to "finance" the giveaway, would end up with a number of unspeakable bookkeeping entries. More important, all other bookkeeping entries in the nation—or engraved paper representing same—would be made to look ridiculous. Such full and purposeful production would make a mockery of the Paper Economy. (And not a moment too soon.)

I am talking about the creation of real things which would not otherwise be created. To do this you have to "steal" the value of existing paper in order to create more things than that paper allows for: as if there were only so much "value" available or permissible, and one had to choose between Paper and Thing for its manifestation. The Federal government "stole" some paper one way and another from 1940 through 1944—physical output increased 57 per cent. At the end of 1944, the Navy had 46,000 ships, not counting little ones—thirty-two times its 1939 size. In three wartime years, we produced 44 million tons of merchant shipping, four times as much as we started with. From the middle of 1940 through 1943, $62 billion of war facilities were built, something less than half being directly financed by the government. And 96,359 planes in 1944— 16,048 of them heavy bombers. While this was going on, production of consumer goods increased during each year of the War—from $122 billion to $145 billion in the period 1940 to 1945. And there you have the amazing story. The most revealing one that can be told about this nation of ours, and its nutty economy.

Now, a further word or two about organization—also called "bureaucracy."

The main thing is that we are stuck with it. The modern world is not possible without it. So it is not a sufficient position just to be against it. We are so backward in this country that one will still very frequently surprise and anger conversants by assuming that "bureaucracy" was not invented by FDR, and is not limited to Washington, D.C.

The lack of realism in this matter could not be more crucially serious. Back in the thirties, Arnold said: "The use of the individualistic ideal to justify dictatorial business institutions is also one of the greatest obstacles to considering the real problems of freedom of the individual." As long as the autocratic power remains, and its existence denied or hidden behind irrelevant images of Private Property or analogies to individuals, not all of the vice presidents in charge of human relations (ugh!) or the tomes on human engineering (ditto) will help to preserve any of the individual freedom for the preservation of which we daily risk blowing up the planet.

We most urgently require two things—a higher order of organization, and a better running criticism of it. The first is inevitable because of the imperatives of technology, and desirable in order to avail ourselves of the benefits of it: it will come about, but exclusively under military jurisdiction, if the issue is not made active within the arena of domestic civilian politics. Paper will not give us the superior articulation between organizations we need to ensure full and purposeful production. We need this so much that, in the first instance, it is not important who accomplishes it—anything would be better than the current military trend, and the consequent irresponsibility of our industrial leaders who seem satisfied to slip into the cozy, profitable role of military suppliers. Let them take over the civilian government and at least *share* the responsibility of government with the military—if *that* is the direction they insist on taking, and we persist in allowing them to take.

As to our other great need, criticism should lead to bureaucratic savvy: in effect, we need some bureaucracy doctors. For the benefit of the organizations *and* to preserve or develop (and, let's hope, to expand) the freedom of the individual in or under them. We need not just the management consultant firms of today, although they have the practical experience to date; but as Arnold put it, "a science of the diagnosis of maladjusted organizations in an age where organizations have replaced individuals as units." As an example of the doctoring of sick organizations as practiced in his day, Arnold refers to corporate reorganizations —bankruptcies—of which there were many during the thirties. It is the humorous highlight of his book. He describes corporate reorganization as a ritual of sale for debt, on the one hand, and on the other as a struggle for political control of an existing organization. In the paper world, a ritual; in the existential world, a political struggle. He sums up the phenomenon deliciously as follows:

A corporate reorganization is a combination of a municipal election, a historical pageant, an anti-vice crusade, a graduate school seminar, a judicial proceeding, and a series of horse trades, all rolled into one—thoroughly buttered with learning and frosted with distinguished names. Here the union of law and economics is celebrated by one of the wildest ideological orgies in intellectual history.

Perhaps nowhere else do greed and piety lock arms so lovingly. It is something of a testament to human fortitude that the organization at all survives the ritualistic reshuffling of its paper wardrobe under these circumstances.

Wherever there is power over people, the people under it are entitled to have a political relation to it.

As far as people are concerned, the essence of the matter is power. Any and all ideas about property are subservient to that proposition. There is no other proper context for the discussion of big "F" freedom.

Therefore, I propose setting up a Power Review Commission—at least in our heads, if not as a functioning institution in fact. (For those who haven't noticed, this is not a book of practical political suggestions. It is, rather, a book devoted to demonstrating that politics is possible, necessary, etc.—that political suggestions are in order. I may write another book—filled, perhaps, with diagrams.)

Everybody is concerned about the fate of the individual, his liberty and freedom, in a society of big organizations. The danger comes from power overwhelmingly larger and greater than the individual's potential force of assertion. The whole justification for the historical institution of private property, as idealized by Jefferson *et al,* was to ensure the individual's liberty vis-à-vis the state, because at that time it was thought that only the state—and perhaps the church—were great threatening powers. Which suggests the first function of the Power Review Commission, namely, to identify *existing* power centers. It would be convenient if the individual were always threatened by the same enemy—especially if that enemy remained a nightmare-image firmly rooted in the seventeenth or eighteenth centuries. But if we are really concerned about the fate of the individual's liberties, that just will not do: ancient nightmares are not frightening enough. There are also current facts to be considered.

The Power Review Commission should undertake to identify existing power centers wheresoever throughout American society, and then periodically to review the exercise of these powers by the stewards thereof. This would necessarily require acceptance of the idea that the evil is not power itself but the exercise of power in particular ways and instances (and whether the power is necessary, and necessary for what purposes). It would also assume that governmental power is not the only power, or the only power to be feared, being concerned as we are with the liberty of the individual in his varying social roles. As Berle has said, what we are looking for is a means of controlling power—power over power.

I don't know whether the truth will make us free, but it can certainly make us more noble in our degradation. And it may do much more than that. It may finally disgust us with the garish irresponsibility of our institutional elites. Why, do you think, have our corporate leaders and their lobbyists risen in arms against the suggested price review bill? How could they dare to suggest that the public which pays the price-tax which they demand is not even entitled to know the considerations leading to a price rise? This is an unconscionable abuse of power, and somebody ought to be on the job day-by-day to identify and elaborate it as such.

You cannot prescribe for, you cannot even discuss freedom meaningfully, unless you first identify and analyze the locus of power. And how much of it can be made responsible—that is, responsive to something other than itself. There is nothing to be free from except arbitrary exercise of power and (or by) unwarranted power-concentrations.

One of the things our fancy (or fanciful) Commission could do, for example, would be to explore the rigid assumption that the industrial army must be led autocratically. I suspect that it is just not true that industry could not be organized more democratically: directors could be elected by the relevant constituencies, administrators could be changed, as they are in Washington. If democracy works and has any meaning in the state's sphere, it could work as well in industry. The Commission could lead attacks on *unnecessary* power, on administrators who *misuse* their power, and all in all it could help individuals to feel like individuals—not utterly aimless, not merely powerless automatons. You can't do away with the Chase Manhattan Bank, but you certainly can throw an occasional intellectual rock through its vulnerable windows.

Let us begin with the simple facts of the matter. What are our resources, what are our needs, what is being done about them, and who is doing it? What we want is adequate authoritative information. There has been so much fabrication and heated irrelevance that we can reasonably expect great advantage from just that—the Simple Truth.

This early stage in our adjustment to the modern world would include a price review bill (the example sticks in my craw)—to get public disclosure of the underlying factors whenever prices in an important industry are changed significantly. Just the facts. The elements of a kind of planning-statement agency already exist in the government and among private groups. This first primitive organization might be handled by some sort of collegium consisting of representatives of these various groups. The Power Review Commission, being the central bank of our future intellectual concern, should be as rich a bank of reputations as possible. Proposals could be made suggesting necessary action by governmental or private groups which were just proposals, with no power whatsoever behind them.

I am thinking initially of a Power Review Commission which does not take on the role of policeman—because, of course, that would right off give too much power to the Power Review Commission itself. Whether or not effective power were required could then become subject to political decision—regarding what agency, private, public or whatever, was to carry out the required control activity. Most often the type of job to be done would suggest the type of agency to do it. A tremendous amount could be accomplished simply by this truth-telling procedure. It would be based on nothing more elaborate or dictatorial than that the truth be told and made clear to the public. If that is collectivism, then I think we ought to have a lot more of it.

The beauty of the Simple Truth in these circumstances is that the individual *does* have the power to do something about it, namely, he can find out what it is and state it in a clear, loud voice. Jefferson told us to be vigilant, but there is no point in being vigilant about the nineteenth century. He suggested vigilance because there was in his time no automatic mechanism to ensure liberty. There still is none. We are in such circumstance that our modern vigilance can begin with simple awareness of where the power is and what its nature is. The idea that power exists only in the state and it is always bad there, and that either it does not exist in non-state institutions or it is always good there (or both, since our business leaders are nothing if not intellectually greedy), is a calculated deceit, turns our vigilance into hysteria, and misdirects most of our political effort.

Liberty is something people want or else they don't get it. And liberty is *not* the absence of power—either in oneself or in others. Liberty is a special kind of control over power. That is all liberty or freedom ever could have been—a kind of power over power. Otherwise liberty and freedom must be equated with weakness (it certainly is often confused with it), and I am prepared to say that is absurd.

I think we will also be amazed at the wonders that can be accomplished by simple, direct, honest intelligence applied to national problems, even if only descriptively. It will certainly have a marvelous effect on the whole cultural atmosphere, and that in itself is a great deal. This being so; even the non-political intellectuals should get behind this effort to comprehend the power structure of our society.

The truth is always good—but for us now it is also a real and immediate opportunity. All that restrains our future are ancient ideas, irrelevant dogma and the deadening exclusionary effect of existing political synthesis—the jealousy of existing power. That is the greatest currently observable problem, the jealousy primarily of private corporate power vis-à-vis the other, elected government.

16

POLITICS AND POWER

THE REGULAR OBJECTION to further rationalizing the organization of the economy derives from the ideal of Freedom. In the newspapers, American freedom is the one concept that is always understood without any explanation. Elsewhere, freedom (of whatever nationality) is one of the most sensitive and difficult ideas with which humanity concerns itself.

The cowboy is free—and that's why we love Westerns. But the cowboy, an inveterate nature-lover, is mostly free *from*—from the big city and indeed all forms of cluttered civilization (except an essential link, the gun). As a relief from the problems of civilization, cowboy-freedom is much to be recommended. As a definition of freedom to be used in civilized living, it is a dangerous fantasy. Unfortunately, it is so used, widely and pervasively, on and off the screen.

It is a concept of cowboy-freedom that leads us into our deepest national error, the confounding of public and private, and the consequent misstatement of most genuine issues of freedom of the individual involved in the politics and power of our social order. All power contains an awful potential for un-freedom. It is a function of politics to so deal with power—all power and any power—as to limit and reduce this potential. That is, on one side that is the function of politics—the side of those individuals genuinely interested in their freedoms. On the other side, politics is the defense of existing power concentrations by the current power-wielders.

The American property system is a technique for distributing power. The road to power and the arena of power is politics. I would say that our most active political life in this country now goes on in and between the great centers of corporate power: that is where our political energy as a people has gone. And that is why conventionally defined politics is so often flaccid, so denuded of vitality and interest: because the power lies elsewhere.

This issue of freedom—or "the problem of the individual" in a mass organized society—is not dealt with adequately by reliance on a steadfast opposition to Bigness. Especially that noble eighteenth-century opposition to central public government. The consequence of unduly limiting the role of government in a society like ours is that more and more of its functions are exercised by private centers of power, or inherited by the military. No, big government is required to make the corporate system work;

and beyond that, to keep it decent. In this whole ancient anti-state attitude there is today hidden, but only half-hidden, a contempt for and disbelief in the forms of political democracy. Power in a government controlled by voters is more to be deplored, under this view, than power in a corporate system which is not so controlled, only because of this underlying contempt for democracy.

The problem of the individual should not be confused with the problem of the corporate system, because we have already made our commitment to the latter: the very size of the population is based on the technology the corporations administer. What is so puzzling about our situation is that, having made this great sacrifice, we do not insist on getting anything like the full benefit out of it. That benefit —meaning material security, an acceptable standard of living, and sufficient leisure—would in itself go a long way towards solving "the problem of the individual." It is certainly one thing to "solve" that problem now, and quite another to tackle it with the benefit established. It also should be fairly obvious to all freedom-lovers that if freedom is defined as non-interference by the government in standard-of-living and other welfare matters, freedom may well become a very unpopular idea.

The first issue is that industry produce all the goods that it is capable of producing and that these be distributed to people who can use them—both here and abroad. This cannot be done without a more rational organization of the entire industrial set-up, especially in its relation to governmental authority. Here, the more severe difficulty is our attitude toward the paper balloon. We must indulge a more purposive manipulation of the balloon. It is our money/paper religion that is sapping our strength: we will have to put ourselves into the hands of the heretics, who will lead us out of the paper wilderness. This is not as painful as it sounds, once it is realized that we are about to re-enter the Garden of Eden—that there really is enough to go around for everybody. Moreover, the currently annointed need not worry about their sons: in our new world, as the indiscreet senator promised, everybody will go to Harvard.

Not only will the problem of the individual be approached in a fresh context once we allow our technology to bless us, but the opposite face of the problem—that of tyranny, the abuse of power—will also be newly approached. Understand that the largest motive behind the great abuses of power which history records for us was ubiquitously the unfair allocation of scarce resources. People simply will not fight and claw with the same animal passion over the issue of who is going to stroll majestically through the automated system, which is turning out houses or personal helicopters, as they did about who is going to end up "owning" all the American oil. Why must we frighten ourselves by imagining Cesare Borgia in Eden?— he would expire of boredom. The *caudillo* and the Bonapartist manipulate a population by deciding whose greed is to be satisfied and whose is not, there being a paucity of goodies available. (We all count on this kind of "softening" in Russia—why not here in the United States as well?) As the standard of living and the security of individuals rises, we will be "arming" the people against their rulers, in spiritual effect—just as if the Czar had distributed machine guns at the direction of Lenin.

Power which by its nature and circumstance can be abused probably will be abused; but the opportunities for the abuse of power result from the lack of counter-force.

The reason tyrants have been able to dominate whole populations is that these populations were ignorant, they lived on a level of bare subsistence, they became embittered about life and could not enjoy it nor express their native human vitality. Because they were inferior, they felt inferior, and submitted to their rulers. And throughout history those who have not felt inferior have not submitted quite so much, or quite so easily.

The great lesson for us to learn is that the road to salvation does not lie through powerlessness. Power is a dangerous human invention, no question; so also is the powerful attitude of mind toward the universe which has unleashed modern technology. Having accepted the one, we are stuck with the other.

In America, don't look for things to be called by their right names. Our conventional distinction between "private" and "public"—whether of property, power or politics—is intellectually nothing but high comedy. It derives from the fact that vital uncultivated people are so interested in *doing*, that they jettison even minimum respectability regarding the depiction of *what* they are doing. It just isn't important enough to them. In a society ruled under the proposition that money is more real than the things it buys, it would be expecting too much for the important powers, interests, and circumstances to travel the streets undisguised. But there is a serious danger in all this gay fabrication. Politics, for example: after a while, you don't just fail to tell the truth (that's an ordinary part of the game): you lose the capacity to recognize it (and that is an essential cultural failure).

The worst part of this is our advertising culture, paid

for by business and inextricably wedded to the paper-happy
giants. In clucking our tongues about billboards and published junk and other details, we sometimes overlook the
larger horror—that advertising and the consumption-values
it peddles are not distinct from the mass culture they sustain: the ads and the stories and the reportage in, say, *The
Ladies' Home Journal,* are a single, passably coherent culture: a single, internally consistent distortion.

In the secular society (and especially this early exis-
tentialist version) ideology is necessary to rulership—as
necessary as guns. Now while it is quite true that the worst
thing that has happened in this excessively secular century
of ours has been the use of guns to enforce rigid ideology,
the uses of ideology (and the means of enforcing it) are not
to be understood solely by reference to this circumstance.
In America, for example, our consumer-oriented groupism
and accompanying ideological conformity—sustained both
by mass culture and the emotional conditions of mass life—
go a considerable distance toward achieving effects similar
to state-enforced ideology in Russia. It is not that, unlike
the Communists, we refrain from manipulating and exploiting the social mind, but that we do so without the
special aid of guns and also without any serious purpose
in view (the two may be causally connected). What we
have here seems to be something that might be called "voluntary totalitarianism." (Freedom that people do not care
to utilize is not really freedom: it is imperfect organization.
Certainly someone will come along and view it that way.)
C. Wright Mills shrewdly notes: "The 18th century idea
of the public of public opinion parallels the economic idea
of the market of the free economy." Just as we have not
progressed far enough in candor and insight to substitute a

more relevant notion than that of the free market, so also we have done poorly in our occasional efforts to understand the how and the why of the mass mind. Meanwhile we are becoming so deeply ideologized that the issue of the necessity of guns has not had to be met.

Scholars have investigated and noted the gnarled historical roots of specific totalitarianisms. Well enough. But it can be argued that generic totalitarianism originates in the future, not in the past. In the technological future. What science is doing—and clearly before we are ready for it—is to transform traditional social existence into a permanent administered social revolution. The underlying imperative-to-happen here is so great that guns are not a necessity; they are merely a convenience to speed up the process.

"To suggest that we canvass public wants to see where happiness can be improved by more and better services has a sharply radical tone. Even public services to avoid disorder must be defended. By contrast, the man who devises a nostrum for a non-existent need and then successfully promotes both remains one of nature's noblemen," says John Kenneth Galbraith, less bitterly than sadly, in *The Affluent Society*. This horribly true proposition is the quintessence of his book which, although many people found it shocking, was written with at least equal quantities of sweetness and light. His point was to demonstrate that resources are not adequately allocated without conscious direction; that consumer demands are created, they don't just happen; all with the result that we have "private opulence and public squalor"—because there is paper-profit to the one and indifference to the other. In order to make his point as effectively as possible, he gave in to his own considerable rhetorical talent and assumed not merely the actual possibility of abundance, which is indisputable, but the actual existence throughout most of society of what he chose to call "affluence," which certainly can be disputed. But he achieved his rhetorical purpose, and no economist since Keynes has equalled his influence.

For example, he influenced John F. Gordon, president of General Motors, to influence the Company's staff of speech-writers to attack the Galbraith thesis early in 1961 in a speech delivered by Mr. Gordon before the Society of Automotive Engineers in Detroit. It was suggested in this educational endeavor (as reported in the *New York Times* for January 12, 1961) that people with a word or two against fins and annual model changes are "lay evangelists," "exponents of a new austerity," "hair-shirt philosophers," etc., who "would have us believe that the United States is sacrificing social benefits for material indulgence," etc.

> We must demonstrate to the world [Mr. Gordon declared] that the free enterprise system can be more creative than any other—not only that it can create more and better material goods and services, but that it also can create the purchasing power to absorb this output at the same time producing as a by-product more social goods and services than any other economic system.

That's social goods "as a by-product," friends. *As a by-product.*

This is the strong, authoritative voice of illegitimate government in the United States—the private government that does not care what it produces so long as it creates a favored paper-position for itself by producing it. And be assured that it will not abandon a paper-successful formula until forced to do so by paper-considerations. Or some pressure from outside the paper system.

There is not much to say for big business from a cultural point of view. But one's feeling about this, and also the animus generated by contemplating all the lost opportunities, should not lead one astray. Private government has created our productive society, with public government as a decidedly junior partner. If the corporate and financial powers had been legitimate, if we had known what they were doing to the traditional property system, we might very well not have allowed them to do it so effectively. So something must be said for autocratic ruthlessness in carrying out great historical revolutions. (But not too much.)

In any event, we have gone about as far as we can with our frightening heritage of mindlessness. What happened was something like this: while the intellectuals and other ideologists on all sides were word-locked in the capitalist/socialist debate, the non-owning and non-theorizing managers were effecting the revolution which created our present system. This group was able to come to power and accomplish its task because the social mind was elsewhere, and didn't notice them for what they were. Unfortunately, the managers thus came to be terribly dependent on this convenient mindlessness. Which is why they try so hard to perpetuate it. But the system they created cannot be run: a) by themselves, without sharing power; and b) mindlessly. There must be ideology; and it will be an increasingly awful one if our business rulers persist in their devotion to the early mindlessness to which, it is true, they owe a great deal.

It may be that we are about to abandon our historic mindlessness. The current collapse of traditional economic, legal and political theory affords us the greatest possible opportunity to do so. The fact that private property no longer explains anything of importance allows us without embar-

rassment to contemplate creatively the legal disorder encompassing the current disposition of material things. The
unabashed failure of the image of free competitive markets
returns to us one of the great issues of history in a pristine
form—the grand *quid pro quo* of human exchange and relation. The rediscovery of the existence and importance of
private governments gives us a hungered-for chance to spell
out a reasonably descriptive political theory, and to abandon the collage of hypocrisy and appendant nonsense of
democratic formalism. And about time, one might say—
since political buying and selling, the illegal provision of
necessary goods and services, and the forceful creation of
industrial complexes, have characterized our national existence at least for a hundred years, and are a more important
as well as a more interesting set of historical chapters than
the simple succession of administrations in that artificial city
on the Potomac.

Most big property is not private or individually owned
—it is *organizational* property, owned and operated by organizations. If an individual has title to big property, then
that is, we discovered, largely formal—since such big property ends up being handled very much as organizational
property is. Title to paper ensures mostly unequal distribution of consumer goods; it is less and less a controlling feature. And perhaps most important of all, we noticed that
the *things* owned by organizations which own and control
most of the important things are not the major source of
their power. The really important factor about the really
important organizations is the trained people in them. That
is where our look at the current American property system
has brought us. And, in order to get here, we found it neces-

sary to snap and snip more or less continuously at the conventional image of the property system which was discovered to be still a practically effective if intellectually inept misrepresentation. By and large, we found the property idea a useful tool of understanding; but at the end, the tool wore out, and we were left with the central concepts of power and politics.

I have used the term "politics" very broadly (out of necessity it must be redefined for the modern organized world) to refer to the relations among people in groups wherever there is an issue of power. Under this definition, activity can be political and politically significant even (especially?) when there are unwilling and unaware parties to it. To the extent that organized administration replaces received tradition in determining behavior, the term "political" replaces the term "social" or becomes equal to it. (More and more frequently in our world, tradition does not play its customary role but is merely another given element available for *exploitation* by one administration or another: traditions of all kinds are being chewed up in the maw of administration.)

So we have the politics of administration replacing traditional factors such as, for example, the ownership of property. But the profound human emotion of or for ownership does not subside so easily; it reappears without invitation and quite inappropriately in strange places. As an important illustration for our theme, it is investing itself in the job-as-property. We would very much like to *own* our jobs—and also to *own* our position in the society of welfare and other advantage. This point is worth pausing over.

Top corporate executives typically have choice long-term employment contracts as well as many lucrative

"fringe" benefits. The contracts and benefits afford them
substantial security, but they do not amount to "owning"
the job—any more than union seniority and grievance procedures mean the assembly-line worker "owns" his job.
Some of us want and need the security of a sense of ownership so much that we kid ourselves into the belief that we do
indeed own what we need to own. For example, a woman
who needs to feel that she possesses her husband will literally
think and feel a "property right" in him. This happens to be
a property right that the courts recognize; but they have not
come around to accepting much of the ownership quality in
our job tenure.

Eventually they will, however, because insofar as we
move away from private property and are bureaucratized,
we become defined as a society of job-holders—all of us,
from the quarter-million-a-year executive to the subsistence
laborer. In a certain fundamental sense, both are proletarians:
an increasingly comfortable proletarianization is America's
gift to the modern world.

Now we can belong to the job as proletarians, or the
job can belong to us as individuals. This is what could happen: as jobs come more and more to be *owned* by the job-
holder, there will develop an increasingly elaborate
structure of rights and duties with regard to jobs-as-property. A system of *law* will probably develop, just as
happened in the epoch of bourgeois property after the
transcending of feudal forms. Although there is an ironic
twist to the phrase, the new age could be based on proletarian property forms. I think this is a more likely outcome than that the human race should manage to dispense
with the sense of ownership and property entirely—dispense, that is, with identity in depth between self and thing.

Meanwhile, union members are as much concerned with seniority rights as with wage demands, the secretary home-furnishes her office niche, and the medium-level white-collar worker simulates the mercilessly strained quality of belonging by measuring the size and newness of "his" desk against all comers. (Note that many advertisements for new typewriters, postage-meter machines, etc., are directed to the office worker rather than to the boss.) In a decision nicely handed down on Valentine's Day in 1961, the NLRB ruled that a truck driver had been properly dismissed for kissing a dairy company employee "against her will" (she was married, but the Board did not base the decision on this factor). So I think we can look forward in general to a new set of problems on the job—especially as the job becomes a way of passing the time as much as a way of producing the wealth of the world.

As we get away from the self-emphasis of the property idea and the possession need as it concerns *things*, what will take its place? The only area left is the relation to self and others. We will return, in other words, to the primitive mode—before the invention of property—but this time sadder and wiser, as well as better fed, it is hoped, and without emphasizing possessive enslavement of the person. Economics will give way to politics and psychology, the search for power over oneself and others—perhaps for the pure creative joy of it. The capacity for this had better be more fairly distributed than property has been, or we may find ourselves in a bigger mess than before. Anyway, at that point, the human race will have arrived at the age of puberty, and so can start taking notice of itself in a coherent way. Then more and more people can live by the *true* ideology, namely, awareness of one's own experience.

Capitalism was certainly right about one thing—it put motivation into the forefront, it made the human being's emotions that important. That was wonderful—but capitalism had a naive faith in this approach, and we simply do not live in a naive world. Capitalism was the first dynamic effort to make the individual and his powerful mind the center of history—to adjust history to that centrality. But now we have entered a new age. Mind has now become so powerful that it can no longer be left to the wayward fortunes of individuals. It has been institutionalized. But all due fanfare for capitalism—without that, we would never have braved the foreseeing of freedom.

The sense of community, our deepest need, does not begin with self-denial—it begins with an ineluctable desire for something more than simple self-fulfillment. Capitalism set the stage for a new and greater sense of community. What is wrong is that its self-emphasis has lasted too long: it transcends itself poorly.

The measures of democracy are two: 1) effective majority rule or, conversely, the responsiveness of power-centers to major constituencies; and 2) the extent and quality of techniques available to out-of-power groups for communicating new facts and ideas to existing majorities or power-wielders. On the first criterion, it is demonstrable that we have since Roosevelt's death and the end of the War experienced a very serious decline. And on the second measure, we began at such a low level that genuine improvement has come easily, and also has a way to go before rising to significance.

Those who do not believe our democracy is in decline —or may even be insulted by the suggestion—rely on (or are victims of) the pervasive popular meaning of democracy, that is, an absence of obvious tyranny. What autocracy we have, and it is considerable, is so much a part of the system that it is no longer noticed; for the rest, substantial comfort is taken from the Twenty-second Amendment and its sparkling guarantee against monarchy. And behind these considerations lie the most convincing assurance of all: we *must* be a democracy since we obviously have no effective leadership.

In the safekeeping of the early European bourgeoisie fighting strong monarchies, democracy came to be conceived in an absurdly negative fashion. This character was preserved by the later denizens of strong private government deceitfully perverting their predecessors' victory over central government. So democracy has been understood as non-rule by non-leaders. But just as freedom can no longer be conceived (much less preserved) as disorganization, so democracy itself is about finished under the definition of non-rule. Very simply, it makes dictatorship much too attractive, not to say inevitable. Modern society unled is a terrible danger to every member thereof.

Most of the power-centers in America are not subject to political activity, properly denominated; so that both the power and the related politics are called by other names, when they exist, which does nothing for the situation culturally. The greatest such other-political force in the nation is that of the Rear-guarders—the determined activists of concerted non-rule by certified non-leaders. Of these, none was greater than Eisenhower—the almost perfect non-leader, undoubtedly the last of the species, and the end of a magnificent American epoch. Eisenhower was as much of the American farmer's idea of the nineteenth century as we are apt to see in these nervous days. President Kennedy is a leader, in nature and in concept: his problem is that the American political system, lacking a crisis of earthquake proportion, is constructed to prevent leaders, not bring them to the fore and welcome them to their work. What he will do, measuring his demonstrated practicality (existing power) against his assumed ambition (structural changes), will be the most widely discussed political issue through November 1964 at least, even—or perhaps especially—if he does nothing.

Whenever anything happens politically in America, it happens first in the Executive, then in Congress, and when the change has already been effected in fact, the deal is concluded by shaking the dead hand of the Judiciary (until the political deadlock following Roosevelt's death, that is). The key to this impossible system is the middle term, Congress. The business of the Judiciary is to formalize accomplished political facts, and slow or fast it always finally gets down to business; and the Executive can initiate as it will, but always without real structural effect until it has carried the Congress, usually by the lowest possible means. The issue is that Congress of ours—and never more so than today.

While Congress has lost its power to rule affirmatively, which it had in the nineteenth century, it is perhaps exercising the greatest power in its history these days in its role as non-ruler. (Burnham suggested that the primary locus of sovereignty lay with parliaments under capitalism, and shifts to the executive under managerialism.) Congress represents a middle level of power, not the important national elite power, according to the view of C. Wright Mills. He refers to "the semi-organized stalemate of the middle levels of national power," implying that we have checked and balanced ourselves into a form of political paralysis. But the issue is whether Congress represents local interests which are still powerful enough to make themselves felt through the special and peculiar machinery of Congressional elections; or whether this backward force is used and manipulated by true elite groups as part of the over-all rearguard action. It seems to me that Congress as blockade-agent is much too useful to have come about by accident. The basic pattern of checks and balances in our history is not really between the different departments of government, but between the banks, the industrial leaders, and the official government when it is effective. The role of Congress now is to represent business and financial interests, the non-governmental powers, and through this representation to hold down the power of the national executive. (A long time ago, Congress represented the farmers.)

In the public sphere, non-rule by non-leaders; in the private, autocratic baronies. And the effectiveness of public government sabotaged by mediocre personnel ensured by low salary levels. So much so, that in order to get high-level work accomplished the practice has grown of creating non-governmental agencies to handle it: over 350 non-profit corporations, also called "think factories," have been set up in the past decade; along with educational institutions, these absorb $400 million in Defense Department contracts.*

---

* A particularly hypocritical and dangerous aspect of this public/private nonsense is the official attitude toward strikes by government workers: the underlying idea is that all work for public agencies is "essential" and so no strikes can be permitted, whereas the prohibition covers *all* government work, including municipal sports stadia and asphalt plants, but *no* private facilities, including basic industries and advanced technical installations. And always, of course, the no-strike burden falls on the workers, thus defends a status quo, and without supplying adjudicative machinery which is the only feasible substitute for domestic violence.

There are in truth scores of extremely effective measures to ensure the dominance of private autocratic government which have been incorporated into our political system. It is the essence of our system, and there are three big props to it immediately noticeable: 1) the downgrading of all real political activity—"politics is dirty"; 2) the disastrously unrepresentative nature of our basic democratic instrumentality, the Congress; and 3) the deep tradition of exploitation and non-leadership suffered or enjoyed by our privileged, powerful groups. Of these, the first is comic, the second is disgusting, and the third is tragic. The lack of respectable class and elite leadership is the important factor, the truly shameful factor, the ultimate American tragedy.

Politics is dirty, Congress is undemocratic, our class leadership is inept. The Soviet confrontation is bringing on a great domestic crisis. Without a major creative effort, the result is all too clear: nuclear war, a military-industrial dictatorship, or both. Only a few years remain to present this crisis in its true dimension.

Politics is dirty, for one reason, because so many people engaged in it seriously are compelled, by the economics of the situation, to earn an "illegal" living. It is delightfully ironic that basic politics is thus financed exactly the way serious art and intellect are cared for in this nation. Neither is sufficiently commercial to begin with, and so each must pick up extraneous change along the way in order to survive. And obviously it has been the dominance of money-making enterprises that has placed both activities—the crumbiest precinct politics and the most ecstatic symbolic reaching—in the province of theft, illegal or legal, the latter going by the nicer name of charity.

A study made at the University of Michigan showed that more than half of the adults in Wayne County (Detroit) thought politics dirty and dishonest in 1956. But we hardly need surveys and studies to find out what everybody already knows, or soon learns: politics is dirty. As an inverse consequence, all outsiders engaged in it are exceptionally moral, frequently to the point of painful irrelevance. (I am more impressed with the fact that most people are *not* moral, than I am with the fact of potentially how nice things would be if they all were. If morality is nothing but the World-of-the-Could-Be, then it should be understood as a religious exercise and not confused with those directions we give to ourselves when we actually want to do something, and actually have to make a choice among alternatives.)

Politics is dirty, and Congress is undemocratic. The one leads to the other. Congress is supposed to be our basic democratic instrumentality: apart from spiritual effluvia, Congress is the structural reason why we are a democracy, along with a more or less popularly elected Executive.

But Congress—especially the House of Representatives (which is a kicker, since the Senate was planned to be the fraternity of old fuds)—is our most significantly reactionary institution. Which shows how much things have gotten out of hand. The backward quality of Congress is readily apparent; so also are the reasons. It over-represents white farmers, hardly bothers with Southern Negroes at all, and makes a joke of affording fair representation to the 70 per cent of the population which is politically so misguided as to live in cities and suburbs. (The situation is even worse in the state governments, which is why the Rear-guarders always favor leaving problems to the states, which is so much more democratic, you see, than having the Federal Revenooers take a hand.) In a recent Congress, a Representative from San Diego had a constituency of over a million, while a fellow from a rural district in Michigan represented less than 200,000 people. The system of misrepresentation which so shamefully favors the nineteenth-century farmer over the twentieth-century city-dweller is the basis of one-party, no-contest rule in numerous districts —Democratic in the South, Republican in other rural areas.

But the quality of political activity and of the Congress is just a backdrop for—indeed, it is the result of—our leadership. I refer not to heroes, not even to villains, but to class and elite leadership. The people who have the privilege and the power are supposed to run the society—that's part of the deal. When a society has to recruit someone off the street to run things—or allows that someone to recruit himself—it is already in deep trouble. That is confessed incompetence.

Now what about our class and elite leadership? By and large, I would guess that they are a very capable bunch —with limited vision. Leaving the rentiers aside, they know how to do what they do, and they do it energetically: our failure has never been a lack of intelligence or energy. Considering how little tradition sustains them, the performance has a substantial amount of what we might as well go ahead and call dramatic magnificence. But as a cultural enterprise—a nation and a people relying on and utilizing a continuity of culture, class and otherwise—this country is a farce and a failure: it never got off the ground. Probably there was not time—hardly time for us to become a nation before we began participating in the rule of the world. It is easy to be misled by the existence of our dis-

tinguished group of colonials, New England and ante-
bellum Southern culture, isolated giants like Lincoln and
Wilson and Roosevelt, etc. And of course there were
always cultured individuals around, many of them original
and worth-while. But they weren't ruling anything, and
didn't have much to do with those who were: the Adamses
were an early exception. No, the American nation as a
coherent something covering the continent is a recent invention. Until the immigration stopped after World War
I, we were in essence a frontier town—the greatest ever,
to be sure—but hardly a nation: more a gang with a raw
style for exploiting a continent, the elements of which
style had been drawn together hastily (mostly for the
benefit of farmers and conspicuous spenders) from polyglot
European sources. The best that can be said for our current
national culture is that there are a lot of things to eat, and
a lot of distractions for the period when you are not eating
them. This is the creation of big business, both the in-
gestibles and the distractions. It ought to be ashamed of
itself.

We are capable of a great deal more—and many of us
are determined to get it. Given time, I would join in
dreaming the American Dream all over again, this time with
a little more savvy. But time is running out. For the promise
of the Dream to survive—more likely even for the nation
to maintain an area of discretion in its relations with the
rest of the world—we must carry to further completion,
and soon, the domestic social revolution begun with the
establishment of the Standard Oil empire and the building
of the railroads, brought to fruition by Morgan and the
other bankers, and then salvaged and redirected by the
New Deal. Only our class and elite leadership groups can

accomplish this. It is up to them. And it is among the leadership groups that the most vital and fateful struggle for the nation's future is now going on. That's appropriate, because: 1) they have most to lose, the greatest stake; 2) there is no time for anything socially more profound; 3) they have the monopoly of information necessary for decision, and can easily call on all the educated brains in the country. No other group can, in adequate measure. But they have only a few years, at best. Then a major *undirected* crisis, with consequent polarization (the cadres of the Right have already begun). And in the wings, the inevitable-unless: military dictatorship as the response to a series of international failures, and as an alternative to surrender. No civilian administration could either push the button or deal with the area of the former nation thereafter.

Our leadership has been too democratic, in its selection; and for purpose, too much concentrated on the self-protection of money, for themselves and even more for the second-level cadres from which they rose. The first is not so terrible, but the second is downright ridiculous. They misconceive their leadership function: they are leading a great nation, not a couple of million guys-on-the-grab. The constituencies have been improperly identified. Also, to concentrate so much on money, while there is no scarcity of the things money buys, is either: 1) incredibly piggish; 2) based on a disastrous misunderstanding of what money is; or 3) as I have argued, derived from an historical backwardness which resists the finer meshing of our two spheres of government, the so-called public and private. In other words, it is the selfishness of autocratic power—which supports Congress as blockade-agent, for example, instead of directing the use of all of the immense power of the elites to educate-for-necessity the backward constituencies on which the petty chieftains of county-power depend.

Our leadership is too democratic: the trouble has been that the anonymous farm boy *can* become president—of the nation or even, if he's very lucky, of General Motors —and without being educated along the way for leadership of constituencies made up of more than farmers. Well, this has all been said before: leadership is the problem of problems in a democracy. Clearly, one can do nothing more helpful for a democratic polity than to seize every occasion to attack, ridicule, and by any rhetorical device to undermine, the innate and persistent and malevolent tendency of the democracy to demand the world in its own exact image, to envy and isolate superiority wherever discovered, to elevate and adore any home-grown replica. This point is so crucial for the health of a democracy that attack, and again attack, is essential.

Instead, we have a characteristic pandering—the blintz and pizza eaters who run for office in New York City, for example. It is both funny and disgusting that someone with the name of Rockefeller has to cultivate a football-hero slouch, and that his boyish smile—past the age of fifty, yet!—should be his greatest political asset. And scientists are sold to the public because they play catch with their kids in the backyard. One has to have elements of superiority in order to contribute anything as a leader; but our public leaders especially have to lie about it in order to get in a position to do so. All this is a little bit too funny.

Take General Eisenhower, for example. A more beautiful-looking modern soldier no one ever saw: his crisp assurance, his soldierly but humane appearance, were—

in the newsreels from the European Theatre—a warming symbol for most of the nation. (He was a much better military actor than the World Conqueror of the Pacific, for sure.) But then they had to go and say he won the War for us. I don't believe it: when Marshall and Roosevelt dug down and found an untried regular Army man to stand in front of the European troops, they were looking for and came up with a very special item. He was not exceptionally experienced either as a field commander or as a top staff man. But they were looking, imaginatively, for a certain kind of public relations figure. In that, he was one of the greatest. And he looked marvelous as President, too—as American as apple pie. But as a national leader in a complicated and continuing crisis . . . well, we will be paying the price for a long time to come. (The best one-line summary of the General's administration, toward the end after the shock had worn off, was the following report from the *New York Times:* "Augusta, Ga., April 16—President Eisenhower devoted nearly two hours today to studying position papers on the summit conference.")

The General seems really to have believed in what he called "fiscal integrity" (meaning an unwillingness to try very hard or disturb the paper system very much to achieve full production)—it was not just a slogan whispered in his ear by George Humphrey. That is why he bought Mr. Dulles' bargain-basement policy of massive retaliation—and if the Russians need more than the historical leeway that gave them, they deserve to lose. But when you are all done with the story of the stand-still foreign policy, the inept not to say disinterested handling of recessions, and the golfing jokes—the main achievement of the eight Eisenhower years still stands out in shining relief: the New Deal was not repealed. Which means it never will be without a convulsion bigger than an election. Rear-guarding, yes; old-style reaction, no.

The true non-leader leads neither backward nor forward. It was so surprising that it was actually a shock when the General warned against the military-industrial complex and the scientific-technological elite in his farewell address to the history books—until one recollected that he could now afford to notice important matters since no one could any longer accuse him of having to do anything about them.

President Kennedy is not a born non-leader—he is the squirming victim of a system of non-leadership: he has to learn the lesson of non-leadership freshly every day. The significance of our current President is that he will execute and administer within the given conditions, drawing eclectically on the best ideas and talent available. Eisenhower relied on old ideological materials—basically a farm boy's morality—in order to accomplish the rear-guarding purpose of his supporters. President Kennedy is operating under the ideology of executive efficiency and shrewdness, with nothing much else to boost him along. If he fails, we have then experienced the failure of the best, most important, most readily available executive elements in our society in a position and with the desire to use the power available. After him, the executive gold-rush is over. The Kennedy administration is our last chance to avoid a major national ideological crisis, which would necessarily pose the issue of survival of the nation. To live through such a crisis in an international atmosphere structured by Soviet initiative should be frightening to any intelligent ideologist, from whatever side. President Kennedy is shrewd: the point to be determined is whether or not he's shrewd enough. Or more profoundly, whether the development of American society has already, *sub rosa*, achieved what it needs to achieve, and all that is required now is for some vital shrewdness to bring it into the kind of existence which is apparent as well as real. *Has the managerial revolution progressed to the point where a bunch of fast, shrewd managers can make the resulting social order work satisfactorily?*

President Kennedy has an almost unbelievably fortunate background of qualifications for an American leader. If anything, he is over-qualified for the job, having inherited and been trained to an excess of political and other practical savvy. He would appear to have an excellent intellectual endowment, the kind of first-class education that is available only to the wealthy (it is not just a question of being able to afford the tuition at Harvard), a frightening quantity of energy, and so on. I wonder only if he has the imagination, for which all the rest is only preparation; or has it been trained out of him by knowing too much about how too many things are done in our society? He seems potentially as unprejudiced and experimental as FDR (but with more intellect and less genius than our nonpareil of a modern democratic leader). Indeed, he is so clearheadedly unprejudiced that he is rather difficult to understand. He obviously is not a believer in the rags and tatters of New Deal ideology which he uses carefully to get votes. Nor does he seem to be one of those like Senators Humphrey or Douglas, or many of the political intellectuals around him, who are seriously engaged in trying to make the New Deal tradition coherent and up-to-date. He speaks most feelingly of "responsibility"—not the General's fiscal responsibility, but some kind of social or at least executive responsibility. That may be as much of an ideology-for-belief as he has: one would certainly be entitled to deduce so from the character of his administration through the first two years.

With this equipment, acting on a concept of leadership for which he was perhaps overtrained but which happens also to be the best such concept readily permitted by the system, how will he deal with the coming crisis? And perhaps more important, *when* will he begin to deal with it? And what will he say? Is he capable of developing a liberal managerialist ideology which will inspire both the managers and the managed?

It is all up to him. The issues comprising the crisis will have been met and passed, however well or poorly presented to the people, before he leaves office. If he lives.

If it was a military crisis, we would know just what to do. We would do what we did in World War II, what we have always been prepared to do—flip over the ace in the hole, straighten out the world in short order, and get back to being Americans again as quickly as possible. That would be *our* kind of crisis: so much so that a broad stratum of opinion in the country insists, against all evidence, in seeing it in this traditional fashion. But the crisis is very obviously not military: we may be able to deter the Communist nations from a nuclear attack by our military deterrent system, but we cannot deter them from Communism either by that system or by war itself. (This was Dulles' tragic mistake.) To deter Communism requires 1) an alternative to Communism and 2) our great power available and applied to the support of that alternative. This is war, but a new kind of war; it is a social revolutionary war, with only minor military engagements.

As soon as one gets past the military illusion, one is

confronted with an amazing realization: what is called for is to "mobilize" the nation to fight a social war which will go on without interruption for decades, and in which neither the method nor the objective is primarily military. And then the awareness slowly grows: *that means permanent structural changes in our own society*. To "mobilize the nation" for such an engagement means to initiate a domestic social revolution. Or, if you see it as I do, to quicken the pace and intensify the conscious direction of the domestic revolution that we have in fact for some time been undergoing. No wonder jaws fall agape and there is quick retreat to the security of the military illusion: it is required that the most conservative nation in the world devote its great power to leading a world social revolution —beginning at home.

We can stop fighting this war, and we certainly do not have to win it. But note that there is no viable alternative. We can neither stop the world social revolution nor give it a direction by military means: we could blow up the world, ourselves along with it, and thus put an end to the world revolution along with much else besides. But that's all—and that, literally, is not a viable alternative. Of course, we could always surrender—or at least try to. Surrender in this war means to leave the social battlefield of the world to the Communists. The best that could be achieved by this would be increasing isolation and, at the end, engulfment.

The world revolution is simplicity itself to define: the members of the human race have decided that they don't want any longer to live miserably and die young. They are convinced that the means are available to achieve this objective. This is quite a decision: it is, from here on out, the alpha and omega of world politics. We notice it less in this country because it has progressed so far here—because it is in our bones.

The issue between ourselves and the Russians is the direction and character to be given to the development of the world revolution. (And incidentally, we had more to do with starting it than they did.) If the issue were their espousal of the revolution and our resistance to it, we would lose hands down. Their greatest achievement to date has been to peddle this characterization successfully. We have unfortunately assisted them to achieve this advantage, by emphasizing the military aspect of the conflict. But the only military achievement possible in this situation is for one side to keep the other side from resolving the issue by military means. Note that such an achievement is not itself a resolution of the issue.

The main point for us to understand is that the crisis of the world revolution is for us primarily a domestic crisis. The revolution in its technical aspect has progressed so far here that we have been able to indulge ourselves inordinately in misrepresenting its character, and thus postponing our response to its social, organizational, and ideological aspects. We have overplayed the golden opportunity to kid ourselves. The resulting confusion I have called the Paper Economy. This charming, bubble-headed system is certainly good enough for us, we are convinced; but clearly it is not good enough for the rest of the world—and *it* is fairly well convinced of that. Moreover, we cannot lead the world away from Communism by offering it a state of confusion, even though we may have prospered under the Paper Economy and consequently are very fond of it.

The Paper Economy is inadequate in confronting the world revolution both practically and theoretically. Practically, because it does not make available our full productive power for waging the social war for the world—the power that was unleashed in another kind of war in the early forties. Theoretically, because it cannot comprehend this war except in military terms. Notice the close connection between the two, both domestically and in external relations: the Paper Economy survives at all only because of military production—structural and dynamic advantages (rather, necessities) are achieved in this way that would be impermissible in any other way. And the same military motif or ideology which is the best "resolution" we have domestically also dominates our conception of the foreign aspect of the problem. In both spheres, the military gambit can be nothing more than a holding action subject to slow or fast but certainly inevitable attrition. Or disaster: in the world, by nuclear war; at home, by military dictatorship.

Take, for a moment, the example of foreign aid. Properly conceived, it is neither propaganda nor a form of bribery—it is these only when it is a minor adjunct to military policy. It is, simply, the export of revolution, for us as well as for the Russians and Chinese. The material part of foreign aid is easily lost to the pockets of the local elite, or just in the general shuffle, if it is not handled as a part of the revolutionary package. The revolution being exported is mostly the social accommodation to technology; it is not limited to the technical factors alone. Technology can only exist and prosper in a society that is prepared to use and maintain it—to create these conditions, and to restrain the elites from growing fat on the seed-grain, is all part of the package. These factors are mirrored in the personnel of an aid program. What foreign aid requires is not just technicians, any more than we manage here with technicians alone. It requires the export of revolutionary cadres. And these must be conscious as well as capable managerialists: not just smart bankers, because we are not just interested in the security of the loan, so to say. (And certatinly not just the non-profit enthusiasts making up the Peace Corps.) The aiding nation, through its cadres on the scene, must take sides in the internal political struggles of the aided nation. There is no help for it, it must be done. If that is for some reason impossible, then just distribute some food to the hungry people—directly, of course—build a show-dam or two to keep pace with the Communists, and maneuver for the creation of an elite that can be dealt with. Or have the CIA subvert the corrupt or incompetent elite. What else? We are talking about social war—*the permanent administered technological revolution.* Of course, we should be reasonable about all this: it is not essential that we rather than the Communists administer the revolution in *all* areas—any more than in that other kind of war one had to win all the battles on unselected terrain.

(Incidentally, the validity of the perspective I have been presenting does not depend on anyone's, including myself, liking it. That technology-too-soon has brought about the administered revolution for the modern world is no source of satisfaction to me. Managerialism elevates the administrative intellectual, with his vulgar scientism and half-mad functionalism, where capacities of humanity exist only after a place has been found for them in the more important statistical series. I am proud to be an old-fashioned humanist out of the mainstream, and personally go to some lengths to preserve as much antimacassar and overstuffed irrationality as I can safely manage. But like de Tocqueville viewing the march of democracy some time ago, we must see the whole thing as inevitable. Much as we may be revolted by the spectacle, we should be disgusted more by the lack of clarity and candor in observing it. Which, also incidentally, is a classic humanist response to major movements of history.)

As the *New York Times* says every Sunday, the fate of the free world depends on our domestic political decisions. This is the crisis, and it must be presented to the people by a responsible element of our class and elite leadership, preferably led by the President who represents the best elements thereof. There is no time for anything else.

For several hundred years now we have been experimenting with the first really big non-religious society in the history of the human race. The results have been phenomenal for creative adjustment to objective experience. But spotty elsewhere: our souls are nearly dead. This untutored existentialism cannot go on much longer without leading to even more profound convulsions than we have already experienced. We are going to have to become more useful to each other as human beings: we may manage without God, but not much longer without each other. Without a sense of community, society is absurd and detestable—and all members of it will detest it, somewhere in themselves, even if they do not kill because of it. Without community, we will have increasingly convulsive returns to de-civilized animalism, whether Communist ant or Fascist hyena or some new variety.

The historical religions were illusory means of sustaining (and exploiting) the sense of community. Religion relies on the fear of death and sacrifice of sexuality as a basis of morality: it then states the illusion that the morality thus derived *is* community. Neither the fear of death nor the need for some kind of morality can be dispensed with merely by disbelief in God and the dogma of His spokesmen. On the other hand, any large point of view that accounts for both serves the purposes of religion. The sense of community does this. The sense of community is our expectation of the willingness of others. This is an act of faith at all times; and sometimes it rises besides to the proposition that all us modern existentialists have suspected and feared—that the alternative to religion is heroism.

Only an illusory communion can be based on sexual sacrifice. Mankind made the sacrifice and elevated the illusion only out of necessity, out of material scarcity; and because most people didn't live very long anyway. Americans now live more than twice as long as most other people, and all the sacrifices to scarcity are occasioned by nothing more fundamental than bad habit. Abundance and the leisure it creates are unthinkable without a revolution in sexual mores (which suggests a reason for our strange resistance to abundance). After all, the sexual repression engineered by early capitalism was purposed to engender the ethos of hard and unremitting work, preferably unpleasant. Now the work of capitalism has been accomplished, and we have a world of non-work on our hands.

Once having transcended the tyranny of things, especially as seen through the symbolism of paper, we will be squarely up against ourselves—the ultimate reality. Any aristocrat of the past or wealthy individual of today could tell you that there is no self-discovery without sexual freedom: it is one of the first things people buy after the necessities. So it is clearly going to be more difficult for us to spend our affluence than it was to make it.

But sex, just as money was, is properly only a way-station on the road to human fulfillment. The opportunity to emphasize people rather than things leads back through all the human arts—back, back to the queen of arts, child-rearing. *In the new world a-coming, we will all be Moseses and mothers.*

If a loving mother's wish for her child were equal to the fact, we would need to suffer neither history nor the revolutions and other disasters which comprise it. Mothers are potentially the greatest revolutionary force of all: they would, with each generation, give personal birth to the kingdom of God. And theirs is, in fact, the ultimate power: from them we learn all the lessons past forgetting. If they had their wish, no other revolution than fulfilled mother-hood would be required. And, in truth, no revolution of any kind ever achieves its end until it alters the relation of mother and child—affirms itself in that.

Having said my piece for motherhood, I can now con-clude this book about the American economic order. (Ex-cept for the following Postscript.)

17

POSTSCRIPT ON THE SOVIET-AMERICAN CONFRONTATION

WHAT IS MOSTLY WRONG with current popular thinking on the nuclear confrontation is that almost everyone feels a responsibility to take an *official* position immediately, before having thought through the awful problem. As an example of this, note that threatening to push the button and actually pushing it are two quite different acts. Threatening the act may achieve something in relation to the Soviet Union, and also may keep it from achieving certain of its ends which we properly oppose. Pushing the button will achieve nothing for anyone. The moment the button is pushed, everything we are struggling for in the world has been lost, and domestically we are transformed into the most disaster-

oriented military dictatorship anyone has ever imagined.
There very likely will be no government at all at that point,
and any government there may be will operate by machine-
gun.

I am not now saying that it is advisable for us to cease
threatening to push the button because the threat may lead
to the act: I am simply pointing out what strikes me as one
of the most neglected facts in all current discussion of this
ultimate problem. Most of us in America believe we would
never push it first. Assume the Russians for one reason or
another had done so: there is no point in our responding in
kind at that time. It would, in effect, be an act of monu-
mental pique. But if this sort of thing is discussed, most of
us feel that the Russians might then consider pushing the
button first—just because we dared to mention it. So it is not
discussed. The following discussion of the Soviet-American
confrontation bypasses this consideration.

The human race has a long way to go before it can
conceive of life—I mean the resolution of serious conflict
—without a resort to ultimate force. But it is demonstrable
today that the resort to ultimate force is an act of suicide.
(In this sense, the essential politics of our day cannot be
understood apart from the psychology of suicide.) Which
nicely indicates the extremity and the stark originality of
our circumstance. We are deeply and disastrously involved
in what Mr. Churchill christened the "cold war." I want
here to discuss war aims and consequences: because in this
"war," 3 billion individual lives are at stake, the existence
of what we ha e familiarly called civilization, and for all
we know the actual continuation of life on the planet.
Therefore, the discussion of war aims and consequences is
unequalled in importance by any other previous discussion
of social policy.

I submit that a war of this kind cannot be fought and should not be threatened for merely national interests. If Russia and the United States were identical in their social systems, the cold war would be pointless—and our reason for engaging in it compounded of ignorance and suicidal need. But if we continue to take this immense risk, then we must be very clear about the reasons for doing so, about the particular difference between Russia and the United States for which we risk the future of the human race on this planet. We must be very candid and clear-spoken about the *precise* nature of this Great Difference: as a corollary proposition, we must own up to the existing and potential similarities between the two great power blocs. (Everybody else in the world will.)

Even then, having been lucidly clear about war aims and consequences, we must still integrate this clarity with the murky fact that a nuclear war can be threatened but cannot be fought. We must first know exactly why we are engaged in a struggle with the Soviet Union, and then we must devise limitless means of pursuing our aims in this struggle short of engaging in, or over-risking, the nuclear holocaust.

To rephrase the proposition: there is no conceivable justification for engaging in this deadly struggle other than the preservation of superior elements in our social organization. None of these elements can be furthered or preserved by nuclear war. The new end therefore suggests the new means. The Soviet-American confrontation is a struggle of social competition and it is fought not by military means at all. The most that can be achieved by armament is a standoff—and this is significant only as it affords *time*. The time is to be used to fight the war of total social competition, which is not a military engagement.

The Communists have challenged us to a war for the planet, and whether we accept the challenge or not, the planet will be unrecognizably altered in fifty years. If we do not fight the new kind of war to which the Soviets have challenged us, this great transformation will be carried out increasingly under Soviet auspices. This war is not a military encounter on any known historical model. It is a war of *total social competiticn*—a totally new kind of war. Unfortunately, we cannot engage in this contest as we did in the Second World War, as a battle of armament production. We have experience in that, it suits us politically, and we were an unqualified success at it in the early forties. (The year before the War ended, American armament production accounted for nearly 45 per cent of all such production of all belligerent nations, Allied and Axis.) In these industrial terms, we are more powerful today even than we were then. But the new kind of war cannot be fought by means of armament production. What is required now is quite similar in wealth-effort to what was required then—full use of our industrial capacity, and free delivery of the product thereof. But not ships, planes, tanks, and bombs. And that poses the deep political difficulty. We are called upon to give away useful material instead of destructive hardware. Can we manage the problem politically?

In this Postscript, I want to outline some of the primary points of comparison between the American Paper Economy and the Soviet system; and to elaborate briefly some of the necessities of the non-military war of social competition.

Perhaps our great defeat to date in the cold war has been our failure to see just how multiform it was becoming, and to foresee that it must eventually become total—encompassing all imaginable forms of comparative competition, from medical care to mighty rockets, from Taiwan to the South Pole, and beyond this planet altogether a quarter of a million miles to the moon.

In America, the cold war has been widely misunderstood to consist primarily of the balance of nuclear terror. That, and something called "propaganda"—which need not be taken seriously because it is "just words." The fault for this can be laid squarely in the historical lap of Mr. Dulles, with his shortsighted *ad hoc* maneuvering and overblown, lawyer-like phrases. Under Eisenhower, the cold war was fought unimaginatively and with a hold-the-line objective. The line has not been held because in the nature of the game it could not be held on that basis. The line through Europe has been maintained, but as the Russians conceived the conflict that is clearly only one theatre. We have lost everywhere else, most noticeably, of course, in science education, rocketry, Asia, Cuba. But these are only the beginning of our defeats if we do not learn how and determine actually to fight the new kind of war.

The early debate in this country concerning our inadequacy in the cold war was carried on mostly in terms of budgeteering over conventional armament and scientific research. This narrow perspective, in conjunction with self-exhilarating noises about "liberation" of Eastern Europe and "massive retaliation" as the noblest form of suicide, have been our substitutes for policy and realistic conception since Korea. At least Truman and Marshall built a NATO when building a NATO was important—and fought a limited war in Korea when that, too, was probably important.

Any real policy must begin with the proposition that

nuclear war shall be considered an impossibility. The contrary proposition is not policy at all, but literal madness. Even assuming that after such a war the planet and part of the civilization on it continued, what would have been achieved? It is not even clear that there could be a "winner" in the sense of one of the great powers surviving in a position to dictate the terms of the reconstruction—or even participate in it effectively. Could such a war be fought for "freedom"? If there are no other ways to fight for freedom, then probably it is a lost cause—or it is a cause which must be left in the hands of the Russian people and the bulk of subject humanity where, in any event, it very possibly belongs.

Unfortunately, it is not a mere belaboring of the obvious to reiterate the underlying assumptions of the ghastly stalemate of annihilation in which we are caught and which so many of us call the cold war. A congressional report estimated sudden death to 50 million Americans in a surprise nuclear attack, and serious injury to an additional 20 million. Our own department of annihilation has assured us all along (presumably not just to comfort us) that a lot of Russians would accompany us to the other side. And what if, somehow, there were more than one attack on each side? if the war lasts longer than half an hour? . . . This image of destruction is real. It must be accepted as a primary structural fact in any conception of our new world—the permament background of everything that men hereafter do or fail to do on the stage of history.

Our understanding of history is, from this moment, totally rewritten. Man is now permanently active in history —he even has the capacity to do away with it altogether. Thus, the future has arrived.

The present balance consists of an exchange of homicide-plus-suicide threats. The threat appears to be indispensable, the war is clearly impossible. So we are faced with the reality of impossible alternatives. Moreover, it is too early for unilateral surrender on either side, and probably inadvisable in any event. What would be surrendered would be the power and the right to participate in the governing and developing of the planet. Neither side is really capable of doing this alone; and to encourage a dictatorship of the world by an incompetent power, attempted or achieved, seems eminently to be avoided. So also is a nuclear holocaust—and its source, uncontrolled technology.

In the present balance of impossibilities, there has been brought into effect an implied anti-suicide pact. Delicate, tentative, but nevertheless existing. This is the true power-foundation of the coming world government. It is fundamentally an alliance between Russia and the United States; it is obviously the most important alliance in world politics; and like all alliances, it is inevitably directed against non-parties. Thus the nature of war has been turned inside out, so that it now *begins* with an agreement between the warring parties, and is carried forward on two complementary fronts: a) in any and all non-military areas; and b) by strengthening and extending the agreement which marked the onset of hostilities. In other words, modern war consists from the beginning and entirely of a long, hard process of *phased surrender*. So disarmament, for example, is not properly conceived as an end to the war, but rather as a particular—and very important—theatre of combat. Success in this theatre would mean a significant deepening of the war-agreement, achievement of further substantial surrender, and of course an increased assertion of the power of the alliance against non-parties.

All of which adds up to "negotiation"—difficult, complex, unending. We must negotiate, or accept the impossible alternatives of nuclear war or unilateral surrender. And the basis of negotiation—all negotiation, any negotiation—is the definition of reality in terms of power or commitment, with an implied understanding that each party to the negotiation will face up to agreed-upon reality. Before we get to the question of power, what commitment do we share with the Russians? Let's be safe and assume none, until proven— except the commitment to avoid self-destruction, because that is already proven. For commitment, read morality— which is significant in conflict-situations in the real world only to the extent that it is actual shared commitment. And one is never sure. That is part of the nature, the burden of morality. One is never certain that it is, in fact, shared. All morality requires taking a chance. (Otherwise we spend all of our time killing each other.) To lose is to lose, to take a chance is to take a chance, and no cheap satisfactions of indignation or righteous superiority are to be contemplated. So much for shared commitment as a basis for negotiation: it is the *end* of the process, not its beginning.

Now power. Power as a basis of negotiation refers necessarily to existing power. Most frequently, parties cannot negotiate as to future-existing power; what they ordinarily do is wait until the future has arrived, and then sit down to negotiate about their mutual understanding of it. During this hiatus, they go out into the field and create realities—as a basis for future negotiation. This is the pattern of the next fifty years.

It is a process of defining reality in primary terms.

Primarily the terms of power. That is negotiation. When the same parties negotiate about a sufficient variety of matters and do so over a sufficient period of time, an habitual pattern which can be relied upon may be built up. That is the element of commitment with its proper place in negotiation. But often, upon analysis, it will be seen to consist mostly of habitual assumptions as to existing power in the currently accepted definition of reality. Take, for instance, the steel strike of 1959 and the resultant lackadaisical negotiations. For years the parties had negotiated successfully with each other. Then one of them unilaterally decided not to negotiate but to revert to a test of basic strength, to see whether a redefinition of the reality of power would lead to any significant changes in the negotiating assumptions. The next decade of negotiations in big steel was then being determined (apart from obvious changes in political power). The test of strength may or may not have been worth the effort: that could not be known ahead of time.

The United States and the Soviet Union can afford only limited tests of strength. That is the essence of the difference between their negotiations so fateful for the world, and traditional negotiations among other parties. We are compelled to comprehend this essential difference. A great deal depends on our doing so.

The nature of the new war: a largely symbolic struggle for superiority without the advantage of any actual sure tests of strength which might facilitate the course of negotiations, *i.e.*, the process of creating the shared reality of a world order. This will hold for a long time—maybe even to the millenium, which must be at least 50 or 100 years away. And always studiously avoiding real or accidental nuclear

war. (And if they talk long enough, they may just happen
to agree on something—and we will have accidental peace.)

What will they negotiate about? About everything—
the whole planet. Berlin, the Middle East, Southeast Asia,
Formosa, and eventually India and Africa. And South
America. And scores of other intermediate situations. They
will negotiate about all possible matters as they mature for
negotiation, or are matured by one power or another for
purposes of negotiation. And remember—one cannot
negotiate on the basis of morality, on the basis that I am
right and you are wrong. That is a way of stating a proposition, not a way of negotiating about it. One negotiates exactly because one cannot dictate and cannot wait: because
the unilateral proposition is inadequate. Russia and America
will negotiate so long as and to the extent that this is true of
each. In certain essential matters, it *is* true of each now.

Negotiation is not preaching, it is not propaganda, and
it is not the direct expression of power. It is the creation of
a universe of discourse in which a common reality can be
defined. It does not involve a universe of moral discourse
unless there are existing shared moral factors in the reality
being defined and discussed. (Which suggests a neglected
opportunity in our grand and fateful negotiations with the
Russians: where it will not cost us the world if we are
wrong, we might take a few chances and offer them the
option of responding in kind to our voluntarily taken moral
position: that is, be as witnesses to our own morality and
thus invite them down the same chancey path. This is a
moral position in addition to the usual table-thumping.)

We must all ponder what it means to negotiate, because
clearly we have entered upon a stage of prolonged negotiations with the Soviets, and our lives depend on the process

as well as the outcome. Now the dominant popular *idée fixe* about "negotiation" is that it's practically treasonous even to contemplate doing it except from what has been called a "position of strength." Unfortunately, there will never be enough of these to go around—just as none of us has ever been in a poker game with enough aces to satisfy everybody. Mr. Churchill, who is to be blamed for popularizing this catchy idea, never took it with the single-minded devotion of his single-minded followers (it strikes me this was true of a number of his *bons mots populaires*). In other words, one negotiates without the absolute certainty of victory—the same way all games are played. While negotiating, however, one certainly bends all effort toward preserving and expanding any and all positions of strength. And here we come up against the second most unfortunate popular idea about our fateful negotiations—only military positions of strength are taken to be such, or even taken at all seriously. (But this is just a corollary error generally accompanying the military illusion, so we need do no more than note it here.)

The net result of the fifty-year negotiations will be a *line*—a gerrymandered line drawn around the globe. In places it will be as stark and absolute as a Rouault outline; elsewhere it will subtly waver and flicker. Jockeying for influence and position, then negotiating sessions, occasional firing, more deal-talk—and out of all this finally a line drawn wherever one needs to be drawn, and drawn with as much definition as may be needed.

What else could this coming negotiation come to? Whether or not the raw areas of the world are necessarily a power-vacuum, they certainly are such as long as the Communists are expanding aggressively. There is not much question of that. It would be silly to think that we can "negotiate" about their ceasing to be imperialist, about their becoming "good" nations. That is preaching or dictating, not negotiating. America, even all the West, has the power only to negotiate, and to create favored positions from which and about which to negotiate—we do not have the power to dictate. And we cannot fight. Neither can they.

There will be a line, but it would be nonsense to draw it on our own initiative in thick black crayon carefully tracing our national borders. Especially since the line in essence is economic and social, not military.

Nothing would please the Soviets more than a revival of the Fortress America idiocy. That would be like a postdated check made out to surrender. We would by that abandon the main war, and assume a last-ditch position for a war that can never be fought to anyone's advantage.

The main war is the economic and social competition to which the Russians have challenged us. At the opening of the American Exposition in Moscow a few years ago, Khrushchev at one point in his wild, running debate with Nixon smiled nastily and said: "When we catch you up, in passing you by, we will wave to you." And then, in an astonishingly provocative fashion, the crude wily bureaucrat waved his pudgy hand under the nose of the well-groomed orgman. Perhaps a hundred million people witnessed the event on television shortly thereafter. We should take that as Khrushchev's declaration of war—opening the new and greatest theatre of combat in the cold war. The one that will be decisive.

So the big point we can now get to is: What does it mean to compete, and what is the comparative nature of the competitors? Apparently one of the nice things about this great new competition is that, like charity, it begins at home.

The question, *How good are you?* seems to be the big bomb in the new non-military war for the world. How good are you—and prove it to the world. This *could* become the most worthwhile form of warfare ever devised.

Both countries are equally committed to industrial production as a way and a purpose of life. From this one complex of fact, profound similarities follow. When two such industrial organizations compete, even profounder similarities are due to develop as the competition continues. There are not that many different ways to make steel or generate electricity: scientific technology, we all know, is frightfully objective—meaning not particularly responsive to human differences. When a steel mill is built in India, the Indians must adapt themselves to steel-making. It doesn't work the other way around: the other way around, you simply get inefficient steel-making, which is a waste of time. If we have a superior steel mill, the Russians will copy it; if they develop a superior rocket design or means of propulsion, we will have to imitate them.

There are and can be, however, significant social differences in the organization of production. When men go into a steel mill, they are not free to treat it like an amusement park; they must organize themselves to operate it in its own terms, for the purpose of production; but they do not all have to wear exactly the same clothing or think exactly the same thoughts. Functionally similar, but not in fact exactly the same. They must be so organized socially as to be capable of producing steel efficiently. That's all. (Unless they produce so much so easily that they are then free to concentrate on nonsense like paper-position, as in America today.)

The chief purpose of the Russian manager is to produce

goods. That is *not* the purpose of the American manager, who is charged with tending a balance-sheet rather than meeting quotas of production. The self-interest of the manager in the other country is clearly tied to this purpose: the Russian receives bonuses for exceeding his quota. In *The Red Executive*, Professor David Granick says:

> The Soviets have adopted the concept that earnings should be tied closely and immediately to production. For workers, the piece-rate system of payment reigns supreme. For managers, monthly bonuses make up a major part of income and are tied to the operations *during that very same month* of the production unit for which the executive is responsible.

The American, on the other hand, increases his income when the balance-sheet is properly tended. This is the most important difference between the two systems—remembering, of course, that the current phase of Russian industry is far behind us, and they have never been forced to deal with the problem of surplus. It is just barely possible that there is something about the preservation of power against the onslaught of surplus which, making the power less than compellingly necessary, would lead the Communist Party bureaucrats to sabotage the production of a mature industry (to preserve their unnecessary power) just as the American paper-manipulators have done. But this we will not know until the Russians are truly faced with the problem.

The emphasis on production is experienced by the Russian manager as soon as he begins to work. He typically has plant experience. But the American manager may be a financial or administrative man from the very beginning and never even get a good solid look at the inside of a factory. More Russian than American managers have a formal college education—almost all of the Russians have engineering degrees, even though they end up doing administrative work which might be handled in the United States by a lawyer or a business school graduate.* Granick says, "I would expect Soviet industry to be more receptive to new technological ideas than are American firms"—because more Russian top managers are engineers, and their training leads them to be more receptive to theory in any event.

In America, the control factor lies in the financial-business part of the organization—not in production itself. In Russia, it is clearly and simply the Communist Party, which begins to have its effect in the shop and is omnipresent as a control factor from the bottom level all the way up to the Presidium. The human relations curriculum in American business schools is supplied, in Russia, by practical activity in the Communist Party, which the Russians begin to experience while getting their engineering degrees. The elite quality of Russian management is thus secured: "While management is recruited almost completely from Party ranks, only some 4 per cent of the total population are Party members." In America, money, class, family and educational status, and money, fulfill a similar purpose in much looser fashion.

The two main things about America are that it is a very big country and, unlike Russia which is also a very big country, never had a strong central authority. This tradition of central authority in the one and the contrary

---

* This takes some of the curse off the fact which has so much exercised the American worry-bird, that Russians turn out about three times as many engineers annually as we do.

tradition in the other is very likely the essence of the two responses to technology. Alexander Gerschenkron, a Harvard professor expert in these matters, is quite perceptive on this point. Beginning in 1929, he tells us, Stalin made a great effort at centralization of the industrial organization. He precisely characterizes the resulting order as follows:

> The official view of the Soviet economy is premised upon the assumption of unrestricted knowledge and foreknowledge on the part of the central planners. Needless to say, this assumption is far from realistic. . . . The fundamental ignorance of the central authorities restricts their ability to enforce their will. Obversely, it is the knowledge of the manager that assures for him his area of freedom.

In other words, there is something like the decentralization of our "markets" in Russia not because of the absence of central authority, but because of its limited effectiveness.

The Soviet manager operates more independently and is much freer in fact than is allowed for by the theory or the Plan within which he functions. For example, Gerschenkron asserts that managerial disobedience is *required* to fulfill the Plan. But he says this cannot be recognized openly because to do so would contradict the posture of the dictatorship. According to the letter of the law—meaning productive and administrative policy embodied in the Plan—most Soviet managers are criminal, since to operate at all they must break the rules. For example, a breach of "company policy"—such as shipping defective goods—is a punishable offense in the Soviet Union.*

---

* Notice how this illustrates Thurman Arnold's theory of the *sub rosa*. And notice also that there is a problem of "legitimation" in Russia as in the United States. Here, it concerns corporate power vis-à-vis the legal state. In Russia, it is the actual as opposed to the purportedly legal authority of the plant director. "In actual fact, plant directors have possessed great authority," says Professor Granick. "But in theory, they have not; and so they have constantly struggled to legitimatize their power."

Recent reforms in the Soviet Union have amounted to legal recognition of the enlarged scope of managerial discretion. In 1957, the central control was modified and partly abolished, and a very significant decentralization of planning and administrative authority was brought about. The Soviets have a term of art for what we in this country would call small business or bustling free enterprise—they call it "local industry," meaning not planned from a central position; and under these reforms the scope of this sector was also broadened. Gerschenkron believes there is a characteristic cyclical swing to and away from central control in Russia. I wonder whether there is any connection between this movement and our business cycle. With the difference, of course, that ours would be the inverse of theirs—it is only after the excesses of decentralization have occurred here that the central authority is called upon to patch up the picture.

A main point of Gerschenkron's essay is that Russia is not as "socialist" as it pretends to be, and that "profit" in Russia has a similar role to profit in this country. The role of "profits" in the Soviet Union "lies in their serving as an index of the degree to which resources have been used in accordance with the Plan." (The central Soviet authorities use pricing in order to enforce allocation of scarce resources by the manager.) If the plan is exceeded, the enterprise makes an "additional" profit. That is so like General Motors planning for profit! Except that General Motors' "plan" is for itself alone, and is not integrated with other such plans or with a national plan. (All of the foregoing, of course, is based on the inevitable irrelevance of who owns the industrial establishment. There are certain imperatives in operating these combines effectively, whether they are called commissariats or corporations, and it is

impossible to operate an industrial technology effectively
without the substantial intervention of state power. And
there you have it.)

The industrial differences between the United States
and Russia are not limited to "Planned" on one side and
"Markets" on the other. We both plan, and we both plan
badly—they from too much centralization, we from too
little. In America, major industry is planned—markets are
internalized and dealt with administratively—but these plans
are autonomous for the particular company (which is often
enough a financial rather than a production unit) and the
purpose of the plan is quite frequently to curtail production
rather than to administer the full use of available technology. In Russia, on the other hand, there is also considerable factory autonomy—that is, effort directed toward
self-preservation of the unit, which undoubtedly also operates to achieve less than the fullest production.

We can assume that there is considerable waste in
the form of misuse and under-use of productive capacity in
Russia. (This may be identified as the issue of "negative"
competition.) For a particular period, Russian waste may
or may not equal American waste—but it is of a different
kind. For example, Khrushchev himself has complained
(it is apparently a very big problem) that parts of a new
enterprise will be completed before other elements—a
plant may be built, and the machinery not delivered, or
vice versa—so that considerable capital investment may
stand idle for a long period of time. Late in 1961, G. I.
Voronov, an important member of the Presidium, complained that "hundreds of thousands of motor vehicles stand
idle without tires," because a new tire factory was delayed

in completion. One can take whatever glow of satisfaction from these Russian difficulties one pleases, but they are just not the same sort of thing as American under-utilization in steel capacity, year after year after year. In the Soviet-American confrontation, therefore, these elements of Russian waste are only a *temporary* advantage to the Americans.

The great shortages in Russia are in raw materials and machinery, including replacement parts. There is considerable waste, for example, in maintaining and repairing machinery, since individual factories will even fabricate their own replacement parts. (In the United States, the original supplier would send in a repair crew in the case of heavy machinery.) Under the gun of meeting the quota, Russian factory managers employ people to scour the industrial landscape in the search for needed material. The Soviet press on occasion will attack these practices (especially since they involve fat expense accounts) and this type of semi-legal activist is called a "*tolkachi*"; he engages in bribery and other sharp practices. It is not clear whether there are more *tolkachi* in Russia than there are salesmen in the United States—I doubt it.

In the summer of 1961—as another example of comparative waste—the Communist Party's economic magazine revealed "that last year almost 80 per cent of the 130,000 'new inventions' reported to the Soviet Government turned out not to be new at all but to have been invented and patented earlier, either in the Soviet Union or abroad," according to Harry Schwartz of the *New York Times*. But note that we typically have trade secrets in the United States which are never disclosed to competitors.

There is a substantial amount of featherbedding in American industry—sponsored by both management and the unions, in the front office and in the plant. The so-called profit motive here too often leads us to produce at much less than capacity, or to produce nonsense, or not to produce at all. As J. K. Galbraith has stated it:

> Our peacetime concern for production, central though it is to our thoughts, is selective and traditional. As a result, at any given time both our total output and its rate of increase are only a small part of what it might be, perhaps indeed only a minor fraction.

We must get straightened away on the fact that the competition with the Soviets cannot be carried on in terms of the money value of production—it is not a statistical game played with GNP figures. GNP includes the billions we spend on cosmetics, on refrigerators that don't frost up and do make ice cubes automaticallly, and tens of thousands of other such things. In the new kind of war it may be significant that we are a nation on wheels and the Russians are not; but our industrial effort toward planned obsolescence of our automobiles, with the weird and ephemeral style changes which only some Americans can even understand, is hardly a sign of our superiority. It is built-in waste, like the waste resulting from bureaucracy which we assume about Russia. And waste equals waste. We cannot depend upon *their* waste to lend *us* superiority. We know our own waste, that it results from Madison Avenue's forced feeding of the nation along with our huge unused productive capacity—from an excessive emphasis on profitable consumer goods and a paucity of "unprofitable" state services like education, research, urban renewal, and so on.

It isn't necessary to go into details on the differences in standard of living between Russian and American managers: both are privileged in the national circumstances and, of course, the Americans are much better off in absolute terms. But we may note that a consumer's "income revolution" is now under way in the Soviet Union. The main beneficiaries of it are people similar to those who have cut the better part of the cake in the United States, although there is a spill-over to the larger mass of workers there just as there has been here. But Granick states: "Roughly 80 per cent of all urban Russian able-bodied women work at full-time jobs, while the American figure is 28 per cent, with an additional 10 per cent working part time." Household appliances and other consumer delights go first to the technological and administrative elite. But in Russia the main problem is housing—they are behind us abysmally in this regard. (Allen W. Dulles stated: "Our housing investment is roughly twice that of the Soviet even though living space per capita in the United States is already four times that of the USSR.") And residental housing is obviously the most fundamental investment in preparation for a consumer's society. They have an immense problem there, but meanwhile are moving ahead in other areas: they are second only to Britain as an importer of tobacco, having bought more than 200 million pounds in 1960, which was 70 per cent more than the amount imported in 1955. In 1959 the Soviets introduced installment buying on a limited scale. They are very firm-handed bankers, however, and will deduct payments from payrolls. So the Russians are taking care of broader sections of their elite as consumers. But Gerschenkron says: "It is doubtful that a consumption economy can be established in Soviet Russia." He suggests that rising consumption levels in Russia "would leave the Soviet dictatorship without a social function, without a justification for its existence." (Anyway, we can hope.)

Soviet economic competition has been the subject of an investigation of the Joint Economic Committee—hearings were held and papers submitted late in 1959. Walt W. Rostow, an economic historian from MIT who has become an important White House advisor, submitted a really exceptional paper in which he summed up the contributions of all the panelists by saying:

> Our dangers do not lie primarily in the size of the Soviet economy or its overall rate of growth. Our dangers lie in a particular allocation of Soviet resources; in particular Soviet policies; in the way we Americans now conceive of our problems on the world scene; and, consequently, in the way we allocate our resources, human and material.

Clearly correct: the competition is not a numbers game. Nor do the Soviets misconceive it as such. Rostow notes:

> The professional Soviet literature on "catching up" with the United States suggests the objective in the next decade is to equal or surpass American production in certain key sectors related to military potential (e.g., steel) rather than to exceed American levels of GNP. . . .

The simple straightforward significance of the Sputnik episode was that in utter disregard of our statistical-to-1975 advantage in production, the Soviets outdistanced us decisively in the most advanced scientific-industrial area. They accomplished this with half our GNP—by means of superior organization and the concentration of resources to an end. There is no reason why they cannot do this again. Russia is still a poor country compared to us, but we now must accept the fact that our superior wealth is not an automatic guarantee of other superiorities. They are increasingly able to surpass us in crucial areas. It should be recalled that they accomplished the same result before Sputnik—in equalling our armament on half our GNP. So whatever theories we may hold about the superiority of market decisions over bureaucratic ukase, we must admit the facts in front of us—that not all bureaucratic decisions are wrong or incompetent.

We used to think of our productive capacity—whether used, unused or misused—as the source of our great power. With a little time for conversion, GM will produce thousands of tanks, Ford will fill the air with thousands of American aircraft, the steel mills will turn out the steel for millions of tons of shipping, and so on. Yes, but there won't be any time, this time. Or more properly, the time is now —and the products are not tanks, planes, and ships. The products are everything we can use to make ourselves superior to the Russians, and everything the world can use to be induced to follow us instead of them. Apart from maintaining the military stand-off, that is all that our superior industrial capacity can mean in the new context. We have to use all of it, and we cannot continue to misuse so much of it.

For example, it is not enough that we *could* create a scientific establishment equal or superior to the Russians. They have it and we don't. There is only one cure for that —create it. Not tanks and planes, but schools. Not Liberty ships, but laboratories. Otherwise, we lose the war—just as surely as we would have lost the war against Germany and Japan if we had not stopped making cars and refrigerators and started producing war materiel. (And the corporations dragged their feet at the beginning of that war, too.)

Although the critical awareness is growing, not everyone who should understand really does understand the true nature of the competitive situation. A few years ago, *Fortune* concluded a survey of executive opinion on crucial issues of the day with this awesome statement: "Only one executive voiced concern over 'the real possibility of conflict with the USSR.' Only one declared he was worried over 'Communist world domination.'" At about the same time, speaking of the power and achievements of Russian technology at a conference held by the CED shortly after Sputnik, Professor Jerome Wiesner said: "When I really feel gloomy I think that five years from now they will be obviously superior to us in every area. But when I am optimistic I feel it will take ten years for them to achieve this position."

One of the problems encountered in comparing the two economies is the necessity of relying on Soviet statistics. These involve categories and definitions different from our own, and also our belief that they include pure fabrications for purposes of propaganda. The detailed issues cannot be gone into here, but I may just mention that Professor Granick has said: "Nevertheless, given an awareness by the user of the problems involved, the statistics are considered by most authorities as reasonably reliable." But there is an even better way of bypassing this initial problem in comparison: we can rely on the public statements of Allen W. Dulles—statements issued when he was CIA head. I think it is self-evident that he is not to be doubted on the up-side.

In the spring of 1959, Mr. Dulles addressed the Edison Electric Institute on the subject of "The Challenge of Soviet Power." This was an extremely important and revealing speech; but the sting and import were somewhat lost because the speech was headlined as a counter-statement to Khrushchev's boast that the Soviets would equal our production by 1970. Mr. Dulles said they wouldn't. He did not say *when* they would, he did not say they would *not*, and he gave every reason for supposing that eventually they *could*. He expressed the opinion that, beginning with 40 per cent of our production in 1959, the Soviet Union might achieve 60 per cent of U.S. production by 1970. But he added: "By 1965 Soviet output of some basic raw materials and some industrial products will be approaching, and in a few cases exceeding, that of the United States. Most prominently, these products will be the kind that are needed for industrialization in the less developed countries."

As for ratio of growth, Mr. Dulles said that in the seven years through 1958 "Soviet industry has grown at the annual rate of 9½ per cent"—which is the CIA's "reconstruction and deflation of Soviet data." This rate was three times ours during the period; and he asserted clearly that if our rate of growth remained that low—between 2 per cent and 3 per cent a year—"the United States will be virtually committing economic suicide." This statement was made by the head of our secret intelligence agency: it may well be looked back upon one day as the great turning point in the thinking of our elite groups.*

Professor Rostow in his paper noted two contributing factors to the high rate of Soviet growth which may *not* be expected to continue into the future: 1) they must begin to devote more resources to replace used-up facilities—this becomes more expensive the more facilities an industrial nation

---

* Mr. Dulles, incidentally, did not rely on GNP figures without a breakdown: one of his examples in comparing the two economies was to point out that "while the Soviets last year were producing only one automobile for every fifty we produced, they were turning out four machine tools to our one." And more of the same.

has; and 2) any country begins its industrial advance with a large pool of existing technology, and naturally when this has been applied its technological increment is merely annual and much harder earned.

We may take whatever "satisfaction" we can and will from considerations such as these. But not too much—because they will not be decisive. Of infinitely greater concern must be the profounder factors. Like automation, which I referred to earlier as the Soviets' "secret weapon." An item in the Communist Party's draft program issued in 1961 concerned the building of huge automated steel plants. These are technologically feasible. (Notice also that unlike the American steel industry they will "use up" existing steel plants rather than ignore them, as they create the new, more modern facilities. They are not afraid of steel. It is not "inventory" to them, as it is in the Paper Economy.) In December 1960, a panel of mathematicians connected with a research institute of the Martin Company issued a 350-page report indicating that the Russians were mounting "an all out scientific program in the field of automatic control," that is, automation. Very astutely the report stated: "It seems clear that [the Russians] . . . intend to make the effort and it is unwise to assume that they will not be successful." Remember that the problem with automation is that it is too productive—a real problem for us, a blessing for them. *Automation is Russia's secret weapon.*

Along this line of productive growth, Professor Rostow notes that a 6 per cent rate of increase in Soviet GNP puts $12 billion annually at the disposal of the Soviet government, while a 3 per cent rate of American growth puts only some $15 billion at the disposal of our whole economy. There is no reason, for example, that the Soviet Union could not determine that in one year the entire increment would be devoted to foreign aid. Technically, we could devote our entire short-fall of production (percentage of unused capacity) to foreign aid—something on the magnitude of $60 billion in one year—but our political and social machinery for accomplishing this is so old-fashioned that it would produce a major convulsion: it could not be had without a declaration of war, of some kind.

Professor Raymond Vernon of the Harvard Business School says:

> The Soviet bloc enters the development field with one resounding advantage over the United States—namely, the fact that all its capital and all its technology are effectively at the government's command. . . . The Soviet bloc is in a position to ship investment goods and technicians abroad with an indifference to profits and to recruitment difficulties which no private investor can match.

Meanwhile, American direct private investment abroad goes overwhelmingly to Canada and Western Europe and some oil and mineral countries in South America, especially Venezuela. The character of our capital outflow has the effect of extending the period of primitive accumulation in the underdeveloped world—and opening the door for Soviet penetration through more direct and useful offerings. Our private investment is not planned—and it is not really the "development" of underdeveloped areas.

Among the difficulties of effective American competition in the development of these overseas areas are the inhibitions against cooperation among corporations in an industry, and the difficulty of recruiting personnel. The antitrust laws are a big down-side factor here, along with the general unwillingness of business organizations to reveal their best know-how to domestic competitors—which is a necessity in any cooperative effort to export such know-how.

The baronial structure of American business, along with the system of dual government in which the Federal power is always at last less than adequate, is our great weakness in competing with the Soviets in the newly avid areas. How far will a big corporation operating in a foreign nation go in cooperating with the State Department in devising and executing policy? If the "policy" is for the corporation to make money, the State Department becomes a very junior partner. But how much institutional and profit interest is the business organization prepared to sacrifice to the national interest? In effect, just about none—unless the Federal government underwrites the whole endeavor; which means the corporation looks to Washington instead of, say, the Indonesian masses for its profit. I find it very suggestive (and indicative of the *domestic* character of our crisis) that American industry will have to learn how to work more efficiently with itself and with the government in order to accomplish effective competitive export of technology— and in so doing may even learn how to do the same thing back home. Wouldn't that be nice?

While there are obvious political differences between the two countries, the basic social power in each has much in common: it lies in the managerial control of the economy. The managerial class in Russia, whether in or out of the Communist Party, has considerable independent significance. (It has been reported that the British view Khrushchev's maneuvers as being responsive to this controlling group, and have based their policy on this belief.) The social power of the American managers is not to be doubted. They have had less official political power than their Russian counterparts chiefly because they still believe in absolute limitations on the role of the state. But when a regular war is declared, for example, they just naturally go in and manage the state, too.

Of course we much prefer our awareness of the differences between ourselves and the Russians. So the striking similarities flowing from the commitment to managerialism are little remarked. And note that in both Russia and America managerial power is justified by irrelevant notions of property. In Russia they say the people own everything through the state, and here they say the people own everything through the private corporation. In each case, the ownership of the people is merely technical and in fact they own nothing because they control nothing. But we are supposed to be a democracy. The Russians are not burdened with that requirement. We are a democracy, however, only with respect to *public* affairs—and the great centers of business power are said to deal with *private* affairs.

We have too high an opinion of ourselves, and too low an opinion of our enemies, just as if this were an old-style national conflict. But the cold war is not a conventional contest fought over national boundaries—or, in fact, from behind national boundaries. It is total social war, and the total citizenry is involved in it not only because they may be destroyed by nuclear bombs, but even more because both the means and the end of the war are social and political control over the great bureaucracies which are an ineradicable part of the new technological world. This means some measure of control over the managers. We have developed no techniques for calling our own managers to account—

to us, the democratic polity—for their stewardship of the economy and properly conceiving this war, that has been our greatest failure in it. The corporate managers in America are as little willing to engage in politics—in ideological argument and factual justification before a public—as are the Russian managers. The method of suppression is different, but the results are exasperatingly similar.

We cannot struggle successfully against the Soviets without more effective organization at home, and there is no point in struggling against them if our bureaucracies are to be as little responsive to the people as theirs. There is a world-wide struggle of all peoples against bureaucratic control, and therefore against managers. The only good reason for our struggle with Russia is that we do not want the profound defeats of the Russian people vis-à-vis their managers to become a pattern for world development. Here in America, we have suffered fewer defeats—we have joined fewer battles—but we have not met the final issues of the integration of the great bureacracies with state power.

Managerialism in Russia and America: the differences lie in the fact that we are not yet completely bureaucratized —and in the means of control of the population by the bureaucracies, and of the bureaucracies by their ruling figures. Simply, the Russians utilize varying degrees of terror. But bureaucracies are bureaucracies, with or without terror. Moreover, the terror in Russia is required mainly because the people there do not yet have our standard of living. It goes along with the primitive accumulation of capital, which is a horror for the mass of the people whether or not accompanied by totalitarian state rule; as Engels described it, the effects were shockingly brutal in nineteenth-century England. The Russian model is primitive accumulation by bureaucratic means, backed up by terror. But if one compares nineteenth-century Britain with twentieth-century Russia, the sharpest difference will be in the cultural quality and style of life—freedom or lack of it—of the two ruling and privileged groups, not in the condition of the masses. If the Russian experience has been worse for the masses, this is probably because it has been bigger and quicker, rather than inherently more "evil."

Industrialism, the mass productive society, achieves its most profound effects with or without terror. In American organizations—corporations and other governments—we have a bureaucratic conformism which often seems like "voluntary" totalitarianism. Voluntary in the sense that no terror, no organized extra-legal police terror, has induced it. Totalitarian in the sense that so many aspects of personal and spiritual life are "controlled" or relevant to social rule—from opinions to ways of living. This would seem to result more from the stark bigness of industrial organizations than from terror and wrong ideology. It suggests that terror in Russia has a *special* role, and that there are underlying similarities between the two countries which have to do with factors more basic than political ideology and historical accidents. Even the special rapacity of the Russian ruling class may be based on special circumstances, including their deep belief in our inherent weakness.

But of course important differences remain. The difficult thing is to figure out which ones are temporary—no managerial ruling class is as yet fully consolidated—and which are to be more long-lived. Any historical analogy is little better than an historical analogy, but to work the Russian-English one again: no matter how one feels about the Victorian hypocrisy of the English rulers, the Moscow

Trials were a unique event in history. The technique of falsification, like technique in so many other fields, has become historically incomparable in our day. All societies lie to themselves, and all ruling classes have taken over the role of cheerleaders in this ignoble effort. But the Soviets have developed something new along this line, and America has an important opportunity to avoid repeating it—on the chance that it will not turn out to be temporary in Russia.

Both countries are bureaucratically organized. Because of its size, because of its interdependent intricacy, modern industrial society is necessarily bureaucratic. So many people, so many resources, so many small diverse parts in such a large, complicated machine—necessarily bureaucratic. Bureaucracy results from modern industry, not from an evil impulse of the Communist or collectivist soul.

The issue is not merely organization and the controlled direction of production, because that is inevitable; the issue for the world is planned democratic control, or Soviet-type bureaucratic-terror control. Since the purpose of the new war is to preserve the freedom inherent in a democratic system, the time to fight for democratic planning is now and the place is here. (We cannot blow up the world in favor of the past.)

We lose if we don't organize, and we lose if we don't organize on democratic lines. The struggle against totalitarianism is not a simple we-they combat. It is, most profoundly, a struggle against the conditions of modern life—ours as well as theirs. The war begins at home.

For the ordinary person in both Russia and America, the main thing in life is a job for an economic organization that is probably so big he doesn't know where it begins or ends. In any event, he will work for something much bigger than himself—something that he controls by mass political action, or thinking nasty thoughts about his immediate superior, or not at all. George Orwell's *1984* was not merely an image of the future Soviet society. It was a nightmare common to all men in bureaucratized societies—England and America, as well as Russia. We understood it, and it became a common image, because it touched fears that had been generated by our own experience—not because it finally "explained" Communism to us. *1984* was a nightmare of adjustment to mass industrial society. The nightmare exists everywhere and it flows over into daylight reality wherever there is conformity to the great impersonality, and whether or not this conformity is induced by terror. Terror is only organized fear: there is a great deal of fear in America, some of it organized and more of it still unorganized.

If the ultimate problem in mass productive society is bureaucracy, then we must each become exquisitely sophisticated in our perception of the thing as we see and experience it. It must be defined, clarified, understood, analyzed—in all its aspects—as nothing else in our entire cultural history. All our intellectual and moral effort should be devoted to the humanification of this one monster. Because it is an inner animal that can be combated in no other way. If the cold war is not merely a conflict between two super-states, then this individual effort to master the Bureaucratic Effect is clearly one of its primary battlegrounds.

Notice how such a battleground is overlooked as a matter of course in this country. If there is one true lasting ideology of managerial society, I suggest that it is applied science, utterly believed in as a comprehensive view of man. (One should recall that Marxism is supposed to be scientific.) If this is so, the similarities between Russia and America are even larger, and spiritually deeper. Notice further that what we currently envy the Russians for is their scientific elite. Industrial society—not democracy—is based on the applied scientific, administrative view of man. Just like the Russians, we are loaded with it here in America, too.

The difficult problem is to relate managerial control to state power in each nation—but on the run, so to speak, since Russia is excessive and we are immature in the use of state power. And the situation remains fluid. When you talk about the state in Russia you are talking about everything. In America, to view the power system comparably, you would have to talk about the state *and* corporate and other property-power over the economic machine. And then you would also have to explicate the intricate relations between state and economic powers in America—our eccentric system of dual government. Now, we are freer than the Russians to the extent that our two-party system actually functions to allow for democratic control over the state. We are not freer than they are when we lack democratic control (either directly or through the intermediary of the state) over the economic power centers. On balance, we are of course much freer: and naturally we are nicer people. But we are also weaker, we have not yet engaged fully in the coming struggle for a higher level of organization. It is the quantum of freedom achieved at that higher level that is decisive—not the freedom enjoyed by virtue of lack of organization: because the latter is not durable—especially if the cold war is to continue without a loser.

During World War II, the United States remained a substantially freer society than Russia or Germany or Japan. Were we a less democratic country during the War than we have been since? The answer to this question might indicate our capacity for freedom at a higher level of organization.

One more point about the role of the state (which was first noted two years back in the third chapter). Whether property is owned entirely by the state, or by corporations or by individuals, *all property exists at all only insofar as it is sustained by force of law*, and force of law is a function of the state, backed up ultimately by guns. In this sense, private property was never private—and not since the feudal barons seized and held property by their own force has there been perfect privacy of property. The bourgeois system and the national state were concurrent developments, and necessarily so; the national state was required to exist in order to make bourgeois property tenure feasible, to allow markets to happen, and to ensure the free exploitation of labor. The state also presided over the seizure of natural resources. All this indicates the central role of the state even under genuinely free enterprise capitalism. There never was the kind of freedom in privacy of property that the capitalist ideologues like to talk about. And the whole point made about the state in this book has been that its role in the currently functioning economy is and must be greater by far —in kind, not merely degree—than even it was when the continent was given away.

Now if, in order to fight this new kind of war, we have to abandon certain features of capitalist property or free enterprise ideology, then we either do so or we lose. The Second World War could not have been fought without price controls, material priorities, and the more or less gently forced cooperation of capital and labor. The Great Depression could not have been overcome without revising old ideas. If these techniques are again required, then we must have them.

To the extent that the "free enterprise" system says of itself, in the self-serving way of all systems, that more will be produced under it than under any other possible system, the statement may be tolerated or ignored. But to the extent that as part of its ideology it insists that there shall be no interference with its blessed workings, then it is still one of the more dangerous myths loose in the world. On that basis, we would have lost World War II. On that basis, we might as well give up now—Russia will walk all over us.

The unwritten rule in current American discourse that no comparisons of similarity may be indulged—that the existence of democracy here and totalitarianism there prescribes only black-and-white appraisals—is an intolerable intellectual condition for us. We cannot save the difference unless we define it precisely. The beginning is to admit that our democracy is not perfect—and neither is their totalitarianism. Also, as noted, there are profound forces at work on both of us that start outside, go deeper, and will end up going beyond either political system. We should recognize these social-historical similarities *exactly because* we value and want to preserve the political differences. Moreover, the chief *cultural* difference is just this, that we can be more honest about the whole thing. Perhaps most important, real probing would bring us within talking distance of the rest of the world, which is genuinely interested in this vital comparison—and what's worse, interested as if the answers were not so obvious as we, refusing to compare, like to think they are.

When we compare, and otherwise view our unique circumstance realistically, we note that in the course of the competition we are bound to become more like them, where they are better or more powerful; and they must become more like us for similar reasons. That is the iron logic of long-run competition. A simple illustration would be the mile run: over a long period, the competition to run a mile in the shortest possible time resulted in all the top runners training in the same way, eating similar foods, and actually running very much alike—they even look alike. The only way the force of this logic can be broken is to cease the competition, or for one party to become a loser. But in this grandiose competition between the United States and the Soviet Union, there must not be a loser. Any loser would be tempted to risk nuclear disaster. Or else he would have to acknowledge his loss by surrender. Putting the worst eventualities aside, there will be competition without a loser, and in the end we will both be substantially similar in power and most other qualities that would appeal to each other and the rest of the world.

It may be that one day, decades away, whether because there is a loser or for some other reason, a terminal point to the competition will be reached and it will be transposed back into military terms. God help us if this happens. We are entitled to hope that by that time such a measure of prosperity and world organization will have been achieved that everyone will have too much of a stake in the world to contemplate destroying it. Here, we are reminded of the ultimate world problem—population control: since the objective is to create a world in which everyone will have a stake, the number of people cannot be allowed to exceed the number of existing "stakes." (Also, if the world is ever to be run democratically, power must be distributed—roughly and eventually—on the basis of a head-count: and we wouldn't want the United States of the North Pole or the Union of South Pole Socialist Republics to grab power by the simplest of expedients.)

The Russian challenge to compete offers us a bright, new perspective. In an abstract sense, of course, we did not have to stand by nursing our budget while the Soviets rebuilt their war-devastated areas and created armament and a scientific establishment equal or superior to ours. We could have bought the allegiance of most of the world with a real Point Four program, and established our own unattackable superiority by thoroughgoing domestic reconstruction. But we didn't. Now we must. That is what the challenge has already accomplished.

Many people who refuse this challenge and perspective do so in reliance on two contradictory beliefs: that Russia's growth will result in mellowing, and that they will not, in fact, maintain a faster rate of growth than America—since they lack the genius of capitalist initiative and are over-burdened with the dunderheadedness of bureaucratic control. The simple truth is that there is indeed waste in their centralization, but there is also terrible waste in our decentralization. Also, the worst they do is to demand too little consumption by their masses or too much production by their managers, all with the purpose of building up the capital plant and using it at full capacity. Our worst is under-production and spotty expansion, all in pursuit of paper-profit and excessively privileged consumption.

We have noticed several times in this exposition that the state played an essential role in the accumulation of capital in America. Although there were great excesses and conse-quent hardships for the mass of the people, we were probably fortunate that it was done the way it was. Certainly we avoided a Stalinist terror, there were no 4-6 million victims of an enforced collectivization, no slave-labor camps where millions toiled under a five-year life expectancy. The labor gangs of Irish immigrants who built the railroads lived long enough to leave progeny prospering throughout the nation. But now the capital has been accumulated—there it is, the greatest collection of it the world has ever seen. What now? One system to accumulate it, another to use it. In each, the role of the state differs. The state facilitated its accumulation, and now it is charged with the responsibility of presiding over its proper use. That's all we're talking about.

Whether we use or fail to use our productive plant, by revising or failing to revise the role of the state in the economy, we meet our fate domestically—and just as if it were real. How can we possibly base our policy on the assumption that the Russian bureaucrats will make enough convenient mistakes to balance out our misdirection and weakness? What difference does it make if Khrushchev's seven-year plan takes fourteen years instead? Their rate of growth and utilization of existing capacity are greater than ours—even if it isn't as good as they say it is. If the seven-year plan takes fourteen years, all that does is give us *time*— and what are we going to do with the time if we get it? We cannot rely on their actual errors, and certainly not on our dogmatic ideology ensuring the inevitability of their errors —not in the face of their actual achievements to date. (Note that the popular press frequently "exposes" Soviet statistics by pointing out that fabulous rates of increase exist because they begin with practically nothing. This is an excellent debating point, but should not be used to obscure the fact of real growth, and at a greater rate than ours.)

It would be wonderful, of course, if Russia eventually mellowed into something like a consumers' democracy. The fatter and lazier they become, the better off we will be. But what if they don't become as fat and lazy as we are? or if they manage to take over the world before that happens? or if it just doesn't happen at all to China? Again, we can hope for it but we cannot count on it.

If one is entitled to hope that the tightness of the Russian situation will eventually ease up for the Russian people, then shouldn't we in America also look forward to a time when the American ruling class (or system, as you please), based on old fortunes and new corporations, will also ease up on its prerogatives and restrictions and come to deal with our abundance more reasonably? What really would they lose by it? Just what the Russian rulers would lose by distributing greater benefits to their masses—power they don't need, power that serves no useful function, power for its own sake.

The most significant show of strength we could make to the Russians would be just this full and purposeful use of our productive capacity—including an increased rate of growth. It would change the entire atmosphere in the negotiation chambers. Our failure to do so is the primary American weakness on which the Communists are counting. With this issue, the imperatives of the cold war have interlocked with the necessities of domestic development, and the world political center shifts to the American scene: our domestic politics have become crucial for the whole West.

In the economic struggle with Russia, we need some new legislation—to dramatize the issue for the people and to commit the government to meeting the issue. It should go beyond the Employment Act of 1946, perhaps to be called the Full and Purposeful Production Act of 196?. The primary requirements of the Act would be to use our productive capacity at all times; to expand it at an acceptable rate, say 5 per cent annually; and to employ it effectively in the social war against Russia. As an example, the Act could make it an issue of national policy that the steel mills be run at full capacity at all times, even if this required the government to finance inventory or stockpile the stuff (at special prices, of course, because the profit motive should serve the national purpose, not the other way around). The Act could spell out purposes of production—as, production for education, production for research, production for foreign aid, and of course production for defense and survival.

This sort of thing could be done—it is not at all beyond our capacity, of either plant or ingenuity. For example, take the steel mills again: inventory financing by the government could be supplemented by an excess-capacity tax, to be paid in kind perhaps, whereby the mills would find it advantageous to run at full capacity. If necessary, the government could build something with this steel; or use its stockpile to dampen a possible true inflation based on short supply; or just give it to India—but only if the Indian economy can make safe use of it. (Eventually, inventory financed by the government could be used as a substitute for gold—after all, it is "worth" more. We can hope that one day the paper issued by thing-banks will replace the zanier kind discussed in this book.)

Profits are not the Golden Fleece—they are a technique for accomplishing two purposes: to expand and perfect capital facilities, and to distribute consumption income unequally, according to property ownership rather than work. However one may feel about the latter, it is probably inconsequential so long as the over-all system actually functions to produce and grow. To take away the luxuries of our privileged groups would perhaps so dishearten them that the whole system would flounder, they being in control of it. So let them keep their high-living habits, the country can afford them—and they create a style of life that entertains a whole nation of newspaper-readers, movie-goers and television-viewers. What the country cannot afford is that their paper-hunger should make them so shortsighted as to allow less-than-full production. If they benefit most from a system, then they have most to gain when it hums and most to lose if it is bested by the enemy system. I don't know why they are having so much trouble comprehending this obvious fact.

So the final problem is how to engage in total social and economic competition and still avoid totalitarianism: indeed, such avoidance is the very purpose of the engagement. There are two ways that totalitarianism could come to America—we have thus far in our public debate concerned ourselves only with the first, the imposition of Soviet will, primarily by means of war. The second avenue of escape from freedom is more truly potential: that is the very real possibility that by means of their higher organization for national purpose, and our lack of it, the Communists will become so powerful in their own right and so compelling a force to the rest of the world, that in a panic of late realization we will remold ourselves in their image, in order as quickly as possible to become as powerful as they (notice the Birchers' use of Communist methods). It will take time and imagination to learn to organize ourselves adequately while providing for the highest possible measure of free participation in bureaucratic industrialism. Our chance to organize without excessive autocracy is *now*. If we have to organize for power in a hurry, the delicacies and difficulties of freedom will be dispensed with as extra ballast. *Now* while we have the lead, *now* while we have the time—not later and too late, in a panic.

But let's state the final problem in a positive fashion. It would seem that the remaining issue for the human race, now that it has decided not to be poor any longer, is freedom. Are we going to be free well-to-do, or ant-like well-to-do? What I have been saying is that the issue is not the simple convenient one of capitalism versus communism. And it is not the issue of freedom, in the sense of lack of organization, as against slavery, meaning merely a bureaucratically dominated society. Because when we—Americans and Russians and more to follow—committed ourselves to scientific industrialism, we necessarily also took on a considerable degree of bureaucracy. The issue is freedom as possible decentralization of power, opposed to slavery as absolute centralization of power. How to decentralize power in a highly organized bureaucratic society is the one true issue. The cold war is a holding action to give the West time in which to come up with fresh solutions to this problem. Otherwise, with the supra-national dangers involved in this war, it would not be worth fighting. (With nuclear war a reality, the pacifists are at last almost correct, for now the Weapon is as absolute as their morality. This being so, the implied pacifist acceptance of surrender is a real possibility, whether we admit it or not.)

And now it must be said that American capitalism— wild, wooly, rapacious American capitalism—is responsible for the survival of this issue and this possibility in the world today. America has always been a great big sloppy disorganized country, and our real freedom has always been so irrationally derived and irrationally used that, well, no wonder James and Eliot, faint souls, left for England. But the corporations and the New Deal and two big wars achieved a substantial amount of central organization, even on this frightening continent stretching from Hell's Kitchen to the Barbary Coast.

The social cost of private control of capital—and non-elected managers of it—is very high. But some of this cost may well have been a good buy historically, for the extent of decentralization achieved or perpetuated by it. We must have all reasonable decentralization of power possible—or we will end up robots. But we have such a large, intricate social economy that it is absolutely necessary that it be effectively and purposefully organized. The profit motive alone is absurdly inept as an exclusive principle to accomplish this.

Let's not, however, compliment ourselves too much on our happy backwardness. For instance, there is no question that the middle class is better off here than its opposite numbers are in Russia. But we are not entitled to think only of ourselves in making large comparisons. There is a cop at the elbow of every worker, every poor man, every place in the world. There always has been. There is no reason for us to be so utterly righteous about the fact that we—the educated middle classes—have put the poor American cop in his place (mostly by underpaying him and turning him loose on colored people). We haven't put the corporation in its place as yet, and that's much more important. When we do, we can crow: time enough then.

Democracy as we believe in it was a result of bourgeois

property and "free" labor; we are now too big to rely on such old-fashioned grounds for democracy. We have the same problem as the Russians, with perhaps more unrealized opportunities: to create a means for democratic participation in the institutions and activities of mass industrial-scientific society. That is the situation. Only one thing besides: the inherent freedom of Western culture available to those very few men who participate in the tradition as free-thinking individuals. They can be counted in the tens of thousands throughout the Western world. But there are 3 billion people on the planet and more every second. I know there are many cultivated intellectuals who believe that mention of these facts in conjunction is not much more than a sentimental reference. But they are wrong.

A final word on this Russian-American comparison: generally speaking, other people are not that different. Our insistence that they are is just one of the means we have for not understanding them—and, consequently, ourselves. We suffer from a deadly drive toward Russophobic paranoia, which is especially dangerous because the cure is apt to be worse than the disease. Paranoia involves a deep identification with the hated object—particularly as its power is revealed by a cumulation of successes. The hate returns more and more to the fear that created it, and the feared object looms so large on the emotional screen that an identity with it, however distorted, is the only remaining means of making the world bearable. There is a deep well of weakness in this posture, as if fear and hatred are welcomed because the truth cannot be faced. (Whatever else they did, the Nazis gave us a perfect historical example of the price that can be paid for paranoid xenophobia in our complex world.) So let's face the truth: 200 million Russians are not just

Stalin, not even just the Communist Party. And neither Stalin nor the Communist Party were big enough to make it possible for the Soviet Union to escape history. They are foolish in many ways, they suffer from a monomaniacal concentration on power which almost equals our American obsession with profits and high living, but they have not escaped the modern history of industrialism and industrialization, bureaucracy and bureaucratization, scientists and scientism. They are no more and no less human in these weird new circumstances than we. We are no more nor less than they—each is just farther along different roads.

Viewing the Soviet-American confrontation without paranoia, it is resoundingly clear that the impasse must be met and can only be resolved as a matter of domestic American politics. Unfortunately, in America nothing important happens except in a crisis—and it is up to our leaders to indicate the existence of the current one, in all its immensity. Professor Walt W. Rostow is exceptionally perceptive about the relation of public-sector spending and crisis, as refracted through this peculiar American characteristic. He notes that we are always stuck with "existing tax schedules— the arbitrary product of the last acute crisis." This is exactly correct, and abysmally inadequate. And it is, along with the larger matter of ensuring full and purposeful production without plenary Federal price-control power, one of the Big Things for all of us to think about. Rostow is superb on the newer and truer character of the cold war:

> The heart of the Soviet challenge lies, then, in presenting us with a situation where our interests may be eroded away, without palpable crisis, to a point where a traditional convulsive American response will no longer suffice. Our conceptions and methods of allocation to the public sector are inappropriate to a world caught up in a technological

arms race and a slow grinding struggle for power and ideological conception in the underdeveloped areas. It is not
the Soviet growth rate we need fear but a mode of American allocation which tends to imprison us at a level of
public outlays determined by our arbitrary response to the
last major crisis.

In the new world a-coming, not only will we all be
Moseses and mothers, but everybody is going to have to do
some thinking. For instance, we all have to think about *conditions* as they come into being—because it is the essence of
the new world that we believe in conditions as determining
existence, including spiritual existence, if any. This so-called
scientific idea is practically all the baggage we are taking
with us in our terror-ridden and terribly human journey
from the old Christian world through this present existential
desert into the new proletarian land of plenty. And let's
think now, because later is too late.

Thinking is, for us, quite appropriate, since we live in a
time of new ideas. This statement may strike the reader as
uncalled for, if not actually rude. But our world is new,
and therefore our ideas must be new: even the old ones are
new in that they apply, however mistakenly, to new circumstances. The historical call for new ideas cannot really go
unanswered: *it is our greatest human responsibility to un-
muddle the days of our years.*

What I say is, why don't we "go to war" for a decade
or two? If we don't, we will lose the world—probably
including ourselves, since we are part of it—to Communism.
If we are not to lose, then we must go to this new war
eventually. If we do so sooner rather than later, we have a
better chance of winning—of preserving our freedoms in
the process. It's that simple.

It's a *new* kind of war.

ABOUT THE AUTHOR

DAVID T. BAZELON was born in Shreveport, Louisiana, in 1923. A graduate of Yale Law School, Mr. Bazelon practiced in New York City as a corporate attorney for a number of years, and was associated with Paul, Weiss, Rifkind, Wharton & Garrison, a large firm then distinguished by the presence of Adlai E. Stevenson as a senior partner. He has also taught literature at Bard College.

An early critic of popular culture, Mr. Bazelon was associated with a group writing for *Commentary* in the late forties. During the last twenty years articles by him have appeared in various literary and political magazines.